The Art of Liste

The Art of Listening

LES BACK

BLOOMSBURY
LONDON • NEW DELHI • NEW YORK • SYDNEY

Bloomsbury Academic

An imprint of Bloomsbury Publishing Plc

50 Bedford Square
London
WC1B 3DP
UK

1385 Broadway
New York
NY 10018
USA

www.bloomsbury.com

Bloomsbury is a registered trade mark of Bloomsbury Publishing Plc

First published in 2007 by Berg
Reprinted by Bloomsbury Academic 2013

British Library Cataloguing-in-Publication Data
A catalogue record for this book is available from the British Library.

ISBN: HB: 978-1-8452-0120-3
PB: 978-1-8452-0121-0

Library of Congress Cataloging-in-Publication Data
A catalog record for this book is available from the Library of Congress.

Typeset by Avocet Typeset, Chilton, Aylesbury, Bucks.

For Pat Caplan, artful listener and treasured example.

Contents

Illustrations

Acknowledgements

There are many people I need to thank for their help in writing this book. Firstly, thanks to Paul Halliday and Nicola Evans, Antonio Genco and Gerard Mitchell whose photographs are included in these pages. Also, I'd like to thank Michael Keith for many helpful thoughts and insights and Phil Cohen, Nora Rathzel, Lande Pratt, Tamina Maula and Sarah Newlands who shared the rewards as well as the frustrations of the *Finding The Way Home Project*. Thanks to my friends and colleagues John Solomos, Stephen Dobson, Chetan Bhatt, Claire Alexander, Vron Ware, Paul Gilroy, Flemming Røgilds, Max Farrar, Caroline Knowles, Roxy Harris, Vikki Bell, Gargi Bhattacharrayya, Lez Henry, Parminder Bhachu, Beverley Skeggs, Alison Rooke, Ben Gidley, Pete Merchant, Ron Warshow, Dith Bradbury, Simon Lee, Tim Connell, Bridgett Knapper and Pete Jones for many tips, encouragement and sound advice.

I would also like to thank the postgraduate research students at the Department of Sociology, Goldsmiths College. I probably learned more from you than I managed to teach during our Tuesday afternoon research seminars. In particular, special thanks to Rachel Dunkley Jones, Emma Jackson, Charlotte Bates, Polly Haste, Anamik Saha, Kimberly Keith, Paul Stronge, Joe Deville, Sireita Mullins, Yasmeen Narayan and Thomas Zacharias.

The completion of this book would not have been possible without the help and generosity of colleagues at Goldsmiths who covered my responsibilities during the summer of 2006. First and foremost I would like to thank Head of Department Celia Lury for her support and friendship, also thanks and appreciation to Abdu Maliq Simone, Mike Michael, Sheila Robinson, Doreen Norman and Karen Catling. Sincere thanks also to Judith Barratt for her keen editorial eye and incisive suggestions. I'd also like to thank Hannah Shakespeare and Kathryn Earle at Berg for their patience and support.

Lastly, I'd like to thank my family: Debbie and our children Steph, Sophie and Charlie, my brother and sister – Ken and Lynne – my niece Vicki and my mother Joan who all played a direct role in the writing of this book. Deepest appreciation and love to you all.

Prologue: Kierkegaard's Ruse

What is sociology needed for today? What kind of place might there be for sociological thinking and writing in an increasingly information-driven society and knowledge-based economy? The complexity of global relations and the interconnections across time and space have led some to question whether sociology is even possible. John Urry writes: 'One could hypothesise that current phenomena have outrun the capacity of the social sciences to investigate.'[1] The doubt cast across scientific authority is not just a matter of the difficulties of global scale and speed of movement. The arrogant claim that science could know the 'whole truth' and legislate for solutions in order to perfect society led to murder on an industrial scale via the Nazi death camps and the atomic bomb. Commenting on the implication of twentieth-century intellectuals in this perfidy, Paul Rabinow concluded: 'The industries and sciences of Thanatos have had a glorious century.'[2] We have our own examples today. There is a direct link between the interrogation techniques, such as hooding and noise bombardment, trained on the 'unlawful combatants' in Guantanamo Bay, Cuba and psychological research on sensory deprivation.[3] The betrayal and perversion of knowledge is not a lesson from the past but a condition of the present. Sociology is not needed to dictate how people ought to live, or for that matter to be a torturer's accomplice. It is for this reason that the certainty to which social science is prone needs to be laid to rest in the graveyard of twentieth-century conceits.

The *Art of Listening* argues for a type of sociology that embraces the commitment to interpretation without legislation.[4] While the scale and complexity of global society may escape our total understanding, the sociologists can still pay attention to the fragments, the voices and stories that are otherwise passed over or ignored. The task of sociology is to admit these voices and pay them the courtesy of serious attention. It is this kind of attention that gives sociology an opportunity to hear those who are not listened to and challenge the claims placed on the meaning of events in the past and in the present. In the aftermath of the attacks in New York on the World Trade Center on September 11, 2001 and the seemingly unending war on terror, the task of careful listening and critical scrutiny is perhaps more important than ever before.

As sociologists we need to reinvigorate our engagement with the social world and reflect on our place within it. *The Art of Listening* is also written out of a yearning to communicate and to rethink the forms that sociological writing might take. As our discipline has become ever more elaborate and theoretically complex the impulse to communicate has been eclipsed by the desire for epistemological sophistication and theoretical elegance. Sociology is often criticized for speaking a secret convoluted language where sociologists resemble the insular Latin-speaking-and-writing scholarly elites of Medieval Europe. A newspaper subeditor once said to me 'You academics must really hate the English language.' I asked him why, and he replied, 'because you murder it all the time the way you write'. He was, and remains, mistaken. Sociologists are really language *lovers*: the little notebooks we carry around are not only ledgers of our thinking but also records of our philology and our love affair with language. The problem is that sometimes this love of language leads us to try to create one of our own and as a result weakens our ability as communicators.

Sociologist C. Wright Mills wrote in the late 1950s, 'to overcome academic prose you have first to overcome the academic pose'.[5] Mills' career was committed to challenging the academic status quo and is worth revisiting in the current climate. He died in 1962 at the young age of forty-five. He was a prolific writer but wordcraft did not come easily to him. His daughters have edited a collection of his letters. In them we find a desperate pursuit of the right language. In a communiqué to his friend William Miller he expresses his dissatisfaction with the early drafts of what was to become his classic book, *White Collar*.[6] 'I can't write it right. I can't get what I want to say about America in it. What I want to say is what you say to an intimate friend when you are discouraged about how it all is ...'[7] One of Mills' central aspirations for sociology was to connect the intimate experience of social life with public issues.

The writing of this book is connected to a similar kind of moment of truth. When the reader's comments came back for my last book,[8] my father was mortally ill. Like many men of his class and generation he had a terrible fear of hospitals. George Orwell once wrote that the working-class fear of hospitals could be traced to their disciplinary nature where hospitals were viewed as little more than a medical version of the Poor House.[9] I didn't want him to die among strangers so I stayed with him through the night. I took my manuscript with me and read it at his bedside. It was a haunting experience. My father never read any of my books. It was not out of hostility or rejection, but they simply sat on his shelves like tomes in another tongue from a foreign world. He would greet each piece of news from campus with contented bewilderment: 'Well, you know what you're doing.' I rarely felt like I did. As I read at his bedside my attempts to write, I heard the sound of his rattling chest and diminishing breaths. In those moments and through the many nights in Mayday Hospital in Croydon – the hospital that I was born in – I changed my view about the value and importance of sociological work and what sociology might be needed for. That painful and disorientating experience marked the beginning of this book and remains a touchstone for all its arguments.

Søren Kierkegaard commented in his book *Philosophical Fragments* that thinking is like a dance. 'Then the dance goes merrily' wrote Kierkegaard 'for my partner is the thought of Death, and [it] is indeed a nimble dancer'.[10] For him, thinking need not involve engagement with others or listening to their voices. Continuing with the dance metaphor, he concluded 'every human being, on the other hand, is too heavy for me'.[11] But, for those who have looked into the face of death, really looked, it might appear that Kierkegaard's words furnish a profound lie. This was certainly my first judgement, particularly after witnessing my father's torturous battle to hold on to life against the brutal, inexorable suffocation of cancer.

The thought of death is unlikely to provide the comfort of a dance floor intimate. Wouldn't we be in a bad state of affairs if we lived with the sound of diminishing breaths ever in our ears? The great Peruvian poet, Cesar Vallejo commented 'nothing is possible in death except on top of what is left in life'.[12] I started to view the importance of sociology as part of an embrace with and connection to the dance of life with all its heavy and cumbersome steps. It is an aspiration to hold the experience of others in your arms while recognizing that what we touch is always moving, unpredictable, irreducible and mysteriously opaque. In the wards of Mayday Hospital people just disappeared, they were not remarked upon, they were mostly working-class people and – like my father – they simply vanished. The buses continued to run, the shops stayed open and life continued without them. There can be 'no gilding over of the finitude' as Michael Young once commented.[13] The desire to hold on to their trace is one kind of warrant for sociology. Much of this book has been written in this spirit. The task is to admit that which is left 'on top of life' and find ways of recording, transcribing and thinking critically about what might be called the layers of vitality deposited there. Yet, embracing sociological life offers no refuge from Kierkegaard's ruse.

In *Circumfession* philosopher Jacques Derrida writes movingly of the guilt he felt recording his mother's illness: 'exhibiting her last breaths and, still worse, for purposes that some might judge to be literary'.[14] Trepidation about being drawn into celebrity confessional or deathbed exposé was the cause of Derrida's angst. He identifies a double bind implicated in speaking in the place of others that is not exclusively confined to mourning. To choose not to represent her and speak only for himself is no solution for Derrida: 'would I not feel as guilty, if I wrote here about myself without retaining the least trace of her, letting her die in the depths of another time'.[15] One cannot find the right words, yet silence is also impossible.[16] Here thinking, talking and describing is always a betrayal – albeit a necessary one – of either the person about whom one is speaking or the things that we know about them but which remain unsaid. This book is caught in a similar predicament, one that is also applicable to the kind of sociology I am arguing for. Much of it is concerned to argue for a sociological embrace with life, albeit one that is damaged. Yet, repeatedly I have found myself returning to life's relation to death, or more accurately the unnecessary deaths that are socially produced. Running from Kierkegaard's maxim I constantly find myself returning to it.

Confronting the quality and organization of life necessitates entertaining the 'thought of death' and this is the philosopher's trick. In the wars waged in the name of combating 'terror' where killing is renamed 'collateral damage', how is this language implicated in defining some deaths as less deathly and therefore less important? How do the thousands of 'illegal migrants' caught fatally at the borders of European states enable us to rethink the hierarchies and exclusions in worldly belonging? Or, how can we approach an understanding of the young 'suicide bombers' who kill themselves and others in order to abolish the distinction between life and death? As a partner in thought, death may offer an orientation to life itself.

Terry Eagleton writes that an acknowledgement of the provisional nature of our lives might lessen the grip of neuroses and megalomania. 'Embracing death in this sense is the opposite to taking a morbid fancy to it. Besides, if we really could keep death in mind, we would almost certainly behave a good deal more virtuously than we do.'[17] Here the thought of death is an injunction to act differently. In the post-September 11 world, actual deaths are copyrighted and used to license hate or as a call to war. The victims are used to justify the creation of yet more victims. It becomes necessary to reflect on the way the dead are claimed to authorize the actions of the living.

The Art of Listening is an invitation to engage with the world differently, without recourse to arrogance but with openness and humility. It is also an attempt to 'write it right', returning to the struggle identified so aptly by C. Wright Mills. Saul Bellow remarked: 'Death is the dark backing a mirror needs if we are to see anything.'[18] It might also be characterized as a consuming silence that we speak or write against. Clinicians and nurses who care for the terminally ill believe that hearing is the last of our senses to leave us.[19] Hearing is our final link to the external world. In what follows, it will be argued that listening is important for this reason; it is a fundamental medium for human connection, which is often taken for granted, assumed mistakenly to be self-evident. However, I argue that the capacity to hear has been damaged and is in need of repair. This is what sociology is needed for, and, as a consequence, why it is a listener's art.

Introduction: Sociology as a Listener's Art

Our culture is one that speaks rather than listens. From reality TV to political rallies there is a clamour to be heard, to narrate and gain attention. Consumed and exposed by turns, 'reality' is reduced to revelation and voyeurism. The central contention of *The Art of Listening* is that this phenomenon is having severe and damaging consequences in a world that is increasingly globalized and where time and space are compressed. Listening to the world is not an automatic faculty but a skill that needs to be trained. This book is an attempt to think about what such training might include and how sociology could and should play a role in retuning our ears to the world. The question that *The Art of Listening* addresses is: how can we listen more carefully? Through a wide variety of examples, the book argues for an imaginative engagement with the social world, utilizing a range of media, verbal and non-verbal forms of representation. We need to find more considered ways to engage with the ordinary yet remarkable things found in everyday life. The scope of *The Art of Listening* ranges from the stories of desperate stowaways who seek asylum by hiding in the undercarriage of jet planes to young working-class people who use tattoos to commemorate lost love.

Many commentators have characterized modernity as an experience of distraction. In a variety of ways, Georg Simmel, Walter Benjamin, Siegfried Kracauer and Theodor Adorno emphasized that modern life scattered perceptions and fragmented experience. Adorno commented – in relation to the appreciation of music – that a 'regression in listening' had resulted in a kind of 'masochism in hearing'.[1] We become deaf not just to each other but also to the sounds all around us. In this opening chapter I will sketch out some of the main themes of the book. I will examine the role of sociology in offering a contrasting form of attention. This is a progressive listening in which hidden connections can be traced, providing new directions for thought and critique.

As the novelist Eudora Welty once put it, writing involves the process of listening *for* a story.[2] Such an imaginative attention takes notice of what might be at stake in the story itself and how its small details and events connect to larger sets of public issues. It is fed by sociological reading and a familiarity with sociology's toolbox of theories. Also, we are eavesdropping on the story as partisans. The suggestion here is not quite the same as taking sides in research, an issue which has been debated at length in sociology.[3] The listener's commitment to hearing places us on the side of the story from the outset. Yet, this is not a proposal for blind acceptance or unquestioning agreement. Being a partisan to the human story in all its manifold diversity does not exclude maintaining a critical orientation to it. As Eric Fromm pointed out in his discussion of psychoanalytic technique: 'Critical thinking is a quality, it's a faculty, it's an approach to the world, to everything; it's by no means critical in the sense of hostile, negativistic, nihilistic, but on the contrary critical thought stands in the service of life, in the service of removing obstacles to life individually and socially which paralyze us.'[4]

So, sociological listening is not simply a matter of transcription, or just emptying people of their expertise and wisdom. Unlike Fromm's psychoanalytic listening, it is not only about listening to one specific voice. It involves artfulness precisely because it isn't self-evident but a form of openness to others that needs to be crafted, a listening for the background and the half muted. Sociology has been diverted by an enchanted obsession with the spectacular, namely, the loudest voices, the biggest controversy and the most acute social concern. It bears remembering that the notion of the spectacular itself is a visual point of reference drawn from the Latin *spectare* – to watch. Emmanuel Levinas in *Totality and Infinity* talks about what he calls a panoramic exposition of being. This is produced in social encounters and embodied in the face of the other. Ultimately, he concludes, 'ethics is an optics'.[5] Yet, ethics is not only about what is seen. *The Art of Listening* argues that thinking with all our senses can change our appreciation of ethics in a multicultural society. Also, I argue that social investigations that utilize a 'democracy of the senses' are likely to notice more and ask different questions of our world.[6]

Remarkable Things, Experts and Expertise

Some years ago a student gave me a copy of Jon McGregor's evocative first novel *If Nobody Speaks of Remarkable Things*. It tells of a street where the residents encounter each other closely, yet remain strangers. We often don't learn their names. One of the book's most compelling figures is a man with ruined hands. We never really find out why this loving father's hands are burnt beyond repair: we know his wife is dead, and we learn other details in passing, but most of his life remains opaque: he is the neighbour you see every day from the window, someone who is at once familiar and yet a complete mystery. Towards the end of the book he offers a lesson to his child:

He says my daughter, and all the love he has is wrapped up in the tone of his voice when he says those two words, he says my daughter you must always look with both of your eyes and listen with both of your ears. He says this is a very big world and there are many things you could miss if you are not careful. He says there are remarkable things all the time, right in front of us, but our eyes have like the clouds over the sun and our lives are paler and poorer if we do not see them for what they are.

He says, if nobody speaks of remarkable things, how can they be called remarkable?[7]

The man with the ruined hands knows his daughter doesn't understand him, but he wants to put these thoughts 'in the air' regardless. What I want to suggest is that sociology's task and challenge is formed somewhat in the same spirit. One key thread in all the subjects contained in this book is the attention to the hidden life of objects and places, the life that is either concealed within those objects or bleached from them by the formalities of power or the forgetfulness of conventional wisdom. It is a practice of scholarship that is committed to a profane illumination,[8] of reading against the grain, which looks for the outside story that is part of the inside story.

I started out as an anthropologist, but I was more interested in what was going on at the local bus stop than some distant shore. The main ethic that I have carried with me from that training in anthropology is a commitment to engagement, of opening up a sometimes very uncertain space of dialogue and encounter with people in their ordinary circumstances of life. I guess I have practised what some people call an 'anthropology of the near', but I don't care much for the term, largely because of its attempts to make the commonplace ethnographically exotic.[9] In 2002 I contributed to a conference on ethnography organized at the London School of Economics by my friend and colleague Claire Alexander. Ethnography is a style of social research that involves long-standing and intense participation in the cultural world being observed. A respected professor of sociology stood up and said boldly: 'the people are the experts in their own lives!' There was a murmur in the audience, not necessarily one of approval. I thought to myself, 'Hmm ... sounds good, nice radical gesture – the people are the experts in their own lives.' I started to think more carefully and came to a realization: being a professor of sociology is no necessary protection from saying utterly stupid things. If the people were experts in their own lives, love affairs would never end, we would never make mistakes, nor do things that injured our interests or did us harm. I am certainly not an expert in my own life, and who amongst us could make such a claim?

At the beginning of *The Sociological Imagination*, C. Wright Mills characterizes the experience of modern life as analogous to a series of traps. Mills suggests that people are 'bounded by the private orbits in which they live; their visions and their powers are limited to the close-up scenes of job, family,

neighbourhood; in other milieux, they move vicariously and remain spectators'.[10] Far from being experts in our own lives, Mills argues that we are spectators, caught up in the web of history, imprisoned by the expectations of
others. Published in 1959, the book is a stirring sociological manifesto and
statement about the promise and potential of sociology. Mills evokes the
atmosphere of an Edward Hopper painting. Hopper's characters appear similarly frozen in place, alone staring out of a window aimlessly, or isolated at
work or in a train carriage, or simply motionless in the street. The task of sociology for Mills is to identify the larger social forces that furnish our most intimate private concerns, to translate the 'personal troubles' of biography into
'public issues' of history and society. This quality of mind, for those who
possess it, 'often comes to feel as if suddenly awakened in a house with which
they had only supposed themselves to be familiar ... Older decisions that once
appeared sound now seem to them products of a mind unaccountably dense.
Their capacity for astonishment is made lively again.'[11] I recognize that quality
of astonishment that Mills writes about. It is the point at which we come to
realize that the order of things is not a product of nature, but rather of history.

Mills names something powerful, but perhaps the scale has been transformed. In a world where there is increasing global interconnection in technology, and movement of information, there are ever more complex traps. The
story of a young man whom I'll call Jonathan illustrates this profoundly.
Jonathan lives in Anerley in suburban south London. He is twenty-five years
old. He was living with his family in Uganda and studying for a degree in
accountancy when his father – who was born in Zaire (now the Democratic
Republic of Congo) – came under suspicion for supporting rivals of the government and of using his transport business to traffic illegal goods across the
border. Jonathan's mother was from Rwanda and he had a younger sister, who
suffered from a kidney condition. They fled to France but Jonathan stayed
behind because he needed to finish his dissertation and get his degree. He was
'interviewed' many times by the Ugandan police, beaten and tortured, but he
stayed to collect his degree. He then joined his family in France using a passport that his father gave him. His parents later returned to Congo where they
were both murdered. Leaving his fifteen-year-old sister with friends in Paris
but promising he would send for her, Jonathan came to London. The immigration offices in Croydon, one of the southern suburbs of London, turned
down his asylum claim first time around; they said his passport was a forgery.
All he knew was that his father got his passport for him. He spent eight months
in detention centres, moved from one to another. He then lived with a friend
of his cousin whom he barely knew; he had been given her telephone number
by a relative in the United States. She took him in even though he was almost
a complete stranger. She told him that while he was in the detention centre his

sister had been taken ill and died. Jonathan sits alone in his room, he suffers from blackouts that sometimes last two or three days, and is haunted by feelings of guilt, trapped in an uncertain present. Some days he copes, others he does not. He has a letter that his sister wrote to him before she died and can't decide whether to open it or not.

The trap is not just a product of his individual choices. This sketch of a life reveals both the increasing interconnection of people and places – what we usually refer to as globalization – but also the thick lines drawn between people that determine who can move freely across the globe and who cannot. We can't understand these traps without understanding the wider political forces that structure the movement of people, as well as the definitions of citizenship and belonging. In order to make sense of this we need to develop a global sociological imagination subtle enough to prise open the public issues in these private troubles. Put simply, if asylum claims had been processed differently, Jonathan would have been able to see his sister one last time.[12]

My point is that the up-close worlds that people experience combine insight with blindness of comprehension and social deafness. Yet this does not mean that these up-close scenes are not worth taking seriously. Ulrich Beck refers to lived 'side effects' in 'the form of the farmer whose cows turn yellow next to a chemical factory'.[13] These 'side effects', Beck maintains, 'have voices, faces, eyes and tears. And yet they must soon learn that their own statements and experiences are worth nothing so long as they collide with the established scientific naiveté.' He concludes: 'People themselves become small, private alternative experts in the risk of modernisation.'[14] I may be labouring the point but this is not some authentic raw voice. Rather, it constitutes partial expertise that is nonetheless essential for those who care to take it seriously.

It is here too that we might start to think differently about the relationship between the observer and the observed and experiment with new forms of observation. This is particularly possible with the widespread and affordable nature of digital cameras and video and even mobile phones. Video Intervention/Prevention Assessment (VIA) based at Children's Hospital Boston provides a good example of a new kind of observation.[15] VIA gives video cameras to young people, asking them to teach clinicians about the realities of their illness. The goal of VIA data collection is to obtain audiovisual documentation of the patient's day-to-day life experiences from the perspective of the patient, in the form of 'video diaries'.

Each VIA participant is loaned a lightweight, handheld video camcorder and asked to 'teach your doctor about your life and your condition'. Seeking honest portrayals rather than professional production values, a field coordinator instructs participants how to operate the camcorders, but does not teach film-making technique or visual style. Participants are encouraged to tell their stories, taping anything and everything they feel reveals their lives, dreams, successes and frustrations. What is so striking in the narratives is the way they combine rich insight into unspectacular details of living with serious illness with a yearning to communicate with their audience. There is an intense sense that the participants feel that 'I need you to know this'. Participants grab the camera in the middle of a traumatic attack of breathlessness or a bloody coughing episode and record it.

Thousands of hours of video footage is painstakingly logged and then analysed by a multidisciplinary team including clinicians and social researchers. The expertise of the patient is made accessible to the clinicians, often challenging their medical practice. At the same time Jennifer Patashnick, coordinator of VIA, comments that the video data often raise issues about the gap between the patients' 'stated knowledge and their behaviour'.[16] The videotapes reveal the patient doing things that hurt themselves, consciously and unconsciously, sometimes out of frustration within the confines of conditions such as cystic fibrosis or acute asthma. On other occasions their 'bad choices' are a matter of refusing to be governed by doctors and medical authority. The patient is both expert and neophyte simultaneously. This complex combination is what I want to suggest sociological listening needs to engage with.

Scientists or sociologists also have to accept that their view of the world similarly combines insight and blindness. To me, to develop a sociological imagination is to attempt to see and listen on both of these horizons simultaneously,[17] to pay attention to both the insights and the blindness in the accounts of the people who live the consequences of our uncertain world, and at the same time have the humility and the honesty to reflect on our own assumptions and prejudgements. Borrowing Monica Greco's beautiful phrase, we must never become 'ignorant of our ignorance'.[18] None of us is expert in our own lives in the sense that the Foolish Professor meant it. Rather, we all possess expertise and social know-how; it's just that the understanding contained in it is incomplete. Perhaps the difference between a professor and a bus driver is that the professor can say stupid things with complete authority while the bus driver is not authorized to make brilliant insights. The difference is of course not about the quest for understanding, but instead the socially determined forms of authority. The bus driver's up-close reading of everyday life contains something worth listening to, but equally this view may be partial or distorted by prejudgements. The same is equally true of the professor. The trick is to make those insights speak to each other in the service of understanding.

I want to propose that, in the half century since C. Wright Mills suggested we are little more than spectators in our own lives, something else intervened.

Through the proliferation of media in our informational society we have become *spectators in the lives of other people*.

Spectators in the Lives of Others

Many sociologists have examined the ways in which observation and scrutiny are tied to government, control and power. As Michel Foucault pointed out, the power of Jeremy Bentham's model prison was based on total surveillance in what he called a Panopticon (all-seeing) structure.[19] Here the prisoner is constantly aware of being open to scrutiny. But the Panopticon was also an elaborate listening device: the guards could listen and look at the prisoners but the prisoners could not see or hear them. Those following Foucault paid close attention to how power works through knowledge, through scrutiny and through the creation of conditions of self that in turn control and self-scrutinize. This metaphor has been applied to a full range of modern techniques of power, including CCTV and the role of biometric techniques – for example, fingerprint examining and iris testing – in verifying people's identities, which is something at the centre of the Labour government's identity card legislation and immigration control strategy.

The Norwegian criminologist Thomas Mathiesen suggests that Bentham and Foucault's powerful metaphor of surveillance also coincides with another kind of structure. It is not just 'the few' who are observing, taping and keeping records on 'the many', but 'the many' that now watch and scrutinize 'the few'. This he calls a synopticon – all-watching – society. It is not only that Big Brother is watching us – recalling George Orwell's famous prophecy. Rather *we* are watching *Big Brother*. Reality TV or 'extreme TV' is perhaps the best example of mass spectating. Mathiesen argues that public executions of the eighteenth century become 'as spectacles, peanuts compared to the executions (real or metaphoric) on the screens of modern television'.[20] Beverley Skeggs and Helen Wood point out that these programmes become moral dramas where lines are drawn between good and bad behaviour, good and bad taste, good and bad husbands and wives, good and bad fathers and mothers with the help of the obligatory expert.[21] The expert can take the form of the nutritionist in shows like *You Are What You Eat*, the beauty coach in the case of *10 Years Younger* or the psychologist in *Family Contract* (BBC1). As far as I know, a sociologist has yet to be included in these programmes. Experts routinely reduce their protégés to tears before they remake them in the required image. This is largely concerned with the assertion of norms of conduct and selfhood, against which the earlier 'bad behaviour' is judged. There is also the excessive impulse to observe others as well as oneself in the rash of reality shows.

The reality TV format renders the mundane and trivial as prime time spectacular actuality. The determining power of the form itself was exemplified by the appearance on *Celebrity Big Brother* of self-styled political firebrand George Galloway. The Respect Party MP had gained national notoriety in Britain for his defection from the Labour Party and his victory in the May 2005 general election, winning the Labour stronghold of Bethnal Green and Bow constituency in East London on an openly anti-Iraq War ticket. He was drawn to *Big Brother* for the opportunity he thought it posed to speak in an uncensored way to a mass audience. Through the Respect website he claimed: 'I will talk about racism, bigotry, poverty, the plight of Tower Hamlets, the poorest place in England.'[22] This was far from reflected in his almost three-week-long stay before the *Big Brother* cameras. The most enduring image was of him dressed in a skin-tight red cat suit, pretending to purr and lick imaginary milk salaciously from the hands of actress Rula Lenska. Reflecting on Galloway's naïveté, Stuart Hall commented that this was the result of his mistaken view that *Big Brother* is 'an authentic site of the popular and that one could go into it and pass a message to the outside in an untransformed way. And the form completely defeated him.'[23] Political egoists and B-List celebrities are easy prey for the format, but there is also something more troubling and destructive at stake in the 'many watching the few'.

Public life degenerates into little more than a contemporary equivalent of the Victorian freak show. Unlike the purposeful testimony offered by participants in the VIA Project which challenges the preconceptions of its viewer, reality spectaculars like *Big Brother* lead to a kind of moral cannibalism where the viewer is invited to nourish their moral probity by consuming images of badness, crime, vulgarity and degeneracy. This is the reality of the headline, the spectacle splashed over our newspaper on a daily basis. Sometimes these include tales of real cannibalism: 'I've Eaten My Girlfriend' read the headline of the *Daily Mirror* on 7 October 2004. This horrific story tells of armed robber Paul Durant, who confessed to eating parts of girlfriend Karen Durrell's body after he murdered her in Spain. I don't want to minimize the male violence and the human tragedy of this case, but stories of this kind frequently seem to command the headlines; they become the topic of everyday talk and the hook on which moral folk wisdom is hung. Martin Amis calls this the 'obscenification of life'.[24]

I offer these examples as snapshots of what I think of as harmful aspects of the public life of the mind. Partly, what I find worrying in this trend is the confident certainties with which judgements are made. In the world of reality TV, tough moral certainties produce a kind of auction of authoritarianism that is pervasive not only in popular media but also in political debates. In a sense, one of the values of the kind of sociological listening I want to argue for is the importance of living with doubt in the service of understanding, of trying to grapple with moral complexity. As Barry Smart comments, sociological thinking involves 'the necessity of learning to live without inherited guarantees or securities and with a pluralism of images and narratives of action, rationality and value'.[25] We don't live in a world that suffers from doubt, but one that suffers from certainty, false certainties that compensate for the well of worldly anxieties and worries.[26]

My hunch is that moral cannibalism produces a situation in which the worst is always expected. 'The white streak in our fortunes is brightened (or just rendered visible) by making all around it as dark as possible' wrote William Hazlitt in 1826.[27] Here Hazlitt points to the pleasure of hating and perhaps this is why the 'bad insider' or the 'unwanted outsider' has become such an important moral emblem or limit figure in today's world. The asylum seeker is always bogus, the single mother always a scrounger and so on – condemnation produces the appearance of brightened fortune. It is not simply a matter of quarrying into people's individual secrets but rather of connecting those biographies with a wider history of social, political and economic relations, to make 'private troubles' connect with shared public issues and global concerns. The solution to those troubles is not in the quality of the individual self, but rather in the realm of vital shared life.

The next section of the chapter contrasts the 'reality rush' of journalistic accounts of social life with academic representations and sociological practice. How do sociological accounts measure up to the competing representations in public circulation and how can we reach for a sociology that is vital and alive?

Life's Portrait and Arendt's Pearl Diver

The measurement of social life is a staple obsession of the conventional mass media. From political polls to eating patterns and the auditing of sexual mores, each new 'fact' is commented upon, assessed and scrutinized like jewels that one day hold the promised preciousness only to be cast out the next as counterfeit. An extraordinary surfeit of data is produced through the insatiable desire to know the latest news from the frontline of everyday life. Even war is as much about the management of information as it is of military strategy and manoeuvre. In May 2006 the suicides of three detainees held as 'enemy combatants' at the US base at Guantanamo Bay, Cuba, was described by US officials as a 'good PR move to draw attention'.[28] For the British Muslim, Moazzam Begg, who spent three years in Guantanamo, imprisonment without charge or trial in a state of suspended life places the prisoners: 'in a worse situation than convicted criminals and [suicide is] an act of desperation'.[29] It is revealing that suicide inside the camp is re-inscribed as 'info-war' by the US military, akin to a propaganda suicide bomb.

Sophisticated techniques such as opinion polls or MORI surveys contribute to this profusion of information often taking in large samples and principally interview based. C. Wright Mills referred to these styles of enquiry as 'empty forms of ingenuity'[30] producing an 'abstracted empiricism'. Deploying an elaborated methodological apparatus, the abstracted nature of these accounts is normally reported in statistical summaries, assertions of proportion and cross-classification. For Mills, they result in thin insight both philosophically and socially. Sociology and sociological research are often placed in an ambivalent relationship to the excess of popular empiricism, either ignored entirely, or confined to a limited 'sound bite'.

Another style of empiricism that works in the opposite direction might be added to Mills' formulation. Rather than amalgamated patterns offered through numerical tables, 'intrusive empiricism' claims to know and judge the very soul of its subjects. It mines their secret failings, which in turn come to define the people scrutinized in this way. The journalistic exposé and reality TV ethnography crackle with controversy and are 'thick on empirical detail'. This intrusive salacious curiosity is aligned with the notion of moral cannibalism outlined earlier. These descriptions are so thick in detail that they occlude and hide what's at stake. They are by definition fast and produced with such swiftness that each is soon lost in a torrent of others. Intrusive empiricism is defined by revelation, occlusive detail, fast turnaround and an excess of 'data'. Although abstracted and intrusive empiricism are largely non-academic styles of fact making, academic research is not completely immune to it. However, what afflicts academic sociology is a counter-movement.

Portraits of the social world in academic sociology often seem *thin on empirical detail*. The sources of this syndrome are various. The high value placed on the usefulness and veracity of social theory moves the object of sociology away from embodied life towards the ethnography of ideas. Metatheoretical assessment emphasizing the re-reading of classical or contemporary theoretical treatises does not require an engagement beyond the library. The integrity of this style of work is beyond question, but it means that a sociologist can have a long and successful career without talking or listening sociologically to anyone beyond the seminar room or conference colloquia. The usefulness of theory lies in its ability to invite us to ask different questions of the social world. Hence the necessity and challenge to combine theoretical enquiry *and* empirical investigation in equal measure. The political and epistemological challenges to sociological authority also contribute to sociology's empirical deficit.

The inhibition with regard to describing others in social science is in part connected to critiques of the relationship between knowledge and power, or what Anthony Giddens refers to as sociology's double hermeneutic. 'The point is not that there is no stable social world to know but that the knowledge of that world contributes to its unstable and mutable character' writes Giddens.[31] The first part of this critique is the claim that sociology produces the object that it then proceeds to dissect analytically. Sociological methods here are not simply the keys used to unlock societies' secrets but actually create society in the process of understanding it. From a whole array of positions, including feminist deconstructionism and Foucauldianism, the sociological 'dream of omnipotence', to use Pierre Bourdieu's phrase, is brought into question. As Bourdieu suggests:

> How can one avoid succumbing to this dream of omnipotence? I think it important above all to reflect not only on the limits of thought and of the powers of thought, but also on the conditions in which it is exercised, which lead so many thinkers to overstep the limits of a social experience that is necessarily partial and local, both geographically and socially.[32]

Reflective frankness about the truths we claim brings inhibition as well as a benefit. Making the social world hold still for its portrait can seem like a gross violence, reducing its mutable flow to frozen moments preserved in the hoarfrost of realist description. Reading doctoral dissertations I am struck by an inhibition that students feel with regard to social description. As a result, little is offered to situate and describe the voices of the people that have been transcribed so faithfully on the page.

More often than not research findings are presented in the form of long block quotations from research respondents. These excerpts are expected simply to speak for themselves. The portraits of the research participants are sketched lightly if at all and the social location of the respondent lacks explication and contextual nuance. Sociological data is reduced to a series of disembodied quotations. This is a completely understandable consequence of trying to avoid what I have referred to as intrusive empiricism, but in the end the texture of the very lives we seek to render is flattened and glossed. Put crudely, the words of respondents will not carry vivid portrayals of their lives. American ethnographer Mitch Duneier makes this point: 'If you are going to get at the humanity of people, you can't just have a bunch of disembodied thoughts that come out of subject's mouths in interviews without ever developing characters and trying to show people as full human beings. In order to do that it is useful to have a character that lives in a text ... '[33] Put simply, quotation is not portraiture and it is the task of sociological writing to bring to life the people we work with and listen to.[34] For this reason I have used photography in this book both to enhance portraiture but also to communicate what is outside language. This task need not involve a singular author or photographer but it does involve writing, representation, evocation and description. Duneier's work provides a very interesting model of shared sociological authorship and combining visual and written narratives.[35]

The gesture towards more democratic forms of research practice may also contain ethical sleights of hand. Commonly today research participants are referred to as 'partners' or even 'co-workers'. Again, something very important is signalled in this move, namely a shift to dialogic or participatory forms of social investigation. Claiming that research participants are empowered through the research process conceals some of the inevitable unevenness of agreement, consent and participation. Similarly, researchers who claim a smooth passage to the ethnographic inside are fooling only themselves. Tacitly this kind of research ethos is coloured by the sentiment outlined by the Foolish Professor earlier. Even the most righteous researcher keeps a firm grasp on analytical control and sociological authority. Perhaps, abandoning radical pretence may be liberating and allow for greater candour about the limits of democracy in research and also, for that matter, in understanding and insight.

Taking dialogic methods seriously can sometimes lead to uncertain outcomes. One example comes to mind from a project on young people's notion of safety and danger discussed at length in Chapter 2. It concerned a young man called Lay. He was born in Nigeria and came to London when he was very young. He lives with his father, who is a security guard, in Deptford. Lay contributed to the project and submitted to the tacit forms of discipline involved in its exercises but his involvement was always playful. He promised to be involved but he never really participated. Faced with a series of researchers he subverted the ethnographic game. Initially he worked with my colleagues Lande Pratt and then Sarah Newlands. Both found it difficult to work with him; he was evasive and outrageously sexist. Lay was basically every researcher's nightmare. It got to the point where the research team said, 'we're just fed up with him, you deal with him!'

Lay had a lesson for us. Sometimes there is real value as a researcher in being made to feel a fool. Clifford Geertz describes this as one of the 'psychological fringe benefits' of being a researcher, it makes intellectuals endure the ridicule of others and particularly those people we have the impudence to write about.[36] I conducted the last interview. The purpose of the final session was to sum up the project and talk through issues that had emerged during the course of the year. The interview took place in the summer of 1997. Lay more or less submitted to the terms of the conversation. He said he'd enjoyed getting out of lessons but said such wildly disparate things that it was hard to gain any coherent account of what he felt about the issues 'we' were concerned with. In good dialogic style I ended 'Just to finish with, is there anything you wanted to say but have not had an opportunity to?' Lay paused. With his hand he beckoned his white middle-aged interlocutor forward, as if about to whisper a secret. 'I hate white people', he said. Drawing his hand to his mouth in mock astonishment, he said: 'joke, joke'. Then again, 'They are buttock idiots … only joking; only joking.' Lay is a trickster. He undermines playfully the implicit hierarchy between questioner and respondent. He fed us answers that would confound: for my female colleague it was sexist diatribes and with me he professed to 'hate white people'. In each case I think the words were hollow and their effect confined to the moral tableau of the 'interview' itself. True dialogue also means being open to the possibility that those involved will refuse to have dialogue or the participants whose integrity researchers so strenuously preserve may subvert the tacit rules of the ethnographic game itself. Lay helped identify some of our own illusions about or tensions within the project's participatory research design. We did experiment with the nature of observation through giving young people cameras and audio diaries. Nevertheless the young people produced the data and we wrote about it. Ultimately we fudged the issue of analytical authority which we held onto as researchers. In the end, admitting to the limits of dialogues in research is at the least a more honest way to proceed. Lay helped us face up to some of the delusion we entertained with regard to making the research process more democratic.

While cliché and 'fast food thinking' prevail in public discussions of social issues, one of the things that is precious about sociological judgement in contrast is its slowness of pace. I used to feel that this was a weakness. My sense then was that speed thinking or popular forms of research dissemination through journalism or media were necessary in order to make interventions on the public issues of the day. I now hold the opposite view. Of course this isn't always an affordable luxury. In areas of applied social science sociological production is incredibly fast where research reports and project evaluations have to be circulated to clients who require value for money. Equally, the research audit culture in European universities or 'publish or perish' tenure struggles in the United States mean that academics write in a climate of urgent haste that can affect adversely the quality of our endeavours. Not everyone is so keen to resist the hurry. There are plenty of academics who indulge in the temptations of punditry. I am not at all arguing for a retreat into the Ivory Tower, rather that attentive listening and sociological judgement takes time. A recent example comes to mind, which illustrates this point.

It was just a week or so after the 7 July 2005 London bombings. Many friends and colleagues were struggling to comprehend the significance of these events. The fact that the bombers were 'home grown', seemingly very ordinary young British Muslims, caused dismay in the media leading some to say that Britain's multiculture was the cause of the problem. The imminent threat of a

racist backlash loomed. By a coincidence an academic conference was sched-
uled to take place on Muslim masculinities just a few days later. Some of the
organizers were keen to seize the opportunity created by the aftermath of the
bombings in order to garner greater media attention and coverage. Others felt
more ambivalent about the prospect of speaking so soon after the bombings
and as a result several sociologists pulled out of the event. 'I feel like I need
time to really think about this' a friend told me. 'All the things I felt certain
about the state of British society are now not so clear.' Choosing silent reflection over premature guesswork, my friend was one of the contributors who
withdrew and I think she made the correct principled decision. If sociology is
to have any value it is in the insistence on reflective thinking sceptical of the
way the meaning of such disasters is claimed by politicians and public commentators. The deliberate pace of scholarly work is to be cherished for its
time-consuming craft and the opportunity it provides to point to the things
that cannot be said otherwise. 'Not the least valuable thing about the reflection and thought that takes place in a university is that one has time to do it',
wrote Edward Said.[37]

To sum up, the non-academic and academic accounts of social life discussed here can be formulated as a pair of ideal types. The non-academic is
defined by its focus, often intrusively, on uncovering scandalous revelations,
thick on occlusive detail but containing truths that have short time spans.
Contemporary academic research is characterized by its slow pace, cautious
reflection and theoretical elaboration. The cautious sociologist can unwittingly
end up producing accounts of social life that are thin on description, relying
heavily on their informants' words to stand in for their portraits. There are
strengths and weaknesses in both styles. This is reminiscent of the distinction
made by Walter Benjamin between *commentary,* or the uncritical relay of
information about the material of life, and *critique,* which interrogates myths,
elisions and the enigma of life itself. For Benjamin this is analogous to the different orientations of the chemist and the alchemist to a burning funeral pyre.
The chemist is concerned only with the wood and ash, while the alchemist
focuses on the enigmatic energy of the flame itself. 'Thus, the critic inquires
into the truth, whose living flame continues to burn over the heavy logs of
what is past and the light ashes of what has been experienced.'[38]

Put crudely, the central claim of this chapter is that sociology should cast
itself against the forms of *intrusive empiricism* and *moral cannibalism* widespread
in the mass media. The ethos of sociology in contrast prizes patience, commitment to dialogue and careful and reflective claims to truth. The challenge
for sociology, like that of the alchemist, is to develop a critique that captures
life's light and heat. If the society of information produces an empirical surfeit,
how should we as researchers relate to the profusion of talk and text, image

and sound? What kind of attention should be paid to the ash and flame? This raises questions emerging from some of the classical debates about the analytical status we give interview data or what kinds of truths we are looking or listening for.[39] My concern here is a different one, namely how the development of a sociological imagination also necessitates the art of discernment or a capacity to sift through the piles of information.

In Hannah Arendt's essay on Walter Benjamin she characterizes him as a 'pearl diver' who 'descends to the bottom of the sea, not to excavate the bottom and bring it to the light but to pry loose the rich and the strange, the pearls and coral in the depths, and to carry them to the surface'.[40] The empirical depths collected on life's surface cannot be described entirely. It is a matter of finding amid the profusion of informational debris 'thought fragments' that are the equivalent of the pearl diver's treasure. They do not illuminate the whole ocean floor, but rather they shine with histories and memories that have been transformed by the sociologist's craft.

Sociological listening is tied to the art of description. This is the kind of careful evocation described by Clifford Geertz in his notion of 'thick description'.[41] Drawing on the philosophical writings of Gilbert Ryle, Geertz argued for the type of description that is microscopic and yet concerned with rescuing the content of social life 'from its perishing occasions and fix it in perusable terms'.[42] Thick descriptions of life are always interpretative and do not merely attempt to mirror a simple obdurate reality. They are selective and discerning but also require imagination and creativity. In W. G. Runciman's *Treatise on Social Theory*, he places great emphasis on artful description: 'it is no more a vice in sociological description that it should be literary than it is a virtue that is should be literal'.[43] It is the mutual implication of theoretical imagination and empirical detail that distinguishes the kind of description being suggested here. Conceptual and theoretical work should not climb to a level where the voices of the people concern become inaudible. Rather, theoretical ideas and concepts hover above the ethnographic ground in order to provide a vocabulary for its explication. This is a kind of description that is committed and dialogic but not just a matter of 'letting the research subjects speak'. It is informed by a commitment to patience, accuracy and critical judgement. Thick descriptions produced through deep sociological listening are ones that theorize as they describe and describe as they theorize.

A sceptical reader might ask who this listener is. What kind of presumption is being made about the attentive listener's social background? Is it not the modest witness, or the old 'man of science', characterized by Donna Haraway as the authorized ventriloquist, endowed with masculine humility and the temperament and power to establish the facts? 'He bears witness: he is objective; he guarantees the clarity and purity of objects. His subjectivity is his objectivity', writes Haraway.[44] The listener here is not cast in such a form. Rather, sociological attention need not hide its authority in false diffidence; it is historically situated, reflective, contestable, uncomfortable, partisan and fraught. It can be exhausting and sometimes the sociological ear is simply full and the listener needs time to reflect for a while. In the first instance, the invitation to listen more is issued to sociologists and sociological researchers but it can be extended to include activists, journalists, artists, scholars, publics and even, perhaps, politicians. Its sense of purpose is best summed up as an attempt to remark upon the unremarkable, evidence the self-evident and relate the troubles contained in the smallest story to a larger, more worldly scale.

Private Troubles, Worldly Problems: Summary and Structure of the Book

Before moving on to introduce the structure of the book, I want to return to the nostrums of C. Wright Mills and in particular his invitation to turn 'personal troubles into public issues'.[45] My argument is that in the twenty-first century the quality and scale of these troubles have been transformed in ways that Mills could not have imagined. In particular, the shape of public life with all its troublesome elements does not fit into a stable local or even national entity. The challenge of sociological thinking is how to work in a post-national context where the nation state can no longer remain the prime container of sociological analysis. Put simply, 'the here' of any sociological problem or personal trouble is almost always connected to things happening beyond the boundaries of the nation. Michael Keith calls the connectedness the 'elsewhere of place and the global familiar'.[46] These connections are not as productive or positive as the twentieth-century court poets of globalization imagined.[47] Indeed, much of the discussion of globalization that took place in the 1990s has been overshadowed in the new century by the imperial project enacted by American interests in the name of the 'war on terror'. Indeed, the work of writers like Michael Hardt, Antonio Negri and Paul Gilroy emphasizes both the emergence of new empires and the continued disruption of the present by the legacy of old ones.[48] As much as the here also contains the elsewhere, the now also contains the legacy of the past.

The scale of global sociology is precisely an attention to the implication of our most intimate and most local experiences in planetary networks and relationships. Sociological listening is needed today in order to admit the excluded, the looked past, to allow the 'out of place' a sense of belonging. This is not some quick or blithe or romantic 'one world' ethos in which the wretched are listened to and heard. I am suggesting something much more difficult and disruptive: a form of active listening that challenges the listener's preconceptions and position while at the same time it engages critically with the content of what is being said and heard. It also means entering into difficult and challenging critical dialogue with one's enemies as well as one's allies.

In a sense, the task is to link individual biographies with larger social and historical forces and the public questions that are raised in their social, economic and political organization. It is the search for remarkable things that are otherwise not remarked upon. John Berger commented recently on how the parameters of public discussion are limited to the not too distant past and the near future.[49] A global sociological imagination offers the possibility of refiguring the relationship between the past and the present and the near and the far. The past refuses to stay in its place that is behind us, it is unstable. Equally the present cannot simply explain what is past from the point of the now. Rather as Walter Benjamin points out, 'Then and Now come together into a constellation like a flash of lightning.'[50] Those flashes contain insights and sociological gifts.

Similarly, I am arguing for a rethinking of the relationship between the near and the far. Georg Simmel wrote that the position of the stranger is constituted by what he called the 'synthesis of nearness and remoteness'. I think of Jonathan riding the bus through Penge while the other passengers sitting next to him have no sense of his transcontinental story. Simmel also argued that this union of closeness and remoteness is part of every human relationship: 'one who is close by is remote, but his strangeness indicates that one who is remote is also near'.[51] This oscillation between the near and the far is to my mind the scale of global sociology. It is not just between people and places – it is also within us. Our own biographies contain the traces of a global history whether or not we are conscious of it. As C. Wright Mills pointed out over a half a century ago, we are also strangers to ourselves.

In the following passage from Hannah Arendt's *Essays on Understanding* we can hear the echo of both Benjamin and Simmel. For her, it is imagination that enables us to navigate our way through and this links back to Mills' sociological invitation. She writes:

> Imagination alone enables us to see things in their proper perspective, to be strong enough to put that which is too close at a certain distance so that we can see and understand it without prejudice, to be generous enough to bridge abysses of remoteness until we can see and understand everything that is too far away from us as though it were our own affair.[52]

Sociological listening involves such a movement between the boundaries of the personal and the public. As I have tried to show in this chapter it is important to reflect upon the ways in which the personal troubles are made into media spectaculars and the harsh judgements that can follow from this. Consequently sociological listening needs to protect itself and those we listen to from such forms of violation. Nirmul Puwar puts the challenge in this way: 'How do we listen amid the risks of enacting symbolic and epistemic violence? How do we listen without objectifying and anthropologising the local global?'[53] Each of the following chapters attempts to answer this question and offer ways to engage with the social world through sound, vision and touch. Perhaps, one starting point in avoiding the violations identified by Puwar is to insist that our accounts are always incomplete.

'Reality is always more clever than the philosophy that impotently wishes to reflect it. That is why enlightenment is no seamless doctrinary construct but rather the constant illuminating dialogue that we are obliged to construct with ourselves and others' writes Jean Améry.[54] A survivor of the Nazi death camps, Améry ultimately is a defender of a vision of Enlightenment thinking, reason and logic even in the face of barbarism and the perversion of modernity that produced the camps. 'The light of the classical Enlightenment was no optical illusion, no hallucination. Where it threatens to disappear, humane consciousness becomes clouded. Whoever repudiates the Enlightenment is renouncing the education of the human race.'[55] What I find appealing is that he tried to defend humanism and the legacy of classical Enlightenment. His notion of radical humanism is summed up as a commitment to reason and logic and a clear-eyed unsentimental reflection on the kind of human beings we have become.

This resonates with an idea of sociology as part of this movement towards education and the significance of scholarly endeavour in the process. However, as Paul Rabinow has also argued, the daring light of the Enlightenment is at once arrogant and humble: 'It is arrogant in so far as it acts for humanity with the confidence that it is right; it is humble in that enlightenment is an infinite project whose achievement lies in the future.'[56] We cannot any longer claim to act for humanity with such certainty. Rather, it is necessary to think again about the variegated relationship between near and far and what it means to think on a global scale without the presumption of certain knowledge and the forms of arrogance referred to here.

Jonathan Crary points out in his book *Suspensions of Perception* that our practices of listening, looking at, or concentration on things are implicated in grids of power and knowledge and as a result are deeply historical in character. He describes a moment of suspension: 'a looking and listening so rapt that it is an exemption from ordinary condition, that it becomes a suspended temporality, a hovering out of time'.[57] I want to argue something similar in relation to sociological attention that is both situated in time and place, fixated on the object of attention and yet at the same time ungrounded, mobile and characterized by imaginative movement through the past in and of the present. This is what I have tried to do in this book. While I have foregrounded listening sociological attention is not limited by it. As Margaret Mead commented, it is not confined only to a 'science of words' and or what I referred to earlier as mere transcription.[58] Rather, sociological attention involves a mode of thought that works within and through a 'democracy of the senses'.[59] It is for this reason that the accounts, while arguing for listening, also move between visual, aural and corporeal registers.

One of the ordinary virtues of sociology is its attention to making the familiar strange or to *evidence the self-evident*. The protagonist of Saul Bellow's the *Adventures of Augie March* describes himself as a 'Columbus of those near at hand'[60] and there is something in this that I think applies to sociology. Bellow, after all, has a degree in anthropology but, more relevantly, what I am suggesting is the training of a mode of attention in which the relationship to time and change might be apprehended and lost. The lives described in this book are now out of date and my attempts to apprehend them sociologically are like relics of a world that has already passed. Their time – that of the people discussed and described – moves faster than my capacity to apprehend it.

Each of the substantive chapters of *The Art of Listening* focuses on one issue, or a social phenomenon, drawn in most cases from London's cultural and political life. The intention here is not only to put forward an argument about immigration, racism or the modalities of love but also to exemplify a particular approach to sociological craft. In Chapter 1, a global sociological imagination is applied to contemporary debates about migration and mobility. Challenging the ways in which the notion of the 'immigrant' and 'asylum seeker' is framed at the level of politics and policy, it focuses on the experience of those people who are trapped, often fatally, at the border. In Chapter 2, urban boundaries and exclusions are discussed through an analysis of how young people navigate safe and dangerous places. Through a discussion of the *Finding a Way Home Project* it points to the ways in which 'observation' can be reinvented or rethought in social research. Chapter 3 explores the ways in which emotion and love are inscribed on the body. Here, working-class tattooing provides an example of affinities and expressions of love that operate outside speech and elaborated forms of language and where sociological listening and attention is not merely concerned with what is said. In Chapter 4 a street portraiture project conducted in London's East End offers an example of what might be called 'listening with the eye'. This chapter explores the potential that photography offers dialogical forms of research in which the look and the photograph become a gift that can be reciprocated between researcher and research participant. A photographic exhibition provided an opportunity for participants, photographers, sociologists and local people all to be present in the discussion of its findings. The final empirical chapter discusses the aftermath of the 7 July 2005 London bombings. In particular it argues for the role that sociological listening might play in challenging the political copyrights that have laid claim to the meaning of these attacks and also their significance for British multiculturalism. The book concludes with a summary of the main arguments and a discussion of writing and the nature of scholarship itself.

I have argued that sociology is best envisaged as a listener's art and in this chapter I have sketched some of its qualities and contrasted them with news journalism and the pseudo-realities of extreme television. My own attempt to practise this art is demonstrated in the remaining pages of this book.

CHAPTER 1

Falling from the Sky[1]

Bomb alerts are common at the Immigration and Nationality Directorate (IND) in Croydon, south London. Among the high-rise office blocks the Home Office administers immigration policy, constituting one of the largest employers in this part of the city. In 1938 George Orwell characterized southern England as 'the sleekest landscape in the world'.[2] Croydon at this time was a place of suburban somnolence and tranquillity. Orwell pondered:

> the huge peaceful wilderness of outer London, the barges on the miry river, the familiar streets, the posters telling of cricket matches and royal weddings, the men in bowler hats, the pigeons in Trafalgar Square, the red buses, the blue policeman – all sleeping the deep, deep sleep of England, from which I sometimes fear that we shall never wake till we are jerked out of it by the roar of bombs.[3]

It was not just the howl of Nazi 'doodlebugs' that disturbed the suburban peace. The bulldozers and jackhammers tore away its fabric as the intense pace of the post-war reconstruction and urbanization erased and remade the landscape.

The 'redevelopment' of Croydon started in 1956. At the time central Croydon was also a place of nascent teenage rebellion. 'The youth of Croydon were notorious', remembered Jamie Reid, who grew up in Shirley:

> The place was full of gangs: Pretty Boys, Cosh Boys and early Teddy Boys. Teenagers hung around the city centre and its coffee bars: for the price of a cup of coffee, they could sit around in a Lyons' Corner House all Saturday. They would parade the streets in their drapes: this was their patch. It was obvious that this sort of thing had to stop and the authorities found the perfect justification in one single incident.[4]

The 'incident' was the murder of a policeman on the rooftops of Croydon. The botched robbery involved Christopher Craig and Derek Bentley, both from Norbury. Craig had fired the fatal shot but because he was under age escaped the death penalty. While in the clutches of a policeman Bentley shouted 'Let him have it, Chris!' For this ambiguous utterance he was condemned and hanged. An orgy of panic ensued about 'juvenile delinquency' – Craig was the son of a bank official – and teenagers became an unwanted presence to be 'designed out' of the new centre. In the shadow of the skyscrapers and the stained-glass edifices of commerce, artists and musicians flourished often unnoticed. It is against the concrete surfaces of corporate architecture that Malcolm McLaren and Jamie Reid sketched the design of punk rock. Croydon Art College became a hub of activity precisely because it was engulfed by 'single-minded public space' to use Michael Walser's phrase.[5] In the 1960s' boom, commerce and finance overshadowed all else. Croydon's sterile shopping centres and council estates provided the ultimate expression of capitalist modernism. Yet, they equally provided the perfect canvas for situationist slogans and the stylistic refusals of youth subculture.

During the 1960s, forty-nine tower blocks were built in Croydon and, by April 1971, some 5 million square feet of office space existed in the central area alone.[6] The space was designed for business interests decentralizing from central London. The millions of tons of concrete that made the flyovers and office blocks displaced working-class communities in neighbourhoods like Old Town and depopulated central Croydon. An intense residential segregation was enforced along class lines by building vast council estates such as New Addington on the outskirts. So the movement of people is integral to the nature of this landscape. These transformations were also coupled with an intensification of racism as Croydon also became a kind of urban frontier for the defenders' racially exclusive Englishness.

In the minds of most overseas visitors and migrants, Croydon is associated with the Immigration Office located in 'Lunar House' on Wellesley Road (see Figure 1.1). The high-rises were all erected in the age of space flight. This building is perhaps aptly named; the moon is probably a more hospitable place to visit. Most who have been through its doors remember the experience with disdain. On any given day confused people clutching copies of the London A–Z can be found wandering around trying to make their way to the offices of the IND. Lunar House is notorious for losing passports and documents (Figure 1.2). It was this issue that focused the anger of users and led to a campaign that resulted in an enquiry led by local people.

Concern was first raised by a parishioner at St Dominic Roman Catholic Church in Waddon, named Mary. The IND lost her French identity card and she spent seven hours queuing up only to be dismissed in minutes. The parish priest, Father Ian Knowles, acted as an advocate for her, trying to find out what had happened to her lost documents. Father Knowles concluded that the IND are: 'Unable to take criticism from outside, unable to engage with us as people who are saying – "you've got an important public job to do – we want to help make that better." But [I was met with] hostility, suspicion, playing games, and you think – what are they so afraid of? It's a culture. I've described it before as being Orwellian.'[7] The churches, mosques and temples provided a 'listening post' and a point of last resort for desperate and vulnerable people trying to navigate the bureaucracy of immigration.

Figure 1.1 Lunar House, Immigration and Nationality Directorate, Croydon (*photograph by author*)

Figure 1.2 Immigration correspondence (*photograph by author*)

In the summer of 2005 I was a member of a delegation who visited Lunar House as part of the London Citizens Investigation into the Immigration and Nationality Directorate. We waited in an adjacent building before meeting the senior civil servants. A young British Asian security guard checked our credentials while we waited. It was just a few weeks after the 7 July bombings in central London. I asked him if security was particularly tight. 'We get a lot of bomb alerts but mostly it's nothing to worry about. You see, what happens is that when people send in their immigration applications they sometimes put flowers or flower petals in with the form for good luck. In the Asian community this is quite common, it's like putting a prayer in the envelope', he explained. 'Only thing is when they arrive here the flowers have turned to dust and when we open them we think, "this could be a letter bomb."' Prayers are interpreted as bombs.

This anecdote contains something very telling about the misunderstandings and tensions that surround the issue of immigration and the global movement of people. This chapter will examine how the terms of reference surrounding the immigration debate are coded and determined by the legacies of empire and racism, and how the conception of movement itself might be rethought.

The Problem of the Immigration Line

W. E. B. Du Bois commented famously that 'the problem of the twentieth century is the problem of the color-line'.[8] Some ninety years later the renowned writer and postcolonial critic Stuart Hall remarked, mindful of Du Bois I am sure, 'Diversity is, increasingly, the fate of the modern world ... The capacity to live with difference is, in my view, the coming question of the twenty-first century.'[9] In the years since Stuart Hall wrote these words something else has intervened. It might be more accurate to say that the problem of the twenty-first century is the problem of the 'immigration line'. This is certainly Europe's problem, but it is also a global issue, the proportions of which are only just beginning to emerge.

The immigration line is just as vexed politically, ontologically and practically as the line of colour or race. Indeed, it is deeply implicated in the legacy of racisms past and present and of the foundational principles of citizenship and state formation. The problem of the immigration line is also the problem of the ways in which lines are drawn through and across the peoples of the world. I want to say that this is not about the ethnic or cultural qualities of so-called 'immigrants' rather it is concerned with the ways in which the immigrant serves as a limit figure in political life. The immigration line demarcates those lives that are endowed with the gift of citizenship and those lives that can be cut short with silent impunity. The life that is licensed by the work of the state is linked and implicated in the diminished life of people caught, often fatally, at the border.

In mid-2000 the global population was estimated at 6.1 billion. It is growing at an incredible pace. Up until the beginning of the twentieth century the world had not doubled in population within 100 years. In the twentieth century the world's population increased fourfold and is now growing by 86 million each year. More than 90 per cent of this growth is happening in the poor societies of the world. The human population is more mobile than at any point in its history. Some 90 million passengers pass through London's two major airports – Heathrow and Gatwick – annually. Once flight captured the Western imagination, now air travel is banal and unremarkable.[10] The planes are also carrying cargo such as exotic foods and flowers to our supermarkets. Some political movements have taken this mobility as an opportunity to argue for the normality of movement, claiming as their slogan that 'we are all migrants'.

Slavoj Žižek asks: 'What do protesters who pathetically claim "We are all immigrants" actually want?'[11] For him this constitutes a kind of identification 'which imposes compassion and merciful care for the poor while endorsing the existing hierarchical order'. For him this induces 'a hasty claim that our own predicament is in fact the same as that of the true victims, that is, a false metaphoric universalization of the fate of the excluded'.[12] Žižek touches something here but perhaps there is something else at stake, namely the desire to challenge the distinction between immigrant and host.

Under a succession of home secretaries, the Labour government has reinvigorated the idea that the 'immigrant' is a moral and political problem. During his tenure as Home Secretary, David Blunkett claimed that the problem of integration was that South Asian communities needed to speak English to their children in order to 'overcome the schizophrenia which bedevils generational relationships'.[13] Responding to the public outcry, he disavowed being an assimilationist and professed 'integration with diversity'. There is little doubt on whose terms integration is defined. In this sense the language of 'shared citizenship' and 'mutualism' is merely a way of saying that the responsibility for 'unbridled multiculturalism' is laid at the door of the Black and Asian communities. Social order, another one of the new assimilationists' favourite phrases, is centred on a normative whiteness that defines the terms on which the game of assimilation is played out.

New Borderlands and Pariahs

In Britain and the United States the issue of race and difference is usually located in the social container of the 'inner city'. It is very different in Sweden and France where it is the suburbs that are associated with 'dangerous otherness'. In Britain today there has been a shift in the geography of public concern and small provincial towns on the coast (like Margate, Dover and Hastings) have become the focus of anxiety about illegal immigration and asylum. These seaside towns occupy a special location in the national imaginary as places of saucy recreation brilliantly drawn in the essays of George Orwell.[14] The death of twenty-four Chinese 'cockle pickers' in Morecambe Bay, Lancashire in February 2004 is an indication of this shift. These 'illegal workers' had been brought by gangmasters to harvest shellfish and were trapped by the notoriously treacherous night tide. Sister Gina Tan said during the memorial service held in Morecambe for the dead on 15 February 2004, that: 'They came to this country thinking they were going to have a better life – they didn't realise that the sea would take them away.'[15] These towns where cockles and seafood are consumed as a quintessentially English habit, have become the new frontier for the defenders of exclusive national culture and 'rights for whites'.

The venom and crudeness of the public outcry that revolves around the image of refugees as 'beggars' and their alleged involvement in 'violent crime' is a routine reference point in the media. The general context is that asylum seekers are living below the poverty line, surviving until recently on vouchers that can only be traded for goods and subject to a dispersal policy that is aimed at preventing them from settling in particular areas together. Meanwhile, liberal or even left wing politicians try to justify these measures introduced by the Labour government since 1997 as being 'faster, firmer, fairer'. According to the 2002 government White Paper there is a need: 'to expose the nonsense of the claim that the people coming through the Channel Tunnel, or crossing in container lorries constitute an invasion when it patently demonstrates how difficult people are finding it to reach this country'.[16] So, being tough is a matter of placating the delirium of racist scaremongering. The security of those borders also creates the market of desperation that lines the pockets of smugglers and criminals who are making small fortunes out of illegal traffic.

Another layer has been added to this situation since the attacks on the World Trade Center on September 11, 2001. The figure of the refugee and the asylum seeker has been transformed from a political émigré to de facto criminal, and now terrorist. The levels of surveillance and monitoring have increased considerably with the introduction of electronic fingerprint systems and 'Application Registration Cards' or identity cards. This is in many respects the product of the harmonization on a European level of immigration policy that seeks to deter applications for asylum. The contract for the controversial 'voucher scheme', now being phased out by New Labour, was awarded to a French company, Sodexho Pass International, who also implemented this system in Germany.

Despite Prime Minister Tony Blair's routine references to Britain's 'multicultural nature' and proud tradition of tolerance, a clear distinction is made between the 'border questions' relating to new migration and the domestic settlement around the issues of race and racism. Seemingly incommensurable political commitments can be held at bay within New Labour's political formation. The relic of imperial nationalism lingers and provides the touchstone for the debate on identity and citizenship. Indeed, at the heart of the conception of the state and citizenship is a distinction between a human existence that is common to all of us and a particular formation of human conduct embodied in the citizen.

Giorgio Agamben has pointed out that the Greeks had no single term for life. Rather, they used two terms: namely, *zoe* which expressed the simple fact of living; and, *bios*, which indicated the 'form of living proper to an individual or group'.[17] For Agamben the production of a 'biopolitical body' is the original activity of sovereign power. In Agamben's analysis a stark distinction exists between the life that is created through the language of sovereignty and citizenship and what he calls *bare life*. He claims 'that the fundamental categorical pair of western politics is not that of friend and foe but that of bare life/political existence, *zoe/bios*, exclusion and inclusion'.[18] He also introduces a figure from archaic Roman law – *homo sacer* – to characterize the quality of this bare life, that is, a person who can be killed and yet not sacrificed. There is something here that is deeply resonant with the conditions of the displaced people of the globalized world.

The Named and the Anonymous

The desperation contained in the stories of those people trapped at the border needs to be reckoned with. While we have heard much of the victims of terror since the attacks on New York and London, almost nothing is known of the thousands of people who die in desperate attempts to gain entry to freedom's province. This is often simply a matter of who is named and who is nameless. The philosopher and writer Walter Benjamin, himself an asylum seeker from Nazism who was shown a closed door with fatal consequences, wrote in his last essay: 'It is more difficult to honor the memory of the anonymous [*Namelosen*] than it is to honor the memory of the famous, the celebrated, not excluding poets and thinkers. The historical construction is dedicated to the memory of the anonymous.'[19]

Reckless stowaways are literally falling out of the skies along London Heathrow Airport's flight-path. In the summer of 2001 a young Pakistani called Mohammed Ayaz fell out of the undercarriage of the Boeing 777 descending thousands of feet only to land in a Homebase car park in suburban Richmond, west London. He had sprinted through the darkness of Bahrain Airport and hauled himself up into the cavernous opening above the plane's wheels. He was long dead before he reached British airspace. Or, seventeen-year-old Alberto Vazquez Rodreiguez and sixteen-year-old Michael Fonseca from Cuba who fell out of the undercarriage of an aeroplane to their deaths in a Surrey field just outside London's Gatwick Airport. Sometimes they drop without trace. In the summer of 2002 a man driving round the M25 motorway close to Gatwick Airport saw a human figure fall from the sky. The body was never found; England's 'green and pleasant land' ate it. It is not just that these stowaways fall from planes. They are sometimes found dead at the roadside. In June 2006 a suspected stowaway was found dead on the roadside of the A12 in Witham, Essex. Two others were also discovered severely dehydrated. In the soaring temperatures of an English summer they had been dumped there by the traffickers who had smuggled them into the country in the back of a lorry.[20]

Meanwhile, hospitals suffer from acute staff shortages and search the globe for nurses and doctors. In 2006 it was estimated that 31 per cent of doctors working in hospitals and general practices in the United Kingdom are migrants and 13 per cent of nurses working in the National Health Service were born abroad.[21] There are chronic labour shortages and the facilitation of the global movement of skilled labour is an essential priority. The British government has introduced a Highly Skilled Migrants Programme in an attempt to encourage skilled workers, particularly doctors, information technology workers and scientists, to migrate to Britain. The recruitment of skilled international workers is happening throughout the developed world. In 2001 the United States relaxed the annual quotas reserved for professional and skilled workers, increasing the quotas by nearly 70 per cent. In August 2000 the German government instituted a Green Card programme, which resulted in 8,600 computer and technology specialists entering Germany.[22] Similar things are happening in Australia where there are attempts to attract skilled workers in the new technology fields.

There are huge tensions here between the necessity for global population flows in a context where the British population is ageing and not reproducing itself, and the unspeakability of the people-flow debate. Indeed, the very nature of the term 'immigrant' is overdetermined by the legacy of the way in which movements of labour have been coded racially. Britain faces chronic skills shortages but at the same time the legacy of racism and the discourse of immigration mean that New Labour is reluctant to have that debate. Yet the huge scale of the growth and the demand for labour cannot be hidden.

The London Plan of 2004 produced by the Mayor of London suggests 'that under different migration scenarios London's population could increase by between 690,000 and 964,000. The most plausible "central" scenario suggests an increase of 810,000 to 8.1 million by 2016.'[23] Perhaps the only way to open up these questions is to abandon the language of 'immigrants' and "immigration' in favour of less coded terminology. One alternative would be to speak of the necessity of *global movement*, which is both fluid and not necessarily permanent, within an international pool of labour. This view is starting to be voiced in a surprisingly wide range of places on the political spectrum.

In November 2002 the *Economist* magazine ran a cover story on the issue of migration and economic growth. It concluded that there was an economic case for relaxing immigration policies among the lower skilled as well as the elite global professional class: 'It is impossible to separate the globalisation of trade and capital from the global movement of people.'[24] Economic benefits like filling vacancies in which settled communities were reluctant to work would be achieved through the recruitment of deracinated, work-hungry hands. This kind of sentiment has been echoed in the responses to the estimated 600,000 migrants from the eight former Soviet bloc nations who have come to Britain since the expansion of the European Union (EU) in 2004. In 2006, with the further enlargement of the EU imminent, which would make it possible Bulgarian and Romanian workers to seek employment in Britain, the Business Group for New Europe – which includes Sainsbury's and British Petroleum – signed a letter calling for the British government to resist pressure to limit immigration. For these businesses the great success of the 2004 enlargement was the injection of skilled labour into areas of skills shortage in the British economy. Martin Sorrell, the chief executive of the WPP Group, the world's largest advertising business, commented: 'The Polish plumber has become a much loved feature of British life. The migration has plugged gaps in the labour market and boosted economic growth.'[25] The free flow of migration even dwarfs free trade rhetoric in this version of economic liberalism; for them it is simply a matter of letting mobile workers earn from moving and selling their labour where it is most wanted.

The *Economist* conceded that opening the borders could involve a 'political cost'. This, it argues, is best addressed through an assimilationist approach, and if necessary unabashed and premeditated discrimination:

> Winning consensus for an orderly policy may mean trying to pick the migrants most likely to bring economic and social gains ... It may also mean (although liberal democracies detest the implications) choosing those whose education and culture have prepared them for the societies in which they will live. In Europe, that may mean giving preference to white Christian Central and Eastern Europeans over people from other religious groups and regions.[26]

It is telling that a racial logic is being admitted openly; certain nations and ethnicities are close relatives to the white English and others are not. This is ultimately about a version of whiteness that places Central and Eastern Europeans within a shared, or at least compatible, racial genealogy.

Yet, such a vision is little more than a description of the current state of play. There are literally hundreds of thousands of unnoticed economic migrants coming to Britain each year. A study conducted by Janet Dobson and Gail McLaughlan concluded:

> that migrants from developed countries formed around three-quarters of the inflow from the mid eighties onwards – nearly 80% in 1995–99. Contrary to common perceptions, the biggest contributors to the increase in employed people coming from overseas were countries in the developed world, particularly the Old Commonwealth (Australia, Canada, New Zealand, republic of South Africa) and the European Union and EFTA (Iceland, Liechtenstein, Norway and Switzerland).[27]

These mobile workers do not count as 'immigrants' because the mask of whiteness renders them invisible.

There were 282,000 asylum applications between 1995 and 1999; approximately half of those will have been turned down. During the same period the inflow of workers from developed countries into the UK was 381,000. In 2001 the government published figures that asylum applications were 11 per cent lower than in 2000. This trend was reversed in 2002 when published figures showed a 20 per cent increase. However, it was not the beginning of an upward trend. Applications are falling and the number of asylum applications has halved since 2002 reaching a figure of 33,930 applications in 2004.[28] The legal right to asylum was articulated in the Universal Declaration of Human Rights under Article 14: 'Everyone has the right to seek and enjoy in other countries, freedom from persecution' and this was elaborated in the 1951 Refugee Convention. This right does not amount to universal protection for all human life. Rather, it is the gift of each state underscored by the political *bios* of citizenship and the difference in interpretation between states is very wide-ranging. In 2004, 90 per cent of Iraqi refugees in Jordan were given convention status and granted asylum as compared to 52 per cent in the USA and just 0.1 per cent in the United Kingdom.[29] New Labour's strategy is making clear 'how difficult (some) people are finding it to reach this country'.

In 2005 the Blairite journal *Prospect* opened up a debate about the limits of diversity. This debate has its origins in 1998 and was stimulated by the Conservative ideologue David Willets who argued that at the heart of the contemporary political formation in Britain is a 'progressive dilemma'. Diversity in values and by extension 'culture' he argued would mean that the British people wouldn't be willing to pay for welfare provision. Willets claimed: 'This is America versus Sweden. You can have a Swedish welfare state provided that you are a homogeneous society with intensely shared values.'[30] David Goodhart summed up the debate when he concluded: 'To put it bluntly – most of us prefer our own kind.'[31] While he tried to hedge around the issue of who exactly is included in 'our own kind', this is essentially little more than a nativist ontology that is directly connected to the legacy of new and old forms of race thinking. He continued: 'The implicit "calculus of affinity" in media reporting of disasters is easily mocked – two dead Britons will get the same space as 200 Spaniards or 2,000 Somalis. Yet every day we make similar calculations in the distribution of our own resources.'[32] Goodhart and his kind perform an extraordinary act of historical revisionism when they claim that diversity is the cause for concern. As Paul Gilroy has commented: 'The racisms of Europe's colonial and imperial past preceded the appearance of migrants inside European citadels. It was racism not diversity that made them a problem.'[33] It follows that it is the legacy of racism and not diversity that inhibits affinity and mutuality.

The 'calculus of affinity' has nothing to do with a state of nature but is rather a particular legacy of the creation of a racialized *bios* in which the nation is constructed as the extension of the heterosexual family. Here 'cultural diversity' is about the limits on what can be assimilated. The etymology of the word 'integrate' is to make into 'the whole'. In this sense, it is about being made 'the same' as the social totality. I want to argue that there may be other ways to configure a politics that is agile enough to lay bare the degree to which this is a product of history and not some natural affinity for one's own.

Globalization has produced a tremendous movement of people. It is estimated that some 145 million people are living outside their countries of birth; in 1975 the number was 85 million. The global economic and political elites are able to move across borders at will; yet there remains profound anxiety about the global movement of persons. As Zygmunt Bauman has pointed out: 'the riches are global, the misery is local'.[34]

In his article 'Inequality of world incomes: what is to be done?' Robert Hunter Wade points to the uneven distribution of wealth on a global scale.[35] The richest 20 per cent control 82.7 per cent of the world's income: the poorest 20 per cent have just 1.4 per cent of world income. Hunter Wade claims that this pattern is becoming more marked, with the result that the world will be divided into two zones. The first he calls the *Zone of Peace*, or what we might call relative peace, centring on the informational centres of the Pacific Rim, North America and Western Europe. The exploitation of natural resources is supplanted by the pursuit of technological innovation. We might also add that these places also become targets for terrorism. The second he calls the *Zone of Turmoil*. A rising proportion of the population finds access to basic necessities restricted while at the same time seeing others driving around in Mercedes. He argues: 'Large numbers see migration to the wealthy zone as their only salvation, and a few are driven to redemptive terrorism directed at the symbolic centres of the powerful.'[36] We cannot understand what drives the desperate to hide in the undercarriages of planes without taking account of the extreme economic polarizations that divide our world. There is evidence to suggest that one of the benefits of migration is the redistribution of wealth. The World Bank's Committee on Payment and Settlement Systems found that the flow of funds from migrant workers back to their families in underdeveloped countries was a significant source of income. In 2005 it estimated the total worldwide value of such remittances as over US$230 billion involving some 175 million migrants. For some poor countries the remittance from people sending money home is as high as a third of the gross domestic product.[37]

The Economist is right to highlight 'the line between those whose passports allow them to move and settle reasonably freely across the richer world's borders, and those who can do so only hidden in the back of a truck, and with forged papers'.[38] The deadly consequences have already been outlined, yet, as Paul Gilroy has put it, a lingering 'imperial topography' creates hierarchies between those whose lives are cherished and the bare life at the border.[39] The 3,000 dead of September 11, 2001 are remembered in the exercise of patriotic *Gemeinschaft* and civilized outrage. The unnamed and undocumented migrant workers who perished in the World Trade Center on that day direct us to the development of a broader conscience, which connects with the plight of today's migrants.

What of the 3,000 and rising who have died invisible, stateless deaths at the borders of Europe? What of the wretched at the border and those who fall from the sky?

The Wings of Icarus

Bruegel's famous masterpiece *Landscape with the Fall of Icarus* depicts a scene where a young boy falls into the sea while people are going about the business of their day – be it ploughing a field or watching a flock – indifferent to the tragedy of the boy tumbling from air (see Figure 1.3). In the Greek myth, Icarus took flight from imprisonment wearing fragile wings that his father – Daedalus – made for him. Ignoring his father's warning, Icarus, full of escape's promise, flew too close to the sun, which melted the wax holding the feathers of his wings together and hurtled him downward to a watery death.

While the reference is to Greek antiquity, Bruegel's landscape is a sixteenth-century one. He lived through violent times in which purges against Protestants were taking place all over Europe. His painting outlines a landscape that is indifferent to suffering, the ploughman keeps his head down and the herdsman looks upward as Icarus's legs disappear into the ocean. The picture, I think, is as relevant to the twenty-first century as it was when bloody orgies of religious persecution ravaged Europe almost 500 years ago. Today's Icarus is carried skyward by metal wings that are not melted by the sun but his flight is no less risky. Rather, the fall from the sky is produced under the white heat of globalization.

Bruegel's painting has prompted poets to contemplate the nature of human indifference. In 1938 W. H. Auden wrote in his 'Musée des Beaux Arts' of how 'everything turns away' from 'something amazing, a boy falling out of the sky'.[40] Similarly, American poet William Carlos Williams ends his poem 'Landscape with the Fall of Icarus' with the sober accusation:

Figure 1.3 Pieter Bruegel, *Landscape with the Fall of Icarus*, c.1558, reproduced courtesy of the Royal Museum of Fine Arts of Belgium, Brussels

> a splash quite unnoticed
> this was
> Icarus drowning[41]

Both poets are alert to the *active inaction* on the part of citizens who turn away or play deaf to Icarus. All these issues are pointedly relevant to the anonymous people who are falling from the London skies today. As the modern Icarus hides in the undercarriages of planes and is carried toward Gatwick and Heathrow his corpse passes over Lunar House in Croydon. Yet the stories of those who fall tragically are hidden and appear only fleetingly in the public realm – a newsflash across the screen of conscience.

   On 2 August 1999, Flight 520 from Conakry, Guinea touched down at Zaventem International Airport in Brussels. The 200 passengers, who included businessmen, bureaucrats and holidaymakers, disembarked quickly after the long flight. At 10.10 a.m. an airport worker pulled up at gate B-40 where the plane was about to be refuelled. He smelled something. He brought a ladder and looked into the undercarriage wheel well. He saw a skinny brown leg dangling, with a blue and white sandal on its foot. He called the airport police. They found there the dead bodies of two boys: Yaguine Koita, aged fourteen, and Fodé Tounkara, aged fifteen. With them was found a plastic bag stuffed with birth certificates, school report cards, photographs and an envelope containing a letter.

On the envelope, in Yaguine's handwriting, was written in French – 'In case we die, deliver to Messrs. The members and officials of Europe.' Their message reads:

> Excellencies, Messrs, members and officials of Europe.
>
> We have the honour and pleasure and great confidence in you to write this letter to talk to you of the objective of our journey and the suffering of us, the children and young people of Africa.
>
> But first of all, we present to you our sweetest, most adoring and respectful salutations in the world. To that effect, be our support and our aid. You are for us, in Africa, the ones whom we must ask for help. We appeal to you, for the love of your continent for the feelings you have toward your people and above all for the affinity and love you have for your children whom you love like life itself. Moreover, for the love and meekness of our creator, almighty God, who has given you all the good experience, wealth and power to build and organise well your continent to become the most beautiful and admirable of all.
>
> Messrs, members and officials of Europe, we appeal to your solidarity and kindness for help in Africa, we have problems and several shortcomings regarding children's rights.
>
> Regarding our problems, we have war, disease, malnutrition, etc. As for children's rights, in Africa and above all in Guinea, we have too many schools but a great lack of education and training. Only in private schools can one have a good education and training, but it takes a great sum of money, and our parents are poor and they have to feed us. Nor do we have sports schools where we can practise football, basketball or tennis.
>
> That is why we, African children and youth, ask you to create a great efficient organization for Africa to allow us to progress.
>
> And if you see that we have sacrificed and risked our lives, it is because there is too much suffering in Africa and we need you to struggle against poverty and put an end to war in Africa. Nevertheless, we want to study and we ask you to help us in Africa to study like you.
>
> Finally, we appeal to you to excuse us very, very much for daring to write this letter to the great personages to whom we owe much respect. And do not forget that it is to you that we must bemoan our weakness in Africa.
>
> Yaginue Koita and Fodé Tounkara[42]

The letter reads like hope's spectre and evidence of the human cost of world divisions in wealth and opportunity. Yet, it is not simply a matter of calling for compassion for those caught in this terrible fate. In fact, compassion itself can be a damaging thing, as pointed out earlier by Žižek. Richard Sennett, writing in a different context, has talked about the kinds of compassion that wound, where compassion imposes a division between the magnanimity of those who give it and the compulsory gratitude demanded of those who receive it.[43] Hannah Arendt offers a similar caution when she writes, 'compassion speaks only to the extent that it has to reply directly to the sheer expressionist sound and gestures through which suffering becomes audible and visible in the world'.[44] It is not, then, just a matter of taking notice of the splash made by Icarus or the sound of the jets overhead.

Indeed, we might think about the ways in which the 'grid of immigration' sets up relationships of debt and gratitude. Here, at best, the 'host' is always cast as being gracious and as granting the exile a favour. The 'immigrant' is forced to express gratitude. One of the things that I find hard to listen to is the expression of thanks made routinely in meetings with refugees and asylum seekers. The script is already written regardless of whether one wants to perform the role or not. Meanwhile, the words that ring in my mind are the cacophony of racist complaints about the 'new strangers' that confront one at every turn in the 'host's' world.

It is time to think differently about the global movement of persons, to develop a new language, or at least to try to reach beyond the 'grid of immigration' that constructs the relationship between immigrant and host. Who is not an immigrant in a global world where culture, money, music and even imagination travel without the necessity of physical movement? And if everyone is an immigrant then no one is, and it is here that I have some sympathy for Žižek's complaint discussed earlier. Categories like the 'illegal immigrant' and 'bogus asylum seeker' retain their power and currency precisely because they provide the limit point of who belongs and who does not. As Paul Gilroy suggests: 'The figure of the immigrant is part of the very intellectual mechanism that holds us – post-colonial Europeans, black and white, indeterminate and unclassifiable – hostage.'[45]

It is time to make a case for the normality of movement; at the same time there are difficult questions to be faced. Is it simply about opening national borders and 'putting people to work' as some on the left have argued? The danger here is of creating an unregulated licence for capital to exploit the deracinated and desperate. It is chilling to read that economic analysts on the right come to the same position and conclude with glee: 'migration probably raises the living standards of the rich (think of all those foreign nannies and waiters) and the returns to capital (hence the enthusiasm of employers for more flexible policies)'.[46] In the world of liquid rights and individual insecurity the argument for the liberalization of immigration controls may also play into the hands of unscrupulous and exploitative interests. However, it is hard to imagine a situation for the displaced persons of the twenty-first century worse than it is now. Prey to those who profit from illegal traffic, the indifference of immigration officers and hostile street racists, they are at the sharp end of globalization.

Perhaps the argument for more liberal immigration controls couched within an economic logic is necessary. This may be an opportunity to bring further state-sanctioned border killing to an end, where the bare life at the border is little more than the archaic figure of *homo sacer* who can be killed without sacrifice. It is clear that economic liberalism and the Third Way agree on one thing, and that is the necessity of the project of assimilationism; put simply, that immigrants have to become like the wider society. While both can applaud a cosmetic cosmopolitanism in the urban mix of colours, sounds and flavours, neither is willing to question the interconnection of race and nation that defines the terms of citizenship and belonging. This is ultimately about the legacy of racial thinking and whiteness that continues to provide a privileged passport to those who seek to move across the lines drawn around European nation states.

Conclusion: The Look to the Sky

The jets carrying the bodies of tragic stowaways pass over the offices of the Immigration and Nationality Directorate at Lunar House and Apollo House in Croydon. Before they fall, these bodies pass through the 'immigration line' both physically and metaphorically. The pressure of the asylum system is felt intensely within these austere buildings, whose names celebrate space flights. Every time a scaremongering headline appears in the *Daily Mail* or *Daily Express* it translates into political pressure and reaction inside Lunar House. The irony of the situation is that while a ferocious debate about immigration raged during the 2005 general election campaign, the government policy had been draconian and uncompromising for a long while. Removals of failed asylum seekers had doubled since 1997. In 2004, 12,000 people including children were deported. The backlog of asylum seekers waiting an initial decision is under 10,000, its lowest level for a decade. There is nothing wrong with fast decisions, as long as they are good ones. Part of the purgatory of having to suffer the present system is the waiting and uncertainty (Figure 1.4). The public odium directed at immigrants and asylum seekers is paradoxically not really about the stranger in our midst. Rather, this rhetoric is concerned with the shape and the shaping of the 'us', nationally and locally.

A remarkable story is partially hidden in the dust raised by the public row over immigration. The Immigration and Nationality Directorate is not always a happy place to work. The political pressure to process asylum claims quickly

Figure 1.4 Waiting (*photograph by author*)

results in frequent mistakes. Independent adjudicators upheld 20 per cent of asylum appeals in 2004; papers and passports are routinely lost, causing massive anxiety to those awaiting judgement. Staff in the IND feel beleaguered and this part of the Civil Service has a reputation for the highest number of staff suicides. Even the immigration officers feel trapped in a way that C. Wright Mills would recognize.[47] One frontline worker at Lunar House commented that this imperfect system leaves her feeling 'anxious, frustrated and demotivated' so that she feels disappointed in herself because she 'has to act in an uncaring, unsupportive way when dealing with customers'. Activists and members of the community dissatisfied with how the immigration service works set up an organization called South London Citizens. One of its early meetings was held at Goldsmiths College. In November 2004 they decided to conduct an enquiry into the workings of Lunar House, which I mentioned at the beginning of this chapter. They took the inspired decision to take evidence from both immigration officers and asylum seekers. At one meeting there was the extraordinary moment when an immigration officer stood up in a crowded room and apologized to the users present for the misery caused by the workings of Lunar House. The cynic might say one apology does nothing to change the Kafkaesque workings of the institution, but the enquiry rattled the government and made it take notice. Indeed, I think the South London Citizens group is the realization of what Edward Said would call 'the practice of identities other than those given by the flag or the national war of the moment'.[48]

The alliance between the workers and the users of Lunar House did not continue, however, and the Public and Commercial Services Union – the main representative of IND workers – decided not to give written or oral evidence to the enquiry, citing job insecurity and fear that the workers would being held responsible for the 'political decisions concerning draconian immigration laws'.[49] The employees are placed in an ambiguous position with regard to their economic well-being and the distress and anguish caused by the nature of the system. Some IND employees enjoyed their work and benefited financially and socially from the quality of life that it afforded them. There is also evidence that immigration officers abuse their power. *The Observer* newspaper conducted a covert investigation at Lunar House showing that James Dawute, immigration officer, promised Tanya, an eighteen-year-old Zimbabwean girl, help with her asylum case in exchange for sex. Video, text and mobile phone evidence posted on the newspaper's website showed that over a two-week period the young woman – who had been a rape victim – is promised help. The video camera is the young woman's witness. At a noodle bar in East Croydon, Dawute's intentions are captured on tape. 'I'm very honest and I keep my word', he reassured Tanya. He arranges for a hotel and while the young woman, still uncertain, is reassured by Dawute, 'I will tell you when we are alone ... because we are going to have sex.'[50]

Such cases are extreme abuses of the system. Yet, I would suggest these are simply exaggerations of the inequalities and vulnerabilities that are part of the architecture of the system. There are two entrances for users of Lunar House. 'Managed Migration' receives its visitors through the front door. The sight of people standing in line is blocked from external view by screens (Figure 1.5). Those entering the building pass through a security check similar to passport control at an airport. Asylum seekers, on the other hand, enter the building through an austere entrance at the back; they are dealt with separately and this simply reinforces the distinction between a 'managed' and an 'unwanted' human presence. Inside, users wait in the immigration halls on metal seats that are bolted to the floor. The immigration officers sit behind a glass screen. In June 2005 a senior Home Office official who was showing round the delegation of which I was part joked that the seats were bolted to the floor so that users couldn't throw them through the glass windows. In these very public places users have to explain their claim for asylum, including sometimes traumatic accounts of rape, torture or violence. They are not places for sensitive hearing. A student who gave evidence to the enquiry commented: 'The seating for those being interviewed was unusually far from the desk of the interviewing officer. The only chance of communication was when your body tilted strongly forward and you sat on the edge of the bench. People slightly shorter than me would not be able to speak to the Officer and sit at the same time.'[51] Applicants are literally on the edge of their seats; the whole system is predicated on the idea that human mobility is a problem, that if you move across the borders of a state then you become a problem. Yet, at the same time the mobility of persons is an essential fact of life. Much to the embarrassment of the government and the Home Office 'illegal immigrants' had been employed to clean the IND's offices.[52]

Amid the wave of controversies about the immigration service, Home Secretary John Reid told a Parliamentary Select Committee in May 2006: 'Our system is not fit for purpose. It is inadequate in terms of its scope, it is inadequate in terms of its information technology, leadership, management systems and processes.'[53] Despite such a public admission, there is still little sign of an open public debate about the need for global movement and public investment in an infrastructure that could deliver a humane immigration system in keeping with the complexities of population movement in the twenty-first century.

However, the South London Citizens' enquiry suggests a kind of opening and the development of a global sensibility. Zygmunt Bauman wrote: 'All communities are imagined. The global community is no exception to that rule … '[54] Similarly Paul Gilroy has pointed towards a way of re-imagining a sense of global community through the idea of the planetary, which captures both a sense of movement and a worldly reach.[55] I am appealing to a hope for the emergence of a consciousness of planetary belonging; this sounds very weak, I know, even as I write these words. Jean Améry comments that the only universal human quality that we all carry in our bodies is time: 'Time is always within us, just as space is around us.'[56] It is this sense of time being deposited within us at each breath and on every heartbeat that might provide the meter

Figure 1.5 Behind the screens at Lunar House erected to block the public view (*photograph by author*)

for a shared sense of planetary belonging. A sense of worldly time alerts us to the shared vulnerability in living now without recourse to the clichés of universal common humanity. We are each living this sense of shared global time but from an unimaginably diverse range of vantage points scattered throughout the world.

When we look into the sky what do we see? Is it a window or a mirror? If it is a mirror does it simply reflect back the image of us and the parochial concerns of nations? 'The sky that hangs over our head is no longer domestic', remarked Primo Levi.[57] Raising our eyes to the sky might offer another kind of invitation to see the refracted or deflected traces of global route ways that are drawn in it by the contrail of a jet threading its way toward the horizon (Figure 1.6). Here is one place we find the scale of global sociology. It is only from space that a sense of the globe as a whole can be apprehended and perhaps as we contemplate the sky we will find the impression of a truly global human society.

It is not just a matter of raising our eyes skyward. The task is to link individual biographies and the questions they raise with larger global, social and historical forces. As we zoom in from the global process to the local dispute,

Figure 1.6 'The sky is no longer domestic': a jet passes over the offices of immigration in Croydon (*photograph by author*)

from the jet at 13,000 feet to the town hall meeting below, the distance spanned by the falling body of the unnamed victim of globalization, we find the scale of global sociology. This seemingly uncanny occurrence reveals the profound ways in which belonging and movement are regulated by the immigration line. I have argued here that the conception of human movement through the grid of 'immigrant/host' is implicated in the fate of bare life at the border. As Paul Gilroy comments, the notion of 'illegal immigrant' and the 'bogus asylum seeker' holds us hostage. In order to break free it is necessary to confront the legacy of empire and racism and its impact on the political debate about migration. The task of sociology here is to make explicit the assumed terms of the debate, point to the hypocrisy and double standards of the present system and pay attention to that which is ignored. The following chapter explores the legacy of racism and belonging from a very different angle. This discussion deals with the ways in which people are both defined and situated in the cityscape through racial grafts and divisions. Focusing on the ways young people navigate safe and dangerous places in London, it examines how home and belonging are negotiated and remade in surprising and often counter-intuitive ways. While this chapter has focused on the nature of the border, what follows is an attempt to understand the interplay of racism and multiculture within the metropolitan landscape and the lines that are drawn and blurred as a result.

CHAPTER 2

Home from Home[1]

How do people – particularly the young – make cities a home? How are the spaces of the city marked by colour-coded exclusions and what are the risks involved in crossing its boundaries? In her beautiful memoir *From Deepest Kilburn* Gail Lewis described the London neighbourhoods where she was raised as a 'patchwork of no-go and go areas'.[2] While racists loomed and sometimes attacked, she portrayed the ordinary ways a young black woman navigated inhospitable streets and made them secure. 'I negotiated this chequerboard of on-off bounds easily and didn't really experience it as hardship. The only thing to avoid was the gangs and individuals who were at great pains to keep "their territory" free from 'blacks'.[3] In short, she held in her head a coded map of the area in order both to make sense of it and to move through its hospitable and unwelcoming places.

Racism is a spatial and territorial form of power. It aims to claim and secure territory, but it also projects associations on to space that in turn invest racial associations and attributes in places. Beneath the sign of names like 'Brixton' or 'Handsworth' or 'Southall' are racially coded landscapes, created as exotic or dangerous by turns, that act like a kind of A–Z of racist geography.[4] In this sense racism draws a map, it creates places in the process of narrating them. This shading of place isn't simple or one-way, as Gail Lewis's account illustrates: alternative stories are told and in the process new maps of belonging, safety and risk are drawn. Neighbourhoods are thus made and remade as stories are told about them. Franco Moretti points out that this process also works the other way round: 'without a certain kind of space, a certain kind of story is simply impossible'.[5] These stories have consequences as they open up the social landscape and make potential action and behaviour possible. The aim of this chapter is to interpret this process in contemporary London and listen in particular to the way young people represent and inhabit the spaces of the city.

At the end of Italo Calvino's book *Invisible Cities* his protagonist says:

The inferno of the living is not something that will be; if there is one, it is what is already here, the inferno where we live today, that we form by being together. There are two ways to escape suffering it. The first is easy for many: accept the inferno and become such a part of it that you can no longer see it. The second is risky and demands constant vigilance and apprehension: seek and learn to recognize who and what, in the midst of the inferno, are not inferno, then make them endure, give them space.[6]

The inferno here might be analogous to the city of containers, of segments, of the chequerboard of hatreds and violence – a damaged home. The tactics that young people use that are described in what follows point to moments when refuge and belonging are given space. These openings cannot be reduced to a political manifesto, or some didactic call from the streets. Rather, they point to quiet transformations and fleeting moments in which living with and through difference are realized; or, put another way, which make bearable what might be otherwise unbearable. Hanif Kureishi, commenting on his childhood experiences, said 'for me London became a kind of inferno of pleasure and madness'.[7] London is a place to explore the pleasures of freedom at the same time as it is a city divided by hatred, neuroses and phobias.

What follows is drawn from the *Finding a Way Home Project*, which began in 1996 and focused on two parts of London – Deptford and the Isle of Dogs – and examined how young people navigate the spaces of the city, how they make a cosmopolitan and multiracist city their home. Anne Phoenix has pointed out that the reality of Britain today is uneven drift towards a multicultural future, where transcultural openings and multicultural dialogues exist alongside stark new divisions and old hatreds. Reflecting on the fiftieth anniversary of the arrival of the *Empire Windrush* – the ship that brought colonial citizen migrants to Britain from the Caribbean – she argues that 'the contradictions and complexities of multicultures and multiracisms are a notable legacy of the Windrush'.[8]

The fact that London is a multicultural and cosmopolitan city is now beyond question, but this brings no guarantees. How may we try to understand the ways in which people live in and through the paradoxes and incommensurabilities of racism? There are moments of critical opening to be found if we look and listen for them. The question remains, how might this be achieved and how can we recognize this process when we see it and hear it?

From Exegesis to Dialogue: The Finding a Way Home Project

George Marcus has argued that, in the wake of the criticism of ethnographic authority,[9] it is necessary to abandon the way of narrating culture from the vantage point of an omniscient 'eye' and move towards an account of culture from the positioned or situated 'I' of the ethnographer. In short he argues for 'redesigning the observer'.[10] He also argues for the importance of abandoning or at least unsettling the 'know it all' authority of realist accounts and moving from high-minded exegesis ('this is really how the world is!') toward dialogue. In a sense, this is precisely what we did in the *Finding a Way Home Project* as we offered young people a variety of techniques or technologies to observe (photograph, video or map) their own lives and narrate them (audio diaries and conventional interviews). This experiment in dialogic representation was conducted over the course of a whole school year. Before discussing the findings of the research I want first to describe the methodology and provide some background on the two neighbourhoods in which the research was based.

The project began in 1996 and was a collaborative piece of work that included Phil Cohen, Michael Keith, Tamina Maula, Tim Lucas, Sarah Newlands and Lande Pratt. While many of the materials generated that I am about to use were produced collectively (and I'd like to thank my colleagues for letting me use them here), the interpretations and shortcomings of what follows are my sole responsibility. In the writing and analysis of this work there was both a commitment to hold – however unevenly – to the spirit of dialogue, while at the same time offering critical insights and reflections on what was offered in the representations made by the young people themselves. The research focused on young people aged thirteen and fourteen. Ethnography was conducted in the school setting using the multimedia methodology of cameras, tape recorders and video cameras, and involved working with two Year 9 classes of young people – one in a school in Deptford, south London, and the other in the Isle of Dogs, east London (see Figure 2.1).

We chose these areas because, while they are very close to each other and separated only by the River Thames, they have very different histories of multicultural formation and popular racism. South of the river, Deptford is part of former London dockland. It has ancient connections with imperial trade and expansion: it was here the East India Company was formed. It was also a place where popular racism reared its head.

In 1948 the National Union of Seaman agitated to stop black people working on British ships. Colonial citizen migrants established themselves in the area in the 1940s and 1950s and experienced harassment and violent attacks from local racists. In 1977 the extreme right staged a famous march in this part of London. A few years later, in 1981, thirteen young black people died in a house fire in New Cross in the south of the area. To some degree, as a result of the mobilizations against these events, there is a strong sense that the racists have been run out of this part of London and that Deptford is a

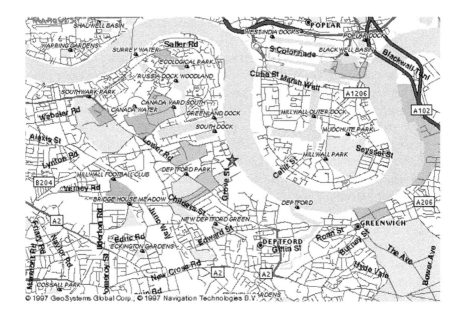

Figure 2.1 Deptford and the Isle of Dogs (reproduced courtesy of GooSystems Global Corp)

harmonious multicultural area. This is signalled by one local resident who pointed out that a piece of National Front graffiti left to fade on the wall – and not removed – was a metaphor for the declining appeal of organized racism in the area. In 1991 around 30,000 people lived in the district and 28 per cent described themselves as from 'ethnic minority backgrounds'. Those people considering themselves black, including Black Caribbean and Black African, made up 28 per cent of the total population, around 4 per cent identified themselves as Irish, 4 per cent identified as Chinese, and less than 2 per cent were from Pakistani, Bangladeshi or Indian origin.[11]

The Isle of Dogs is a tear-shaped peninsula jutting into the river on the north bank of the Thames. The origin of its name is unknown, although there are many myths about it. Some say it is where, in the sixteenth century, Henry VIII kept his hunting dogs. Others say the name dates back further, to a medieval hunting trip, in which the huntsmen were killed, leaving their hunting dogs to roam the area and their ghosts are said to haunt it still. With the emergence of London as an imperial city and the construction of the West India Docks, the peninsula became the centre of the imperial docks. The traces of these connections are everywhere embedded in the landscape; many of the place names have maritime connections. What's interesting about the Isle of Dogs is that it has global connections and yet has an intense sense of locality and insularity.

At the time of the 1991 census the total population was around 11,000. The ethnic breakdown was 78 per cent white, 6 per cent Black African and Afro-Caribbean, 8 per cent Bangladeshi (mainly Bengali), 1 per cent Indian and Pakistani, and 3 per cent Chinese/Vietnamese. In the post-war era another series of folk demons has taken the place of the ghostly medieval hunting dogs whose barks were said to haunt the 'island'. The area has also been viewed – particularly in the work of Phil Cohen – as a microcosm of the politics of nation and race.[12] Chris Husbands argued in his seminal study that East End racism documents a broad catalogue of local racism: from popular anti-Semitism, which helped to pioneer the Aliens Act of 1905 (Britain's first immigration control), through the Mosleyite agitations of the inter-war years, to the dockers' support for Enoch Powell's 'rivers of blood' speech in 1968, and mounting harassment of the Bangladeshi community during the 1980s, which culminated in the victory of the BNP candidate Derek Beacon in 1993.[13] Some saw this victory as the expression of the intrinsic nature of racist culture in East London.

Using the perceptions of the young people, the research set out to examine the adequacy of the understanding racism and multiculture in the opposing representations of the two areas: Deptford as a place where 'race problems' have been supplanted by an emergent multicultural harmony; and the Isle of Dogs as a bastion of entrenched racism. We worked with forty-two young people in Deptford (twenty-three girls and nineteen boys) and forty-seven in the Isle of Dogs (twenty-seven girls and twenty boys) who represented the diversity of ethnic groups present within the two areas.

The ethnic backgrounds of the samples were as follows: 38 per cent of the total were white English (eighteen girls, seventeen boys); 17 per cent were black African or African Caribbean (eight girls, nine boys); 18 per cent were South Asian (ten girls, eight boys); 16 per cent were Chinese/Vietnamese (twelve girls, four boys); 2 per cent of the young people were of mixed parentage (one girl, one boy); and there was one other young woman who was of South American parentage. The school ethnography was in the main conducted by the four research officers employed on the project during the first year. The research was completed in 1998.

The four researchers worked intensively in the school throughout the year. They kept fieldwork diaries and helped out with school activities, in particular an anti-bullying initiative on the Isle of Dogs. For each of the research exercises interviews were conducted either in pairs or individually. One of the successes of the research was the implementation of a multimedia methodology that enabled young people to use a variety of representational strategies to construct their landscapes of safety and danger and included photography, written stories, art work, mapping and video. These research exercises generated over

250 hours of tape-recorded interviews and 11 hours of video footage. What was immediately interesting about the material is that, because of the choice of media we offered them, the young people were able to find the one they were most comfortable with. For some it was the photography exercises, while for others the written exercises and audio diaries proved the most appealing. What follows is largely drawn from the photographic exercises and visual dimensions of the project.

'Youth Gangs' and Local Patriotism 'Talking Big'

Much of the discussion about public safety is underpinned by common-sense assumptions about the 'problem of male youth'. Young men in the inner cities are seen as urban interlopers, agents of street crime and violence. While these young men *appear* spectacularly in news reports purporting to represent 'gang yobbery', 'football hooliganism' or 'race riots', they almost never speak: they are seen but not heard. Academic discussions have centred on whether such characterizations represent a realistic account of the situation or whether they form moral panics whose origins lie elsewhere.[14] Since 1997 the policy agenda outlined by the Labour government has to some extent shifted the terms of this debate, paradoxically by drawing on some of the rhetoric, if not the argument of the common-sense position, in order to respond to moral panics about ungovernable youth by resorting to policies of zero tolerance against crime and antisocial behaviour.

Tony Blair has also connected the issues of youth antisocial behaviour with tackling racism, particularly in the aftermath of the murder of black teenager Stephen Lawrence and the inquiry into his death. At the Labour Party conference in September of 1998 he made this connection clear:

> From tomorrow kids can be picked up for truancy, young children alone in the streets can be subject to curfews, parents made responsible for their children's behaviour. From April anti-social behaviours can be taken to court and punished. Don't show zero imagination, help us to have a zero tolerance of crime ... When a young black student, filled with talent is murdered by racist thugs and Stephen Lawrence becomes a household name not because of the trial into his murder but because of an inquiry into why his murderers are walking free, it isn't just wrong; it weakens the very bonds of decency and respect we need to make our country strong. We stand stronger together.[15]

The government's approach is focused on the management of *risk* through the mapping of crime hot spots and unsafe areas, regulating who is in them when, through child curfews and the invocation of a specific notion of safe space. In this way highly *localized* micro public spheres become the focus of new forms of state intervention through more or less repressive forms of policing and self-government, while at the same time 'community cohesion' and other types of communitarian rhetoric become a catch-all response for social problems that have radically different social qualities. Here white racist violence, the marginalization of some sections of ethnic minority youth and 'black on black' violence is understood as manifestations of the same problem, namely young men who are out of control.

At the same time, young people's narratives, while they sometimes borrow from the vocabulary of policy elites, also draw on their own version of the state of play, which is structured by their positioning within the landscapes that they draw for themselves. While young men appear but don't speak in this public debate, it seems that young women are completely absent. Indeed, the language of community cohesion and strong community may have very different effects for men and women and reproduce gender inequalities both in relation to access to public space and the political sphere more broadly. Iris Marion Young refers to the 'totalizing impulse' in which people are straitjacketed by the communities they are defined as being part of. As a result, the language of community 'denies the difference within and between subjects'.[16] She privileges the city as an alternative theatre for difference that is open to 'unassimilated otherness'.[17] In more prosaic terms, the appeals to community in the multicultural contexts described here may be little more than a mechanism through which adult authority is exercised both inside localities and by state-sanctioned organizations. The picture that emerged within the representations of young people is more complicated than the current policy debate will allow. A good example of this is the way in which youth gangs were discussed in the two locations.

In Deptford there was a strong sense that male youth gangs were distributed as distinct territorial units throughout south London. While talk about gangs was pervasive, only three of the young people interviewed had any direct connection to these gangs. It was claimed that mainly black young people initially formed youth gangs as a response to racism. These gangs were predominantly male but there were also a small number of female members. Gangs had emblematic territorial names like 'Ghetto Boys', 'Deptford Men' and 'Brixton Youth', and at one level they bore the marks of a racist mapping linked to the popular iconography of black street crime and the moral panic surrounding 'mugging'. At the same time, the incorporation of these spatialized gang labels was an attempt to recode these associations. In some of the accounts by young white people the stories about gangs were viewed as a diffuse source of anxiety and threat; at the same time there was a reluctance to racialize these feelings or focus them in some concrete way, for example by invoking the figure of 'the black mugger'. At the end of one interview in which a young white girl had talked extensively and quite fearfully about the threat of gangs, she was asked if there was anything else she would like to say; she replied, after a short pause: 'Yeah, about the gangs and that. It is true that they are mostly black boys involved, but it's not because they're black.'

For the boys in particular, the symbolic nature of these gang labels had to do with claiming a sense of place and identification with that place. To proclaim 'Ghetto Boy' status brought with it both a space of preferred identity and a claim to entitlement. The area around New Cross's Milton Court Estate was referred to as the 'Ghetto' and as one boy pointed out 'To me now to be from Ghetto is an honour.' To recode the association as an emblem of pride changes the coordinates of racist mappings, which criminalize both places and people. Inner urban districts are the canvas on which racist fears and stigma are inscribed. What seems to be happening here is that these inscriptions are turned back on themselves. Local patriotism is a response and a mirroring back of a negative urban imagery that is in turn recoded as positive. Such claims often projected masculine autonomy and also a sense of being placed in a landscape. For example, young men would give the numbers of the local telephone boxes as if they were their own public/private home from home. The talk about gangs became a means through which these young men positioned themselves against the ways in which the places they lived were racially stigmatized. Claiming and renaming place redraws the map of belonging. They are an alternative to the A–Z of racist geography but they do not completely break free from it. The ludic dimensions of the process can be limiting as well as empowering. The local patriotism expressed through such means is a kind of masculine choreography, a local pride that 'talks big' and responds to routine stigmatization. The compensatory pleasures in moves of this kind are important to acknowledge, because there is real fun to be had in countering snobbery and ignorance in this way. Yet, a local pride may also carry 'hidden injuries'.[18] Equally, it is important that conflicts and rivalries that are spoken through these terms can result in violence. In September 2006 former 'ghetto boy' Jason Gayle-Bent was stabbed and killed in New Cross. He was attacked by thirty youths alleged to be members from a rival gang from Peckham. While spaces are reclaimed through 'gang talk', it accepts the territorial limits contained within the white racist mapping. Put simply, it is a version of identity that turns the straitjacket of racist urban associations inside out, but remains held in it.

A black girl complained of being labelled by her male peers in this way:

> Just because you know certain people doesn't automatically make you a part of a gang. Like saying I am like a Peckham Girl. I don't think so! I live in Ghetto and the Peckham Boys think I am a Ghetto Girl but because I was born in Peckham the Ghetto Boys think I am a Peckham Girl.

The association of a sense of identity through such naming is a powerful rhetorical device for inscribing myths of origin in local pride. It can be very difficult to detach these labels once they have stuck. Such identities can be a prison as well as a refuge. It was interesting that the young people themselves, and particularly the young women in Deptford, resisted being defined in this way. Nevertheless, while gang territories were acknowledged to be dangerous places, it was generally agreed that the risk from gang violence was low. Yet, at the same time there was an appreciation of the growth in gun crime and the incidents of 'black on black violence'. In the south London context, questions of violence and gang formation were being worked on and assessed, often critically, within the context of peer groups that were multiracial in composition. There was great care here not to slip into generalizations about race or gender or claims that could be applied throughout the district. The assessment of gang formations and youth violence was both critical and cautious.

The situation on the Isle of Dogs differed considerably. A pervasive sense existed within white youth and larger community contexts that 'Asian gangs' constituted the main threat. Here issues of crime, violence and risk were strongly racialized and associated with a specific gendered and ethno/racial category, namely young Bengali men. Claire Alexander has situated this shift within what she calls the 'rise and rise of the Asian gang'. A new folk devil has been constituted in which a 'complex intersection of age, "race" and gender forms the perceptual baseline for the rise of the Asian "gang."'[19] The diverse experiences of young men from south Asian backgrounds are reduced to a grid of essentialized ideas about race and masculinity. These ideas were articulated forcibly among some sections of the white community activists on the Island. One in particular had on a noticeboard in his office a collection of local and national press cuttings that reported 'Asian gang violence'; this was displayed to visitors.

What became clear in discussing youth violence on the Island was the sense of a divide between black and white youth on the one side and Bengalis on the other. This distinction was kept very much alive in local circuits of rumour and gossip; this in turn enabled young white people to appeal to adult authority and common sense in validating claims about violent Asians. Paradoxically, the Bengali young men who are present in the street or seen 'hanging around' are accused of mirroring the exact forms of masculinity embodied by some versions of white working-class young men. Yet these forms of embodiment – be it acting 'flash' or 'bowling' (to walk rolling the shoulders[20]) – are also seen as threatening because they either challenge 'normal' (coded white) claims to determine conduct, or establish exclusionary zones into which whites fear to venture. Some sections of the white population claim that 'Asian gangs' locally are the prime instigators of urban violence. This has developed to such an extent that it supersedes previous concerns over black male criminality associated with motifs of mugging or civil unrest. It was particularly telling that even local activists from the British National Party claimed 'black and white youth' were equally the victims of police 'double standards' when it came to urban violence, while Asian youth were seen to be getting away with attacks on whites and with violent crime. This shift is not complete and echoes of the 'black mugging' discourse are still registered but locally these formulations are increasingly faint.

For Tony Blair, white racism is understood as the antithesis of community and viewed as the violation of common bonds of decency and respect. In the case of the Isle of Dogs, white racism is articulated precisely through the language of community, a community that is coded implicitly with a notion of whiteness, and with an appeal to 'decency' and 'fairness'.[21] Similarly, Anthony Giddens points to the importance of creating a public sphere in which local democracy and community development can ameliorate dilapidation and engender safer cities.[22] What is striking in the accounts of both Blair and Giddens is that they appeal to some kind of intervention in local affairs yet they lack any real sense of context and the complex struggles over belonging and inclusion taking place in particular localities. What I have tried to illustrate above is how the discussion of youth gangs reveals the shape of some of these inclusions and exclusions. This is not to say that this contrast between, on the one hand, the careful and complex interrogation of the meaning of gangs and, on the other, a racist moral panic, is stable or an echo of underlying structural relationships. Rather, what it reveals are emergent patterns that may be reiterated but can also shift and be contested.

One of the limitations of sociological work on youth is the preoccupation with spectacular behaviour that often focuses on young men. One of the concerns here is to give an account of what lies beneath the contours of the concern about conflict, violence and youth crimes. Attention to the unspectacular disrupts some of the easy essentialisms that have dogged both public and academic debates about the position of young people in the postcolonial city.

Magic, Escape and Places of Refuge

Neil Leach has commented that within cities 'symbolic attachments may be grafted onto physical form'.[23] This process of symbolic grafting came through clearly in the photoscape exercises conducted by the young people in the study. We gave them disposable cameras and asked them to photograph places that they felt to be safe and others they felt to be dangerous. Once the photographs had been processed we then asked them to talk us through the decisions they had made and the stories contained in each image. Vikki Bell has shown that belonging is performative, that is, attachments are established through actions and rituals that unfold repeatedly in any given context.[24] Through such actions places are woven into the fabric of the city, producing specific meanings within urban space. As Caroline Knowles points out: 'Race is generated in the social texture of space, and so the analysis of space reveals its racial grammar as forms of social practice to which race gives rise.'[25] Parks, alleyways, playgrounds and hallways were the environmental features most frequently catalogued as dangerous in both study areas. Sometimes these were associated with vulnerability to hateful or threatening behaviour and sometimes they were simply interpreted as unknown and unpopulated and therefore risky. They echoed the way Gail Lewis described how she moved through the chequerboard of the city in Kilburn. What was telling about the photographic exercise was that we requested a specific act of representation that in turn became a kind of performance of belonging. The images produced were, at first glance, sometimes surprising but, as the young people narrated them, they revealed the subtleties within the everyday maps of risk, danger and refuge.

Figure 2.2 shows a photograph taken by a Bengali girl from the Isle of Dogs. This first image shows the public library in Cubitt Town, east London. The library is a safe public space. 'I feel safe because there are people inside the library', she writes. This choice was common to all the Bengali girls for whom the library constituted a space where they felt both safe from harassment by boys and free from surveillance by their parents or members of the extended family. The second image, taken by her friend, shows the girl posing inside the library (see Figure 2.3). Visiting the library was both viewed as appropriate and approved by adults, but the library itself became a space of freedom. Going to the library was both a kind of 'cover story' where girls could find a place to 'hang out' with friends and sometimes to meet boys, as well as being a place to do homework and work on the officially sanctioned school curriculum. The library was also a place of informal learning where the young people expanded the curriculum on their own terms. Public libraries are places of self-improvement in London and contained in patterns of their use are subtle insights into desires regarding social mobility and 'respectable', or, perhaps more accurately, individual resistances to both adult authority and peer pressure. The library represented a cultural no-go area for the kinds of young people by whom these girls felt most threatened. It was off limits to the informal cultures of authority and recognition found in the street or the playground. In contrast the third photograph (Figure 2.4) shows a playground opposite this girl's home. She had experienced racist name-calling and harassment here: 'I feel unsafe because people there always make racist comments. This is opposite are [our] building.' It was safe enough to photograph from a distance perhaps, but the playground was a potential place of danger that needed to be navigated with care particularly during the daily journeys to and from school.

Figure 2.2 Cubitt Town Library (*photograph by participant*)

Most of the accounts by the young people from ethnic minority backgrounds showed a very sophisticated degree of local situated knowledge about high- and low-risk spaces as regards racism. These findings are very close to the pattern contained in Gail Lewis's account of growing up in London in the 1950s. We also used audio diaries individually recorded by young people and group video walkabouts as ways to represent and perform a sense of belonging. These exercises also provided insights into the strategies of precaution that were used to reduce the risk of racial attack. These young people sifted through a large repertoire of observations, stories, memories and feelings. As a result, their maps of their neighbourhood consisted of a shifting web of association that connected people to places and created a highly textured choreography of safety and danger. As the young people travelled across this symbolic landscape, the crude coding of whole areas as either 'racist' or 'multicultural' broke down into a much more sophisticated and tactically useful map of the streets and public/private spaces they moved through.

To account for these patterns of habitation and exclusion it is necessary to understand the interrelationship between gender, race and social class. Yet, the

Figure 2.3 'A safe place' (*photograph by participant*)

Figure 2.4 Unsafe – playground taunts (*photograph by participant*)

Figure 2.5 'Our landing' (*photograph by participant*)

interconnections between these lines of social differentiation are not mechanistic or straightforward.[26] Avtar Brah has written that the search for grand theoretical schema for understanding these connections has been unproductive. She argues, 'they are best construed as historically contingent and context specific relationships'.[27] It is precisely these context-specific contingent relations in which the interplay between structure and agency can be found.

Figure 2.5 is a picture of three white girls from the Isle of Dogs shown in an austere place that they refer to as 'Our landing'. For them this is a safe place where they come to be together as friends in the winter and which they claim by scribbling their names on the wall, an interstitial space between home and street. During a video walkabout these three girls took us to this landing and they talked about the violence that occurs in the surrounding streets between groups of 'white' and 'Asian gangs'. The landing was a refuge, both out of their parents' jurisdiction and away from the activities of the boys. When asked if they were ever afraid of the violence between rival groups of white and Asian boys they answered 'No. Because they know us.' The young women disapproved of the violence but they also felt protected by the codes of local recognition; here too the complexities of whiteness were also in evidence. The 'white girls' were hostile to racism, yet, at another level, their whiteness protected them – they were acknowledged and recognized as belonging to the Isle of Dogs. They were cast within a white territory, regardless of whether or not they agreed with its terms or parameters of inclusion or exclusion. In this example, whiteness, social class and gender intersect to produce an implicit set of parameters that calculate levels of danger and real risks. The kinds of attachments that are spliced into the urban fabric are context and time specific. Put simply, the same physical structures can have very different cultural and symbolic grafts or cultural mappings. The quality of these cultural mappings is dependent on the social profile of the person making them.

Figure 2.6 shows another picture of a stairwell, taken this time by a Vietnamese girl called Ly who lives in Deptford, south London. Here the landing and the area outside her flat are defined as a dangerous place to be passed through quickly. 'This is my least favourite place downstairs from my flat', she writes. It is a danger zone that needs to be crossed in order to reach the safety of home. In her interview she talked about the threats of harassment that she had suffered from neighbours and the vulnerability she feels in the immediate environs of her flat, where Vietnamese families have suffered routine harassment. Through taking photographs these young people were able to record dangerous places from afar, or as in this case claim those spaces

Figure 2.6 Ly's landing (*photograph by participant*)

momentarily through being pictured within them. It is striking that Ly is pictured here in her least favourite place smiling back into the camera, happy and relaxed.

In a sense, the research provided a context in which a performance of belonging could take place – in this case posing for a photograph. The photograph carries both a history of dread and feeling threatened in this place, yet at the same time the act of photographic representation itself is an assertion of presence. The observational act – controlled and conducted by the young person herself – becomes an assertion of belonging in an otherwise hostile place.

Nigel Thrift has argued that in order to understand the qualities of any given landscape it needs to be situated in time.[28] The quality of the cityscape is transformed by night and day and these time geographies have different consequences for men and women[29] and young and old.[30] For many of our informants the risk associated with a particular place was dependent on the time of day they passed through them. Parks could be safe during the day but risky at night; dangerous figures identified here were particularly drug users or alcoholics. Equally, young women reported being threatened and sexually harassed by older men at night around pubs and clubs. The gendering of these landscapes also intersected with issues of race. For example, almost all the black boys from our Deptford sample claimed that they were vulnerable outside their area if they were alone, particularly in places that were constructed as predominantly white (i.e. the neighbouring regions of Eltham and Welling). These accounts often cited the murder of Stephen Lawrence as evidence: in 1993 Stephen Lawrence was travelling home with his friend Duwayne Brooks when he was killed by a group of whites. The same black boys claimed that this would not happen to a black girl in the same situation. Young black women, one of whom reported being chased and harassed in Eltham, contested these suggestions.

The accounts of the young people also disrupted some of the commonly held assumptions about the two districts in question. At the level of the neighbourhood, the young people in our samples identified specific micro-spaces of racism that did not feature on the adult maps. This complicated the notion that particular neighbourhoods or districts were 'racist' while others were havens of 'multicultural harmony'. In the accounts offered by young people in Deptford it was routinely said that very low levels of racism were experienced in the district and that multi-ethnic friendship groups were the norm. However, within these accounts there was evidence of complex forms of racism that militated against intercultural dialogue and friendship. A young white girl spoke insightfully about the pressure that was applied through her parents to make her withdraw from multiracial peer groups and not have black boyfriends. This was despite the fact that her grandmother was in a relationship with a black man and that her father had similarly been in a mixed relationship. This type of censure on mixed relationships was also manifest in the public spaces at street level.

She spoke of an older white youth who worked as a local mechanic:

> He works down the High Street. I've got to walk past his place to [get] to my Nan's house. He's always standing there like looking me up and down and calling me a 'Nigger Lover' and things like that. He's been out with coloured people and still he calls me one as well. I've been out with three coloured people, and he must have been out with four or five girls and he's the one calling me a Nigger Lover!

Accounts like this disrupt any simple notion of multicultural harmony; in this account, intimacy with black people walks down the street hand in hand with gendered racism. The pressure on this girl to disengage from her relationships with black people was palpable, yet to do so would also violate the norms of trust and association that had become established within the peer group. Here we can also find the disruption of racial categories by gender and the complex combination of anti-racist and racist sentiment.

When we asked her where she would call 'home', she chose not the neighbourhood where she had lived in Deptford, but instead projected herself into the adjacent areas of Brockley, Honor Oak Park and Forest Hill (where in fact she had never lived) because she felt that in these districts inter-racial friendships and mixed relationships were not viewed as problematic. Through an act of imagination the place that she called home, or what might be more appropriately thought of as a *home from home*, is created. She has never lived there, but for her it is a place to be herself outside the surveillance and disapproval of adults and peers. It is also outside the circumscriptions of the domestic sphere crossed by racial contradictions and double standards.

This process of making home *out of home* is both banal and remarkable. In his little book *Sketch for a Theory of the Emotions*, Jean-Paul Sartre writes:

> When the paths before us become too difficult, or when we cannot see our way, we can no longer put up with such an exacting and difficult world. All ways are barred and nevertheless we must act. So then we try to change the world, that is, to live it as though the relations between things and their potentialities were not governed by deterministic processes *but by magic*.[31]

I think the process of making home from home is part of this magic. In the vernacular, the phrase is usually about replicating a home in another place. Here I am suggesting that home is made inside domestic or patriotic inhospitalities. In this sense, it is not a matter of replication or mimesis; it is also a matter of making new space.

In the two areas studied, the linkage between place, identity and entitlement was ordered differently. In broad terms the youth community on the Isle of Dogs showed evidence of racial segregation in peer group formation, dating and relationships and other leisure activities. At the same time young Bengalis had developed a range of sophisticated strategies designed to make this ostensibly white racist place into a space that was both navigable and habitable. This involved constructing a series of 'boltholes', be it in the form of libraries or youth clubs, or other safe urban niches across which safe passage could be negotiated.

However, the position of young Bengalis on the Island was also complicated by the intersection of youth and gender identities. This was a particularly acute issue for young women, of course. For them to be seen within the centres of Bengali community around Whitechapel or Poplar meant that they might become the object of gossip within adult spheres. While these places guaranteed safety in numbers, they were also the spaces under constant scrutiny. It should not be surprising then that a group of young Bengali girls chose to hang out on the Island in an area reputed to be a 'racist place' because its whiteness by definition meant it was beyond the sight of prying adult eyes. If I am not comfortable where I am supposed to be safe, I will find comfort outside those places, even though this might mean going to the places associated with racial risk.

In Deptford, it seemed that the pervasive narratives of multicultural harmony provided another kind of resource to claim entitlement and belonging. It was telling that it was a middle-class boy from outside Deptford who perpetrated the only incident of open racist calling that occurred during our research period. In an extraordinary sequence of events, a multiracial male peer group elected one of its members to confront the boy about his record of racist abuse. Here the rhetorical assertion of 'harmony' was reinforced through policing peer racism. However, such claims and attempts to make safe a non-racist youthful public sphere are always partial and temporary. The local homeland was subject to the pressures of disapproving adults and suspicious members of the local police force. In this sense the stability of the notion of 'multicultural harmony' in Deptford was disrupted by the presence of racism inside and outside the area. The example of the young white girl who is forced to find a 'home from home' outside Deptford because she had a black boy friend and was involved in a multiracial peer group is an illustration of unevenness of racism and complexity of multiculture.

Conclusions: Damaged Homes and Places to Be

I want to return to the question I posed at the very beginning, namely how do young people make the postcolonial city a home? Before addressing this directly I first want to reflect on the different associations contained within this notion. John Berger has commented that the notion of home is quarry to very different kinds of moralists. On the one hand there are those who claim ownership of the definition of home in order to wield power. 'The notion of home became a keystone for a code of domestic morality, safeguarding the property (which included women) of the family. Simultaneously the notion of homeland supplied a first article of faith for patriotism, persuading men to die in wars which often served no other interest except that of a minority of their ruling class.'[32] This sense of homeland is profoundly resonant with our current situation in the world after September 11, 2001 and the wars that have come in its wake. Berger points to another reading of the meaning of home. He says that beneath these dominant interests there is an antecedent meaning. Here home is 'the center of the world – not in a geographical, but in an ontological sense ... the place from which the world can be founded'.[33]

Young people make the city a home precisely through producing a kind of phenomenology of home as a way of centring a sense of place in the world. The maps that are produced to document the contours of safety and danger cannot be reduced to typologies or clunking correlations between ethnic categories or gendered identities and the social qualities of a given place. Each individual young person combined available forms of social knowledge to project a map and find a way through. This is an attempt to name something close to what is *Umwelt* in German, namely the world of our desires, our needs and our activities. As Sartre puts it, this world is 'furrowed with straight and narrow paths'.[34]

These landscapes are complex. They cut through time and space but they are also complicated in the ways in which the interplay of habitat and habitation works. Equally, they are produced through the coding of the urban landscapes with cultural and 'racial' grafts and the ways in which people have redrawn those coded maps in their everyday lives. As Fran Tonkiss puts it: 'The random and fragile connections and disconnections of an everyday life, the shortcuts of memory, the dead-ends and private jokes that steer a subject in space, are like so many maps of the city – written over and folded badly, consigned to routine or made up as you go along.'[35] The results can produce remarkable and counter-intuitive things, be it young Bengali girls who go to a 'racist place' to make a 'home from home' or young men who give the numbers of public telephone boxes as 'home contact points'. We have to listen and look carefully to recognize these remarkable things and find new ways for them to be observed and recorded. *The Finding a Way Home* project was such an experiment and for all its undoubted faults it enabled its participants – however incompletely – to be observers and to draw their own maps of their lives. Inside cities there are still further invisible and mute cities. They are places that give space *to be,* not places of identity or unitary or fixed notions of selfhood, but a space to perform and claim belonging amid the inferno of contemporary city life. Despite the damage done by urban geometries of power and exclusion, young people find refuge and ways through the cityscape and in so doing homes are grown out of home.

In the next chapter I will pick up the themes of belonging, identification and home but this time through focusing on the way memory and structures of feeling are inscribed on the human frame. Through examining how people adorn their bodies I look at the way in which the social landscape makes its imprint on the skin and how love and loss are communicated without being spoken.

CHAPTER 3

Inscriptions of Love[1]

The routes of a life spent in transit are inscribed on his skin. At rest now, he lies motionless, voiceless, in a hospital bed. The nurse interprets the 'vital signs' transmitted from his body. An internal struggle is encoded in these readings like a Morse code message from a vessel in peril at sea. There is no external trace of the great effort going on inside him and the elderly man cannot speak of what brought him to this point. As he lies there, his body represents an illustrated map of his life.

The tattoos that covered his arms and chest each bore the name of a place: Burma, Singapore and Malaysia. Each of them had a record of the year the inscription was made. He had been a merchant seaman and had travelled the world. On his right arm was the figure of an Indian woman dancing with her hands clasped together above her head, her skin darkened by the tattooist's ink. In the sailor's autumn years the figure etched on this pale canvas had turned a deep shade of blue. On the left forearm was an inscription that marked his journey's end: a tattoo of Tower Bridge, London and beneath it the dedication – 'HOME'. It read like an anchor.[2]

The voiceless patient spoke beyond sound. These tattoos told a story of the places he had visited, the voyages in between, and contained allusions to intimacies shared in tattoo parlours around the world. Here the sailor trusted local artists enough – in India and Burma – to spill blood and mark his flesh indelibly. On the surfaces of this failing body was a history of the relationship between the sailor's metropolitan home and the hinterlands of trade and empire. The permeability of that relationship – between imperial centre and colonial periphery – was marked on the porous membranes of his dying body.

The most familiar account of the history of the tattoo in Britain and the West is that this practice was brought back to Europe in the eighteenth century when European explorers encountered the tattooing cultures of the South Pacific and Polynesia. Captain James Cook's voyages gave the English language the word tattoo. He observed the practice on Tahiti in July 1769.[3] It is a variation of a Polynesian term *tatu* or *tatau* meaning to mark or strike.[4] On Cook's second circumnavigation of the globe he transported Omai to London. This man, from Raiatea Island close to Tahiti, became an exotic curiosity in London, in part because he bore the marks of Polynesian tattooing that Cook had described earlier.[5] Cook's ships and the 'specimens' contained within them were unloaded on the south bank of the river Thames just a few miles away from where the sailor whose description opened this chapter lay in his hospital bed.

The emphasis placed on the encounter with Polynesian tattooing cultures has occluded histories of earlier bodily inscription in Britain and Europe. In particular, various historians have shown the connection between tattooing and penal and property rights among the Greeks, Romans and Celts.[6] Also, early Christians in Roman territories inscribed their bodies as an expression of the devotee's servitude to Christ.[7] More than this, there is a connection between pilgrimage and tattooing. Early modern pilgrims to Palestine were tattooed with Christian symbols available in Jerusalem and brought their marked bodies home as evidence of their sacred travels. This practice also occurred amongst pilgrims to the Shrine of Loreto in Italy in the sixteenth century. There is then a strong connection between travel and tattooing.

Alfred Gell has concluded that the stigma associated with tattooing in the West results from a double association of the 'ethnic Other' and the 'class Other'.[8] Tattooing was drawn into the culture and vernacular of the sailors themselves and the cultural world they created. Historian Marcus Rediker has shown that a life on the sea left its mark on the bodies of working-class seamen.

> The tattoo, then and now, often adorned his forearm. 'The Jerusalem Cross' and other popular designs were made by 'pricking the skin, and rubbing in a pigment', either ink, or, more often gunpowder. Seafaring left other, unwanted distinguishing marks. Prolonged exposure to the sun and its intensified reflection off the water gave him a tanned or reddened – 'metal coloured' – and prematurely wrinkled look … thus in many ways the seaman was a marked man, much to the delight of the press gangs that combed the port towns in search of seamen to serve the crown.[9]

Rediker identifies a key paradox. In working-class life, tattooing has provided a way of reclaiming and aestheticizing the body. At the same time these marks sketch the outline of a 'class Other', a target for respectable society to recognize and stigmatize, be it in the form of a press gang, officers of the law, or today's bourgeois moralists.

The painted sailor is gone now; his life has ebbed away. His passing was noted by the registrar of the void who recorded his lapsed life and issued a flimsy certificate. The inscription of his body was an attempt to make an enduring mark, yet he belonged to a class of people for whom there is little place in the official record. 'They are the sort of people', noted Patrick Modiano, 'who leave few traces'.[10] Gruesome exceptions are held in the specimen laboratory at Guy's Hospital, London. Here, pieces of marked skin are preserved in the acrid smelling jars of formalin. The peeled skins are the only traces of nameless men from whose arms they were taken. They show the images of a Hope and Anchor and of Christ crucified, grafts that were taken, or filched, for medical research.[11] This is still happening, although in today's National Heath Service 'progress' demands some payment upfront. Jock Browning, for example, out of Waterloo, London has left his almost completely tattooed body 'to science'. In return he received the meagre sum of £3,000.[12]

Having a tattoo, or being pierced, is a moment when boundaries are breached, involving hurt and healing. It is profoundly a corporeal experience – the piercing of the skin, the flow of blood, pain, the forming of a scab, the healing of the wound and the visible trace of this process of incision and closure. It involves perforating the boundary between the internal and external so that the external becomes internal and the internal becomes external. The tattoo itself can be read through a range of metaphors, for example, the relationships between agency and control, permanence and ephemerality, trauma and healing. Such associations are never straightforward and rarely just a matter of individual choice. As Alfred Gell pointed out: 'The apparently self-willed tattoo always turns out to have been elicited by others.'[13]

The Body as a Political Field

Michel Foucault is perhaps the most eloquent analyst of the ways in which the body acts as a site of cultural and political manipulation. He writes in *Discipline and Punish*: 'The body is also directly involved in a political field; power relations have an immediate hold upon it; they invest it, mark it, train it, torture it, force it to carry out tasks, to perform ceremonies, to emit signs.'[14] Elsewhere he concludes that 'the body is the surface of the inscription of events'.[15] For Foucault, this is both a process whereby the 'Me' of identity is constituted by history and power, but also a site of perpetual disintegration. In this sense the body is 'totally imprinted by history'.[16]

Franz Kafka provides a chilling illustration of a Foucauldian sense of discipline through inscription in his short story 'In the Penal Colony'. In the story, the law of the prison is enforced through a novel tattooing machine composed of a bed, with cotton wool, and, above the bed, held in place with metal rods,

a Designer. Each machine resembles a dark wooden chest. Between the
Designer and the Bed shuttles a skin-writing device on a ribbon of steel called
the Harrow. The Officer of the Colony explains this method of punishment:
'Whatever commandment the prisoner has disobeyed is written upon his body
by the Harrow. This prisoner for instance' – the officer indicated the man –
'will have written on his body: HONOUR THY SUPERIORS!'[17] Prisoners
are not informed of their sentence. The Officer in the story explains why:
'There would be no point in telling him. He'll learn it on his body.' [18] This
chilling tale is not so far from the truth of the ways in which tattooing has been
used as a tool for punishment. Think of the numbers tattooed on the Jewish
and other prisoners of the Nazi concentration camps. Here the tattoo was a
means of regulation, control and initiation into the world of the camp. In the
aftermath of liberation, the survivors have had to carry with them these marks
as a permanent reminder. Primo Levi documents his return from the
Auschwitz in his extraordinary book *The Truce*, writing, as he passed through
Germany, 'I felt the tattooed number on my arm burning like a sore.'[19]

Tattooing continues today inside prisons, but now it is the prisoners who
tattoo themselves. Susan Phillips illustrates this point in her brilliant study of
gangland tattooing:

> No longer tattooed or branded by those who incarcerate them, prisoners now mark
> themselves forever into the stigmatised world of the prison. Tattooing creates perma-
> nent representations of identity that cannot be taken away by the authorities; they rep-
> resent positive affirmations of self in an environment full of negatives. Even if the
> prisoners are stripped of clothes, have their heads shaven, are forced into tiny cells, are
> bloodied by each other or prison guards, tattoos speak of their pasts and carry the
> strength of their affiliations.[20]

Tattooing, prohibited in US prisons, has become a means to wrest control
over the prisoner's body from the grey concrete institutions. Phillips tells the
story of one tattoo artist called Gallo. He was in prison for eight years and
during this time he earned money as a tattooist. Caught by the guards, he consequently had to serve an extra six months. Gallo's body was marked with
gangland tattoos, through which he visibly brought his neighbourhood affiliations into the prison. As a result he received protection and support. Outside,
his tattoos and his physical appearance had a paradoxical allure. On the one
hand, it meant that he was offered parts in hard-core pornography films: for
pornographic film-makers, tattooed gang members apparently provide a
means to titillate the viewer with images of dangerous exoticism. But, at the
same time, his tattoos also marked Gallo out as a target for the police. Phillips
lost contact with him, when Gallo was on the verge of another prison sentence

after being arrested again for possession of soft drugs.[21] So Gallo's tattoos are about both affirmation and damnation, arousing both desire and disgust.

There are connections between Gallo's experience and tattooing in the United Kingdom. In media representations images of tattooed men are associated with violence and football hooliganism. Similarly, tattooed working-class women have been associated, up until quite recently, with sexual deviance, prostitution and criminality. A press report described a working-class community in southern England as a place of 'cigarettes, hamburgers and tattoos'.[22] All of these attributes were connected in one form or another with abuses of the body. In 2004 the term Chav became the new shorthand to describe the disreputable members of the white working class. For young women the signs of Chav style include wearing large gold loop earrings, flashy 'bling' jewellery and clothing brands such as Burberry, Adidas, Nike and Timberland, and having their hair tied back in a tight pony tail dubbed the 'Croydon face lift'.[23] Julie Burchill refers to the class stereotypes as a form of 'social racism'.[24] Others have luxuriated in the anti-charisma charisma of Chavism, resulting in websites that proudly extol its virtues, vices, cultural habits and hallmarks.[25]

The etymology of the term 'Chav' is contested. Some suggest that it is a distortion of the Anglo-Romani word 'charvi', meaning child, while others claim it is derived from 'Chatham girls'. Most agree that Cheltenham, Gloucestershire provided its origin: here local working-class youths were referred to as 'Cheltenham Averages' by the disapproving middle-class students and parents at Cheltenham Ladies' College, and the phrase was subsequently shortened to 'Chavs'. In the venomous popular book *Chav! A User's Guide to Britain's New Ruling Class* the display of tattoos is described as a means for Chavs to announce summer's arrival: 'Most of these will usually feature the name of most recent partner, offspring or dead grandparent. Working on the "waste not, want not" principle, the more resourceful of the species will always try to cover up last year's partner's name with this year's – which usually results in an even more elaborate design feature.'[26] The chav phenomenon has reinvigorated a class prejudice that is primarily and tellingly defined through body culture and style.

These are just recent manifestations of long-standing class-inflected forms of stigma. Part of what I want to do in what follows is look closely at class-inflected forms of embodiment and emotional life, kinship and love. More than this, I want to use this impulse to raise a series of questions about the relationship between the body, language and memory. How does the body become a medium and a fleshy canvas through and on which belonging and structures of feeling are expressed? In what sense does the reliance on elaborated forms of language obscure the modes of expression held within white working-class contexts with regard to emotional life, attachment, love and loss? It is not only that 'the nameless' live and die without trace, but also that the complexity of their emotional lives is lost, ignored or disparaged.

So the project that is contained here is a reckoning with memory, culture and history, particularly of the white working-class communities that traverse inner and outer London south of the river. It is an attempt to approach the biography of 'the nameless' through the medium of the tattoo. Photographer Paul Halliday and I have worked closely together on the portraits that form the basis of this chapter. We worked jointly in the production of these images. We approached people who, for one reason or another, had decided to have tattoos inscribed. The participants were all familiar to us, some were friends and others family members. From the outset we wanted this project to be about an exchange that was both palpable – of giving photographs once they were made – but also a dialogue of sentiments and recollections that were shown as well as written. It is in the showing that the largest part of the story is told.

Speaking and Showing

An implicit impulse in some strains of radical sociology – particularly those inspired by the political projects of feminism and anti-racism – is the desire and expectation that the disenfranchised should speak for themselves. As I pointed out at the beginning of this book, this is a compelling challenge for sociology, but ultimately it is a deceptive hope. The idea itself presupposes the form of interaction in which the voice is rendered. The sociological interview, for example, privileges the idioms of elaborated communication, so often infused with class bias. As the late Basil Bernstein pointed out, class divisions are echoed in language use. On occasions where faithfully, and idiomatically, transcribed working-class speech makes it onto the page it jars the eye. The results can read like a Dick Van Dyke caricature of chirpy Cockney brogue. Bernstein argued that restricted language codes among working-class people result in distinctions that are tattooed metaphorically on their tongues.[27] Within this context working-class people articulate themselves through other means.

The prophetic philosopher Simone Weil once commented that 'affliction' – a notion that she held to be both material and spiritual – is by its nature inarticulate. She writes:

> the afflicted are not listened to. They are like someone whose tongue has been cut out and who occasionally forgets the fact. When they move their lips no ear perceives any sound. And they themselves soon sink into impotence in the use of language, because of the certainty of not being heard.

That is why there is no hope for the vagrant as he stands before the magistrate. Even if, through his stammerings, he should utter a cry to pierce the soul, neither the magistrate nor the public will hear it. His cry is mute.[28]

In order to avoid replicating the plight of the magistrate, we need to recognize that people express themselves through a wider range of cultural modalities that operate beyond the word. Zygmunt Bauman concluded: 'Is it not so that when everything is said about matters most important to human life, the most important things remain unsaid?'[29]

Paul and I have tried to use photography to access the registers of embodied forms of communication. Much has been written about the way the photographic lens operates to survey and govern the definition of what is 'real'.[30] But it is a mistake, I think, to see the lens as only looking one way. This raises the question posed by John Berger, namely 'Who is looking at Who?'[31] An answer is provided in the philosophical writings of Maurice Merleau-Ponty, who argues against the legacy of Cartesian dualism that separates mind from body, subject from object. He makes a case for the importance of developing a sensuous understanding and stresses that 'we are in the world through our body'.[32] Instead of dividing between subject and object, he stresses an intertwining, or a chiasm. For him 'the look' doesn't produce distance, a gap between the viewer and the looked upon. Rather, the look produces a connection. It involves openness to being that is potentially two-way or 'reversible' in Merleau-Ponty's language. 'It is the coiling of the visible upon the seeing body', he writes. 'I lend them my body in order that they inscribe upon it and give me their resemblance, this fold, this central cavity of the visible which is my vision, these two mirror arrangements of the seeing and the visible, the touching and the touched …'[33] This process of intertwining occurs at the moment when the seer and the visible connect. It is made on the stage of everyday life but it also possesses a specific relationship to time. In that fraction of a second when the aperture of the camera opens, a tiny slice of time is preserved in which the relationship between the viewer and the looked upon is caught, and held, in place.

The Lion's Face

Mick looks back at us from the other side of the lens (Figure 3.1). Through his look he addresses us but we have to listen with our eyes as well as our ears. He was born in Lewisham in 1951 and lived as a child in Perry Vale, Forest Hill, South London. Mick shows the two lions inscribed on his chest. They are the totem of his football team, Millwall Football Club, known to friend and foe alike as 'The Lions'. In the public imagination, Millwall signifies everything that is deplorable in English football culture – violence, bigotry and hatred. In his fascinating study of the club and its history, Garry Robson writes:

> The word Millwall, I would suggest, is one of the most evocative in contemporary English. It functions as a condensed symbol, widely and indiscriminately used to express ideas and feelings about an entire sphere of activity and experience well beyond the compass of its original meaning. It has become a byword for, amongst other things, violent mob thuggery, unreconstructed masculinity, dark and impenetrable urban culture and working class 'fascism'.[34]

This caricature holds little resemblance for the devoted fans for which the club provides a sense of belonging and affiliation, passion and love. For within this 'condensed symbol' are the vestiges of an urban history that is largely

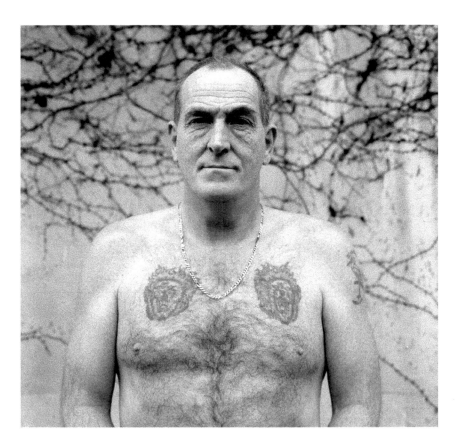

Figure 3.1 Mick and the Lion's Face (*photograph by Paul Halliday*)

ignored by journalists and politicians who are quick to condemn Millwall's fans as proto-fascist football hooligans. Mick's grandmother was from Donegal in Ireland and his aunts live in various parts of Ireland. He started following Millwall when he was nine years old. He speaks of the fun and intoxicating atmosphere of football culture of that time:

> The best times – going to watch Millwall play away was special because the excitement, the adrenaline was there from the Friday evening. Going in the old pubs and having a drink, you know, don't matter what age it was ... we always sneaked you in or they sneaked me in or whatever, but no it was ... it was, the adrenaline was there on a Friday evening, or especially if you was travelling on a Friday evening because in them days you had no motorways and you went overnight, places like Carlisle and Barrow and Workington ... We went up overnight and it was, it was you know, just brilliant, you know, just travelling and letting other people see that you're arriving. You're there like, and you've come all this way like to see Millwall play and then ... the, the high point was at the end of the game, you know ... If we'd won like, you know what I mean, you was over the moon like, you know. Or very disappointed if you lose because the long dreary drive back like, you know ... Well as I say, we've had some brilliant times.[35]

Mick was filmed for a notorious television documentary made by the *Panorama* team in the early 1970s. The programme was an exposé of football hooliganism focusing on Millwall. As a result, Mick's face was plastered up unfairly in football grounds with 'mug shots' of the most wanted 'Millwall hooligans'. The Millwall fraternity was populated by legendary figures like Ginger Bob, Ray Treatment, Harry The Dog, Tiny – who was a black Millwall fan and one of the most respected – and Sid the 'Umbrella Man'. Mick explained:

> Well, we used to go to football matches and when the trouble was on Sid just walked, [he] always had an umbrella with him and as though he weren't causing no trouble. Then when you get the supporters running by like, the opposition he'd chchsh [pull them around the neck], that with the umbrella like and chhh – it was comical. I mean we know it was wrong but in them days it was comical because you was there, you was a part of it.[36]

This world constituted a public sphere of life for these men between home and work, a place that was controlled by them, enjoyed by them, and which possessed unique emotion and electricity.

Mick had the lions inscribed on his chest when he was seventeen in Ringo's tattoo parlour in Woolwich. It was the ultimate gesture of commitment. 'I think it just got it in your blood – obviously in them days you were tattooed up and you had sort of lions put on you, and like Millwall Forever.'[37]

Mick collects statues of lions which decorate his home. At one point he even owned a tame lion called Sheba, which he kept in Bexleyheath, and brought it on several match days to The Den, Millwall's ground. These affinities are about much more than a sporting pastime. It is about a sense of place and of being in the world. It is a form of identification that is acted out, performed and felt both in and through the body. It is something that Mick and others like him struggle to put into words:

> I've ... been supporting Millwall and um – I don't know, I think it's just territory ... just, they own it, it's Millwall and that's it, and it's, and it stays, [coughs], as I say that, that, that's what it is about Millwall, it's just – Millwall is ... it's they're in lights, Les, do you know what I mean, it's, it's there, it's there in lights, I mean everybody sees Millwall, everybody sees Millwall, everybody dreams Millwall.[38]

Ultimately, words are not necessary. This passion and commitment is shown. Yet, Mick didn't want the word 'Millwall' as part of his tattoo. For him the lions carry a symbolic weight that makes the affiliation to Millwall and south London clear, while remaining partially hidden from the disapproving eyes of the uninitiated.

At the time when this photograph was taken Darren was a porter at Goldsmiths College (see Figure 3.2). Like Mick, he grew up in south London and is a lifelong Millwall fan. Like many he has moved out of the capital, in large part as a response to the inflation in house prices. He lived with his family in Walderslade, Kent. He commuted to his job in New Cross, a return trip of seventy miles a day. Inscribed on Darren's forearm is the fighting lion, above which is the club's name and beneath it the club's initials. This is the most beloved of all Millwall symbols. It was the club's trademark emblem up until 1999 when the club decided to ditch it in an attempt to distance itself from associations within the media with violence and hooliganism. This hasn't dented the popularity of this sign in the tattoo parlours of south London. Darren wears the tattoo proudly on his forearm alongside others that draw on styles currently sweeping Europe and America as part of what has been referred to the 'tattoo renaissance'.[39] The two styles sit together, or they seemed to when this photograph was taken in 2001. Looking at it five years later, it is possible that the angular block tattoo that separated the lion from the unicorn is a 'cover up' and the blocks of ink hide an earlier inscription.

Football tattoos attest to the wearer's commitment to their club but are also a mark of rootedness in a particular place. Many have talked about the ways

Figure 3.2 Darren's Millwall lion (*photograph by Paul Halliday*)

in which football grounds become sacred turf.[40] Some football fans take this 'geopiety'[41] literally – they ask to be married on the pitch, or request that upon their death their ashes should be scattered in the goalmouth. Many a night-time guerrilla raid has been performed on stadiums in south London and elsewhere to honour promises – often illegally – and administer unofficial funeral rites. Tattoos work in the opposite direction. What they do is incarnate a sense of place, community and history on the skin of the individual. Steve Scholes, a 34-year-old Manchester United fanatic, has had the entire Old Trafford stadium tattooed on his back. The portraits show an aerial view of the ground in detail along with the words 'Old Trafford Theatre of Dreams'. He told *The Sun* newspaper, 'I just hope they don't do any more building work.'[42] This sense of place with all its associated affiliations is deposited on the body like a

bearing from which orientations to life are taken as the person moves physically through different localities and over time.

It is not just that collective loyalties are written on the body through the
tattoo. One of the characteristics of working-class tattoos is that names of
family members and lovers are often written on the skin. This is particular to
working-class tattooing. Rarely in the contemporary 'modern primitive'
European tattooing subcultures – which are largely middle class – are family
names inscribed.[43] There is something telling in this, which points to the class-
specific nature of such practices. In white working-class culture, the tattooed
names are often the embodiment of filial love and kinship.

In her book *All About Loving* bell hooks writes that 'The men in my life have
always been the folks who are wary of using the word "love" lightly … They
are wary because they believe women make too much of love.'[44] In this much-
needed book, hooks concluded that the lack of clarity over the meaning of love
lay at the heart of the difficulty of loving. Love for her is a matter of will, action
and choice. It is a matter of education. 'To truly love we must learn to mix
various ingredients – care, affection, recognition, respect, commitment and
trust as well as honest open communication.'[45] But what mode of communication is being insinuated here? Much has been made of the emotional inar-
ticulacy of men in general and working-class men in particular. Gary Oldman's
film *Nil By Mouth* is, in my view, the best and most intense expression of
this.[46] In the film the main protagonist describes his father's internment in a
hospital. Above his bed are the words 'Nil By Mouth'. This sums up the son's
relationship to his father.

Speaking casually of love can debase its currency. Julie Burchill has written
that there is a class dimension to the language of emotions.[47] Burchill, an acerbic
and controversial journalist, has argued that middle-class families profess love
quickly leading to a jejune superficiality in emotional matters. There is something in this reproach. We live in the age of the talk show exposé and reality TV
where emotions have been spectacularized. Emotion talk and disclosure is now
a big industry. The ratings for the 'shocking truth' television shows and the circulation of gossip magazines attest to this fact. The lack of emotional garrulous-
ness in working-class culture points to alternative modalities in loving.

On the inside of Darren's forearm, distinct from the fierce Millwall Lion is
another tattoo (Figure 3.3). It consists of two names – Molly and Charley –
that are linked together with a heart and beneath is a date, 26 April 1999. This
marks the birthday of his beloved twin daughters. There is something beautiful and moving in the illustration of parental devotion. Love is given a name;
it is incarnate. But this commitment is not made in elaborated speeches. It is
performed rather than described. It is a kind of illocutionary love, a love that
is expressed without painstaking announcement.

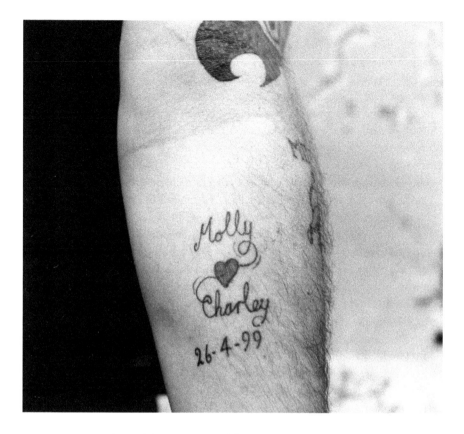

Figure 3.3 Darren's twins (*photograph by Paul Halliday*)

My intention here is not simply to accuse the bourgeois moralist of being blind to these complex sentiments and registers of love. The likes of Michael Collins and Julie Burchill view anti-working-class feeling as the last respectable prejudice, but the kinds of victimology that result from this avoid serious attention being paid to the damage that class divisions inflict.[48] Romanticism and nostalgia is not simply confined to working-class boys and girls who have made good but there is a long-standing tradition of this on the left. Working-class people are not ennobled by class inequalities, but they are often damaged by them. Part of the damage is that the powerful in the dominant order try to make working-class people in their own image, be it in terms of economic life and consumption or national affinity and belonging. It is the nature of the damage that needs attention, even if paying truth the courtesy of serious effort results at another level in the betrayal of the people we are listening to.

What remains unsaid about Darren's tattoos is what happened to him after the photographs were taken. In 2004, with Millwall's old east London rivals –

West Ham – back in the same division after being relegated from the Premier League, Darren was seduced by the allure of his old ways. When West Ham visited Millwall's home ground all the 'Old School' firms of football fans turned out. The police kept the fans apart and a meet had been arranged between rival 'hooligan' firms at London Bridge but it never happened. By mobile phone they arranged to meet in a pub in Stratford. Millwall turned up 'mob handed', twenty-five strong, and the pub was wrecked; a billboard was thrown through the pub window. Darren was arrested on the platform of Stratford Station.

In the run-up to the court case he began to drink heavily. He was picked up for drink driving and he lost his license. He slipped further and further into a mood of resentment and he was pictured on a National Front rally in one of the Medway towns. His wife left him and he is separated from his twin daughters. At the time of writing, he has served the community service that resulted from his conviction for football violence and he is being treated for his alcoholism. Although he could have returned to his job at Goldsmiths College he chose not to. Of course, Darren's story is not just a parable about the injuries of class, and the contrast that Mick's story provides shows that other routes are navigated through life. The presence of racism and resentment and the double-edged nature of local patriotism and pride is at play within Darren's story, as it is more broadly within white working-class life in south-east London. It is the task of sociological listening to render this moral and political complexity without either becoming an apologist for racism or reducing such lives to a caricature of absolute evil and violent thuggery.

The Name of the Father

Michael Young was a formidable public intellectual and a keen listener to everyday life. Author of the sociological classic *Family and Kinship in East London* (with Peter Wilmott) he also founded the Open University and wrote the historic *Let Us Face the Future* 1945 manifesto for the Labour Party, which provided the blueprint for the British welfare state. When he died in 2002, his son Toby wrote a moving tribute to his father. As a young man Toby Young was exasperated with his father's antics and rebelled against his social democratic politics. One Christmas morning Michael Young disappeared to spend some time in an East End cemetery. He had heard that lonely East Enders congregated there to be with their lost loved ones returning to the district for the day after having moved away. By the time Michael Young returned to his home the Christmas dinner was spoilt and his family furious. Toby Young remembered: 'He waited patiently for our anger to die down and then began to tell us about the poor, grieving widows he'd seen pouring tea into the graves of their husbands so they could share one last "Christmas cuppa." Within a few minutes we'd all burst into tears.'[49]

The story caught my imagination partly because of Young's gift for sociological attention and his intuitive sense that something was at stake in the strange spectacle of women pouring tea into the graves of their lost loves. Through the Institute of Community Studies, which he founded and used as his intellectual base, now renamed the Young Foundation in his memory, I found the reference to the article he published in *The Independent* newspaper. Disappointingly, there is no description of cups of tea shared between the living and the dead. Young's ethnographic realism wouldn't allow for such a fanciful piece of trivia, rather the Newham cemetery is depicted through the conventions of modernist ethnography. He wrote:

> No one seemed to be hurrying over their work, for it was work that most of them were doing, gently removing the faded and dead flowers and leaves, brushing or even polishing the stones, planting flowers, putting the cut chrysanthemums into their holders, replacing the old artificial blooms. Where the burial was more recent they were sprucing up the Scottie dogs made of white flowers – a kind of topiary – and the wreaths shaped in the form of names: Dad or Son or Ken.[50]

The resonance of this will soon be clear, but I want to foreground Young's listening ability and his brilliant sociological intuition. Where the uninitiated would have derided the crass floral tributes and plastic graveside flower arrangements, he understood the power of the name in the emotional life of the working classes and their memory rituals. The same processes are at play, I want to suggest, in the inscriptions of love that are made through the tattooist's ink on the skin's canvas.

In her study *Formations of Class and Gender*, Beverley Skeggs demonstrates the ways in which the body and bodily dispositions carry the markers of social class. The young women in her study concentrate on their bodies as a means of self-improvement. As Julie, one of the respondents, says, 'Your body's the only thing you've got that's really yours.'[51] For these women 'letting yourself go' is surrender to the strictures of class, immobility and confinement. Another, Therese, observes: 'You know you see them walking round town, dead fat, greasy hair, smelly clothes, dirty kids, you know the type, Crimplene trousers and all, they just don't care no more, I'd never be like that.'[52] Holding onto the hollow promises of class mobility is reduced to a matter of working on a healthy diet, keeping slim and working out. Skeggs concludes, 'The working class body which is signalled through fat is the one that has given up the hope of ever "improving".'[53] Beverley Skeggs doesn't mention the place of tattooing in her discussion of the complexities of working-class femininity. But I would guess that the tattoo would have been added to the attributes connected with the ignominy of the working-class female body. Up until relatively recently, being tattooed would have engendered for young women accusations of involvement in sexual promiscuity or prostitution and being a 'slag' or 'sluttish'. The tattoo renaissance of the last ten years has changed this situation to some degree as more and more women have worn tattoos and the stigma associated with them has lessened.

On Vicki's shoulder is a tattoo of an angel (see Figure 3.4). She did not want her face shown. On her left shoulder, opposite this tattoo, is a 'little devil'. Her family think these sentinels of the divine and the wicked compete for influence over her personality. She is my niece and lives in New Addington, a large council estate in Croydon on the outskirts of south London and mentioned in Chapter 1. It is a place where the city and the country cut into each other like the teeth of a saw. Approximately 30,000 people live on the estate, with around 19,000 children. In 1956 Sir Hugh Casson, architectural director of the Festival of Britain, said of this estate that it was 'cut off, not only from Croydon and London, but even from life itself'.[54] Early residents called it 'Little Siberia' because it is high up on a hill and exposed to the elements. In the early 1970s Jamie Reid, who designed the art work for the Sex Pistols, published a political magazine called *The Suburban Press* and in 1972 it ran a special edition on the politics of housing, focusing on New Addington. The editorial came to a prescient conclusion:

> New Addington has become Croydon's dumping ground for the working-class ... Your only way out of an estate like Addington is to buy your way out. Work your life away for a taste of middle class life, so someone else can move in to your council house to better themselves. It is ideal for predominantly middle class Croydon to 'hide its workers away' on estates like New Addington.[55]

Jamie Reid predicted precisely what was to happen in the 1980s during the Conservative governments led by Margaret Thatcher, who offered those who could afford it the 'right to buy' with the result that the best housing stock was sold, leaving in large measure only the hard-to-let property in the public sector. Today, the skyline is dominated by the three skyscrapers that make up Canary Wharf. They resemble a giant inverted three pin-plug. Through these towers London is connected to the financial electricity of globalization. In the digital age a 'Cockney' is defined not by being born within the sound of Bow Bells, but rather within sight of Canary Wharf.

Vicki is twenty years old and at the time this photograph was taken she had just come home from her job in a supermarket. I asked her if there was any

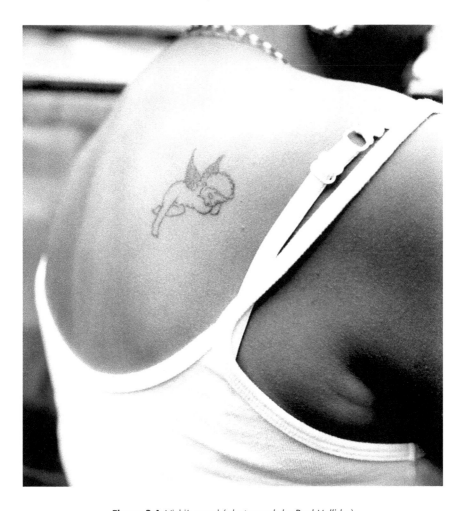

Figure 3.4 Vicki's angel (*photograph by Paul Halliday*)

stigma involved in girls having tattoos these days. 'No', she replied. 'Everyone has got tattoos now. All kinds of things. Dolphins, things like that. They are cheap, too.' I asked her how much. 'Depends where you go, but you can get a small one done for £20–30.'[56] She showed the tattoo on her ankle (Figure 3.5). She was wearing her work shoes. On her ankle is a small red rose with 'Mum' and 'Dad' inked on either side of it. Illocutionary love.

Vicki shows her hands (Figure 3.6). Behind every piece of her gold jewellery lies a story. The third finger of her left hand warms the ring once worn by her maternal grandmother, who passed away ten years ago. Next to the gold rose, on her middle finger is a 'keeper ring', like the one her paternal grandfather wore, this one in fact given to her by her grandparents for her thirteenth

Figure 3.5 Illocutionary love (*photograph by Paul Halliday*)

birthday. The rings on her right hand all carry similar associations and attachments. She bought the diamond lattice ring on her index finger with the money that her maternal grandfather gave her the year that he died. The gold ring on the third finger was given to her by her paternal grandparents for her sixteenth birthday. On the middle finger of her right hand is the large gold sovereign ring given to her on her eighteenth birthday by her paternal grandmother alone. Just two months prior to Vicki's coming of age her grandfather died of cancer.

Her nails are done, professionally manicured. The extravagant artificial fingernails contain a jewel in the centre of each individual nail, a style currently popular among black and white girls in London. The phrase 'dripping in gold' is used as a means to pour scorn on working-class women. It is meant to fix young women and the nouveau riche as brash or gaudy Chavs, and mark them

Figure 3.6 A life in her hands (*photograph by Paul Halliday*)

as inferior within the hierarchies of taste and class distinction.[57] It is a stock phrase in the lexicon of class conceit. Each of the items that Vicki wears carries a meaning and association that escapes the strictures of bourgeois ignorance and prejudice. Each symbolizes a moment passed in living, a register of love or kinship to those near to her, or to the memory of the lost. The story of her young life is in her hands.

There is a tattoo above the gold bracelet on Vicki's left wrist. It is a simple one in a contemporary style. Its presence beneath the gold jewellery signals a cultural trace from the past alive in the present. In the early period of the industrial revolution, workers had ornaments written on their skin. They had few possessions but 'free labour' meant they held sovereign power over their bodies. James Bradley concluded in his study of class and Victorian tattooing, 'Tattoos provided a substitute for jewellery, or other material possessions: a means of articulating emotion to, and forging attachments between the body, the self and others.'[58] The gold jewellery and Vicki's tattoos produce a continuity in which elements oscillate between past and present. They fit together within what Raymond Williams called a 'structure of feeling' that furnishes working-class taste and experience.[59]

Vicki's grandfather, my father, died in 1999 after a long and brutal dance with cancer. After he had his initial surgery I visited him in Mayday Hospital, Croydon. The ward was full of men of his age and background, all smokers, all blighted by the same affliction. Fifty years of factory work left a lattice of cracks on his hands that were hardened with calluses. Standing at a machine for ten hours a day had thickened his ankles and weakened his knees. The regimes of factory work left traces on the worker's body not always amenable to the naked eye but all too plain in the failing bodies in that hospital ward room. Like Engels' famous invocation of social murder, the illnesses found on this ward were the work of similar worldly perpetrators – bad working conditions, poor diet and an industry that profits from the sale of what my father called 'cancer sticks'.

As a young man things had been so very different. He had fancied himself as a bit of a 'spiv', inured to the world and style of the south London gangsters. There are pictures of him posing with his great friend Johnny Graham in the back garden of his mother's terraced home. They are dressed in double-breasted suits, silk ties and long-collared shirts. Dad and Johnny used to get on the train at East Croydon and head for the jazz clubs of Soho, or the boxing gyms, often over pubs, on the Old Kent Road, or to go dog racing at Catford. He carried with him always the humour and love of life that he found in those places.

He served in the Navy but he did not plot his travels in his skin. He forbade my brother and I to have tattoos even though we both wanted them. He 'laid down the law' in the Lacanian sense of a symbolic order, but for him tattoos signified self-damnation and class stigma and undermined his aspirations for post-war social improvement.[60] Like many, his image of a 'step up' was to move to the edge of the city, to the large council estates that offered the promise of better conditions and amenities. In such concrete citadels, working-class culture was deracinated and displaced. Yet, even here the legacy of the past was registered on the working-class body in code.[61] Memories do not have to be consciously held in order for them to be socially alive.[62] Rather, they can furnish a structure of feeling, while remaining elusive, even to those who inhabit them. Our father would not tolerate any carping about progress. For him it was simple. He wanted for his family better than he had known. Towards the end of his life, he looked on in bewilderment as his granddaughter Vicki presented a new tattoo on a more or less monthly basis.

The overwhelming sense of loss following his death consumed us all in different ways. For my brother Ken – Vicki's father – the particular nature of his death cast a shadow over his own future. He is a sheet metal worker and for many years he worked in a factory next door to his father. Now he travels all over the London area, repairing steel structures and erecting steel security gates. The industrial order of Fordist production is fast disappearing in London and a report in 2006 estimated that, between 2002 and 2016, manufacturing employment will fall by 30 per cent from 285,000 to 199,000 jobs.[63] The routines of Ken's working life provide an indicator of how London's economy is shifting: his work ranges from repairing kitchens in fast food outlets like McDonald's, to erecting security gates for warehouses and office complexes for designers and information technology companies.[64] In 2004 the Prime Minister's Strategy Unit produced the London Project Report, which defined the capital's economy as 'rooted in human talent, and expressed through knowledge-based, creative and cultural industries, including tourism'.[65] The capital in the twenty-first century is a place to create knowledge and design things rather than manufacture them.

Following our father's death, Ken went through a period of wearing his clothes, even his glasses. He inhabited his father's absence, in a literal way. He filled out his father's clothes with his own body and carried his garb with an almost identical language of movement and social orientation. Father and son possessed what Bourdieu calls a shared *bodily lexis*.[66]

Like many families in London we have a small caravan on the south coast, a place we have returned to for summer holidays since 1957. In the 1980s my parents brought a second-hand van at Norman's Bay and in the months after our father's death we continued to visit. It was almost impossible to be there. Every place resonated with his absent presence – the beach, the sea and the seawall where he stood to smoke a cigarette and look out on to the waves with the wind pushing back his mane of silver hair. Then one warm summer afternoon Ken said he had something to show me. He rolled up his shirtsleeve and there, on the top of his shoulder, was a tattoo, a graphic imagos, consisting of a swallow in flight, holding a scroll in its beak and on that fleshy parchment was inscribed three letters – DAD (see Figure 3.7).

The tattoo names the object of an illocutionary love. As Alfred Gell points out, this apparently individual choice is in fact elicited by others. In Ken's case they are his family, those closest to him and the spectre of his father. It symbolizes a love that was rarely, if ever, brought to speech, yet it is named. It *is* the name. Psychoanalyst Jacque Lacan claims that from the very beginning of their lives children have distinct relationships to their fathers. This stands in contrast to the immediate physical connection to their mothers that is fashioned at birth and through nursing. Children develop a corporeal relation to

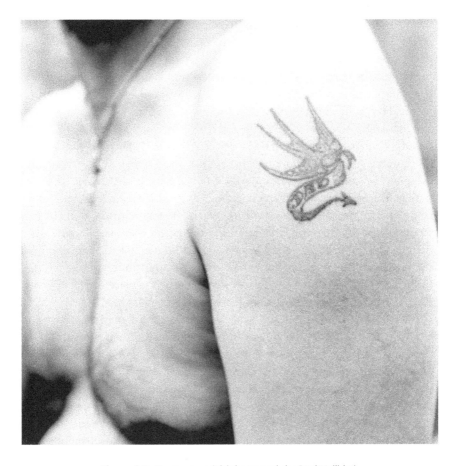

Figure 3.7 Ken's memorial (*photograph by Paul Halliday*)

their mother, while they learn of their relationship to their fathers through language and the word. As Daniel Schwartz concludes, 'the father's relationship to the child is thus established through language and a system of marriage and kinship – names – that in turn is basic to [the] rules of everything'.[67] The veracity of these claims is not the issue here, for what Lacan alerts us to is the symbolic weight contained in the name of the father. The father stands not only for paternity and love but also for a social or moral order.

The inscription of 'Dad' on Ken's shoulder points to the complexities of that moral order. Remember, his father had prohibited him from having such inscriptions. Yet, it is precisely through this debarred line that Ken memorializes his father. Ken's tattoo both carries his father's memory and defies parental authority. In the end, our father lives in part through the breaching of the law that he 'laid down to us' as children. Our father could on occasion be fierce and harsh and, inevitably, as a young man Ken had fallen foul of his discipline. His tattoo thus contains both sweetness and pepper.

Five years on from our father's death, Ken has become like him, not in terms of physical characteristics, or in the superficial surfaces of appearance. The invisible tattoos have been imprinted on his thought, action and conduct. This, to me, is something of a miracle and a comfort. We had not spoken of this. That is until I brought my day job home and turned myself into a putative family ethnographer. All the emotions, palpable support and love demonstrated through the bereavement were never named. I want to suggest that this is much more than a family matter. It can be read as an example of the complexity of working-class emotional lives, which have so often been viewed as indifferent, expressionless and lacking sensitivity.

Within white working-class contexts, men, and, to a lesser degree, women possess a kind of laconic halter when it comes to overfamiliarity. This is certainly the case in south London and its hinterlands, and may be specific to the history of this region and the class cultures that have taken hold. This is not quite the process of 'making the self smooth', or levelling out the internal and external fluctuations of emotion that Clifford Geertz described so vividly in the context of Java.[68] Rather, it is an imperturbable mask that holds still in the face of loquaciousness of any kind. Displays of overfamiliarity and easy affection are met with chilled scepticism. This in part has acted as a defence against external approaches, be it in the form of opportunistic politicians – on the left or the right – or the moral scrutiny of social workers and bourgeois professionals.

The language of love is articulated through acts and gestures within an embodied realm. Here the common-sense maxim 'actions speak louder than words' takes on a literal significance. The danger inherent in this unspoken love is that its communication might be distorted and not received clearly. These embedded emotional affinities can be misinterpreted, assumed, looked past or taken for granted. My essential point is that the lack of speech is not necessarily an indicator of an absence of love. More than this, the expression and communication of love needs to be understood through the range of verbal and non-verbal modalities.

Conclusion: The Colour in the Portrait

In this chapter I have tried to explain that which is not easily accessible to the written word. The key argument has been that within white working-class contexts the body becomes a figure on which emotions, affinities and devotions are inscribed. I have tried to show, through examining the photographs contained here, that the tattooed marks on these bodies contain complex, metonymic interconnections, meanings and symbolism. The colouring of these portraits – which is what I have tried to do through writing – is partial because each contains an enigma. Trying to find meaning in them is like grasping a handful of sand; most of the grains of truth slip through the fingers and I will develop this metaphor in the chapter that follows.

For Lacan, the act of signification, or any form of representation, is inherently unstable. It is what Kirsten Campbell has termed, 'the slide in the sign' or *glissement* in Lacanian language, that is, 'the process in which the signified constantly slides beneath the signifier'.[69] As Lacan argues, it is impossible to 'say it all' because ultimately 'words fail'. Part of this deficit is identified by Raymond Williams in what he calls the slide towards the past tense in cultural analysis and what he refers to as 'fixed forms of understanding'. The complexities of the present resist the categories we use to understand them: something always escapes and remains opaque.

> Perhaps the dead can be reduced to fixed forms, though their surviving records are against it. But the living will not be reduced, at least in the first person; living third persons may be different. All the known complexities, the experienced tensions, shifts, and uncertainties, the intricate forms of unevenness and confusion, are against the terms of the reduction and soon, by extension, against social analysis itself.[70]

This inadequacy in the act of representation is made all the more apparent here, given that the people contained in this study are my immediate family and close friends. What I have offered is very much a first-person narrative in the way Raymond Williams characterizes it. The portraits are inherently incomplete. They are sketches rather than portrayals in which all the shades of experience are detailed. But it is more difficult to indulge in quick judgements and crass sociological objectification when the subjects are your loved ones. This has been a lesson in itself. But the inevitable failure in the act of representation is not necessarily defeat. Ethnographic representation should aspire to better kinds of failure, to paraphrase Samuel Beckett's evocative phrase. This involves being open to the complexities and incomplete nature of present-tense experience, while at the same time avoiding reduction, fixing and closure.

Perhaps this draws attention to the ethics of thinking itself. If thinking is a moral act, what kind of moral act is it, specifically when it involves intimate dialogue of the kind described here?[71] Pierre Bourdieu has written that listening involves an intimacy that is both intellectual and emotional.

> Thus, at the risk of shocking both the rigorous methodologist and the inspired hermeneutic scholar, I would say that the interview can be considered a sort of *spiritual*

exercise that, through forgetfulness of self, aims at a true *conversion of the way we look* at other people in the ordinary circumstances of life. The welcoming disposition, which leads one to make the respondent's problems one's own, the capacity to take the persons and understand them just as they are in their distinctive necessity, is a sort of *intellectual love* ...[72]

The portraits I have offered are themselves outlined through love; these pages are written with it. Making the 'respondent's problems one's own', in this case, contains an immediacy because it has, through thinking, involved a healing and reckoning with personal loss and bereavement. Ken is my brother and his father was my father. But I hope that this discussion also resonates with Bourdieu's contention that sociology should be about a process of *conversion* and transformation in the way we look at other people and their bodies.

The paradox of working-class tattooing is that it can, and does, mark out the painted body as a target for class stigma and prejudice. My argument throughout has been that contained within these inscriptions are complex emotions and affinities. Sue Benson has argued that the conception that the body can be remade and fashioned is a powerful one today. Yet, the tendency to think of the body as something that can be styled and controlled contains a broken promise. Tattooing and other forms of body culture bring this paradox into clear view.

> For in truth we do not own our bodies, they own us, that the only thing that is certain about our bodies is that they will let us down, that in the end they cannot be mastered or bent to our will. In this sense what these practices bring into sharp focus is the *impossibility* of Western ideas about body and self, and of these fantasies of permanence, control autonomy that they seek to negotiate.[73]

The lines in these tattoos touch permanence but cannot grasp eternity. This has a double consequence for working-class expression because this is often the only medium through which their stories are told. There is no place for them, and no prospect of what Derrida calls a 'hospitable memory'.[74] As the cadavers disappear, the traces of their embodied history, of life and love, are lost. They pass through hospital wards to the crematoria, their names remembered in floral wreaths and the inscriptions made on young flesh that will in turn grow old.

As Zygmunt Bauman pointed out, the most important things often remain unsaid and this chapter has emphasized the need to pay attention to the realm of embodied social life that operates outside of talk. Here visual sociology and photography enables us to access and represent the communications written on the body. However, the photographs do not speak for themselves and in order to make sense of them we need to be alert to the interplay between what is inside and outside the frame. The form of sociological attention being developed in this book is trained on listening to what is said but also focusing on what is shown. It suggests a kind of attention that translates across the senses where hearing is looking and looking is hearing. In the next chapter, I argue for a photography that listens through the discussion of a street portraiture project. This example brings to the fore the relationship between the senses and understanding but also the ethics of interpretation and the give and take of sociological dialogue.

CHAPTER 4

Listening with the Eye[1]

When we listen to people, do they give us their stories or do we steal them? At the heart of all social investigation is a dialectical tension between theft and gift, appropriation and exchange. The balance between these forces is more complex than it seems on first sight. The ethical guidelines that govern socio-logical research are an attempt to guard against gross imbalances or abuses of sociological power. Ethics is the art of thinking through which *ought* (that is, guidelines for research) applies to a given *is* (namely, sociological research). In the British context, these guidelines attempt to ensure professional integrity; to attain informed consent and protect the rights of those involved in socio-logical studies and guard against research participants experiencing physical, social or psychological harm; and to guarantee anonymity, privacy and confi-dentiality. They are also concerned to avoid actions that could be deleterious for future sociological investigation.[2] As a consequence, ethics committees have sprouted up to govern all levels of social research from undergraduate dissertations to multi-million pound research projects.

However the 'ethical turn' is not confined to sociological craft, as Charles Lemert comments: 'One can hardly avoid the talk of ethics today – the ethical turn in social theory, the new morality of foreign policy, the ethics of a global environment, biomedical ethics, the clash of civilisation values, etc. Yet the early years of the Millennium are a very strange moment for such talk.'[3] It is curious because of the twentieth-century concern with the damage done by uni-versalistic thinking, particularly in relation to cultural difference. Lemert notes that actions made in the name of universal principles like freedom, justice and equality can result in a masquerade that may conceal implicit ethnocentrism or dominant global interests. The ethical turn is an attempt to address the problem of how to act in the face of uncertainty, risk and moral complexity. Paul Rabinow comments that 'the main mode of regulation now is ethical.'[4]

I am not suggesting here that a concern for ethics is some insidious form of governing control by stealth. Rather, I am suggesting that the bureaucratic ways of addressing issues of ethics limit rather than enhance the discussion of these issues. It thus becomes a matter of achieving a one-off 'ethical approval' from a governing body rather than an open and ongoing discussion about research and thinking itself as a moral act. For example, it is surely straightforwardly a 'good thing' that informed consent be sought from research participants. But how can this be informed when the researcher/writer cannot know how s/he is going to use the fruits of a particular participant's involvement? Neither the researcher nor the participant knows at the beginning of the study, when permission is usually sought, what they are consenting to be involved in and so how can it be truly informed? In this chapter I want to think about the ethical dimensions of research practice, foregrounding the stage on which the craft of social research is practised.

About the Street

What follows is an account of the use of street photography as a means to open up a space of exchange and engender a form of reciprocity between research subjects and observers. It centres on the *About the Streets Project* facilitated by photographer, film-maker and cultural sociologist Paul Halliday whose work was included in the previous chapter. In February 2001 he invited his students at Croydon College, south London to try to produce a visual story reflecting the ebb and flow of metropolitan cultural life. The setting was Brick Lane in East London, a place that Paul had photographed many times over a period of twenty years. This part of East London harbours the trace of many migrants who have made it their home, from the French Huguenots to European Jewry and, most recently, Bengali communities. Brick Lane is also a magnet for weekend migrations from other parts of the capital. On Sunday morning people converge on its markets from the suburbs, often crossing the river to buy everything from leather goods and the fruits of the 'rag trade' to cheap cigarettes. Paul took his students to Brick Lane and set up large format cameras in the street. On successive Sunday mornings, with the market in full swing, they invited people, often laden with shopping, to give their portraits.

My initial involvement with the project was to prime the students with ideas drawn from urban cultural theory, and particularly the work of Walter Benjamin. It must have been a bizarre spectacle on that first Sunday morning in 2001; the 'pavement tutorial' took place just outside the Bagel Bake at the northern end of Brick Lane. I offered the students a potted summary of Walter Benjamin's classic essay 'Theses on the Philosophy of History', while my son sat on my shoulders eating a jam doughnut and sprinkling sugar in my hair.[5]

The photographers set off down the busy thoroughfare holding light meters up to the sky as if tuning into extraterrestrial messages.

After that initial session, three of the photographers embraced the idea and made it their own. Each added a unique contribution to the group effort: Nicola Evans was the coordinating force and calming presence, Antonio Genco the technical alchemist and Gerard Mitchell the urban collector calling people to the lens. Gerry reflected that: 'No one person was in charge. It took away the preciousness of the photographer because we all contributed to the images. It was just a fluke who pressed the shutter and to my mind all these images are ours. It's like an art school punk band – instead of the electric guitars and drums we had a camera.'[6] Over a period of two years the group returned most Sundays with their large ancient-looking equipment to Brick Lane and literally set up in the street. Beneath the cloak of the camera the world was literally turned upside-down, *camera obscura*. The Victorian camera drew the attention of everyone who encountered them. Tourists asked on one occasion if they could buy it. People were drawn to the camera's ancient aura. Sometimes there would be queues of people lining up down the street waiting their turn to go before the lens. This essay is an attempt to right the inverted images and discuss the quality of what they brought back. The large format sheet negatives were prepared before each shoot as if polishing cultural mirrors to reflect and hold still the life of the city.

A Handful of Sand

The brilliantly melancholic writer Theodor Adorno once commented that truth is like a handful of water. I think Adorno chose the right kind of analogy but perhaps his chemistry is wrong. Truth might better be viewed as a handful of sand. Most of the grains slip through our fingers, but something sticks and can be held in the palm. In a desperate attempt to hold onto these pure grains – and in the intense heat produced by the desire to know and understand – a lens is forged. It is made up equally of the grains of truth that form its elements and the hand that fashions it.

I think the metaphor is appropriate to the way the work has been conducted here because the images all share a commitment to connect with the world, to enter into dialogue with it. This commitment produces an intense presence that is evident in each of the portraits. In Figure 4.1, Reverend Paul W. Bowton is pictured in front of Christchurch, Spitalfields. He looks back at us silently through the lens. Set against the wooden backdrop of the door of his church, there is stillness in the image. The photographers asked all their subjects to hold still because of the necessity of using a slow shutter speed that was between a quarter and an eighth of a second. In that moment a presence, or a likeness, is communicated. As John Berger has commented a 'presence is not for sale ... A presence has to be given, not bought'.[7] The stillness needs to be set against the reality of dynamic and sometimes anarchic urbanity. This part of London has undergone an incredible physical transformation in the last ten years. Smoked-glass cathedrals of commerce sprout from the concrete on an almost monthly basis. Between 2000 and 2002 over 40 per cent of all commercial development in London took place in this district. The stillness contained in the portrait is precious evidence of a human presence in the midst of this tumult, where the high-speed circulation of capital fashions the cityscape in its image. But equally, these photographs are not views from nowhere; they are made from a vantage point and they are guided – if not completely controlled – by the photographers' hands.

How much can we know about the people who offer their presence to the lens? This is a complicated question, which cannot be fully answered here – what can be said for sure is that we cannot know everything. Indeed, one of the appealing things about the project was the fleeting nature of some of the encounters that produced these portraits. It was this passing quality that drew Nicola Evans to the method: 'It fits in with my whole obsession with everyday life – just that split second, the face that you recognize, the person that you meet and never see again.'[8] This reminds us of the partial nature of what is drawn in the portrait. The size of the Victorian cameras also reminded those who went before them that they were being pictured. The technology itself militated against subterfuge. Nicola accounted for this in the following way: 'They have to come to the camera, it is not sly – it is really honest. It is really straight up. "Can we take a photograph, yes or no? OK stand in front of the lens."'[9]

The human presence that is evident in these portraits is not necessarily narrated. I think this is one of the great advantages of photography in that photographs need – in one sense – simply to be shown rather than explicated. The quality of the images operates outside of language and the conventions of The Word. Yet, at the same time, there is something to be listened to in these silent portraits. Part of what is compelling about them is that they contain voices that are present yet inaudible. We have to listen for them with our eyes.

Speaking into the Lens

Much has been written about the way cameras operate to survey and govern the definition of what is 'real'.[10] Film-maker Anastassios Kavassos has commented that cameras are like weapons. When Anastassios is filming he doesn't look through the lens. He points the camera and has developed a blind feel for its eye.[11] Others have pointed to the reluctance of vulnerable communities to have the camera trained on them. The photographers involved in this project found it difficult to approach Bengali subjects, particularly young women. This was in part a result of the sensitivities of the photographers, who were reluctant to invite young Bengali Londoners to the lens for fear that it might

Figure 4.1 Reverend Paul W. Bowton (*photograph by Nicola Evans, Antonio Genco and Gerard Mitchell*)

seem like an imposition. At the same time, public space is not open to Bengali women in the same way it is for the rest of the people who live here. Monica Ali captures this sense of gendered confinement in her novel *Brick Lane*, which tells the story of a young Bangladeshi woman. For the protagonist of the novel, the journey from the house to the street is longer than the migration from Bangladesh to London.[12]

This is not to say that Asian young women are not present in the public world of the street. The story is always more complex than can be apprehended in general principles. Figure 4.2 shows two young women – Zarina and Shireen – pictured close to Petticoat Lane Market, laden with shopping. On this particular morning they had crossed the river from Norbury, south London – where they live – to buy clothes. Of all the images in this project, this is the most furtive. It is a beautiful image: the glow of the vibrant pink and blue suits they are wearing somehow transposes to the monochrome photograph – it seems literally to shine. But contained in it is a nervousness that is not present in the other images. Antonio explained:

> We saw these two girls and they were with their father and a younger daughter. We showed them our book of previous photographs and asked them if we could take their picture. We took a family portrait first and then we took an image of the two girls. In a way the first picture was just a kind of family snap-shot. But we really wanted to get the two girls. We said – 'Your outfits are really nice could we take a picture of the two of you together?' The first one was a kind of classic family portrait, the second one seems more engaged in a way.[13]

Perhaps they sensed the ruse, which may account for the tentativeness of the image. But an ethical dilemma is being played out here that not only relates to the issue of consent but also to the way the photograph is interpreted sociologically.

Halima Begum in her study of urban regeneration in Brick Lane found that, while this thoroughfare was a place of Bengali commerce trading on the exoticism of ethnic food and south Asian style, many local young Asians saw Brick Lane as a place of recreation for white people.[14] Brick Lane is viewed as a place where Bengali men work but where whites play. The presence of young Asian women in this place meant they ran the risk of being viewed as morally questionable. This is particularly acute at night and Halima Begum cites a story told by one of her respondents called Shupriya as typical of many of the accounts: 'I was out in Brick Lane with another Asian female friend. This cabbie was standing near his car and instead of saying the usual thing – do you want a cab? – he said, do you want a man? A couple of other boys were standing by and they sniggered.'[15] The implication of this for Shupriya was that being out meant to

Figure 4.2 Zarina and Shireen (*photograph by Nicola Evans, Antonio Genco and Gerard Mitchell*)

the cab driver that she was either sexually available or a prostitute looking for clients. As Fran Tonkiss points out: 'gender and sexuality become visible in the city in the symbolic coding of space, through modes of spatial practice and interaction, in terms of material divisions and exclusions in space, and in the "micro-geographies" of the body'.[16] Participation in Brick Lane's public world is variegated and allows differential access, depending on how an individual body is coded within a complex interplay of racialized, gendered and sexual definitions and associations. Some of these issues may be alive in Zarina and Shireen's portrait but overdetermining cultural explanations contain a danger and a threat of violation. Perhaps they simply wanted to get on with their shopping. The tension played out here is about the nature of analysis, that is how to think about the complexities of the city as a gendered and racially coded landscape without denying these girls their humanity and agency. Perhaps a way to avoid this is to embrace the picture's enigmatic quality, reading it in an open way that can connect to cultural explanations without reducing and flattening the motivations and human complexity of those portrayed. The reason for the photograph's inclusion is not only for its beauty but also as a register of Zarina and Shireen's being there. That presence shines back at us; it is a fragile and precious gift that deserves careful handling.

Part of what I want to argue is that the lens is not always about the control and fixing of subjects. To see photography as merely a governing technology misses the instability and complexity of the drama that unfolds on either side of the lens. In an interview Brazilian photographer Sebastio Salgado commented: 'Sometimes people call you to give the pictures. People come to you, to your lens, as if they were coming to speak into a microphone.'[17] It is a mistake, I think, to see the lens as only looking one way. The figures in these portraits look back. They stare back at us. Cameras in this context are like windows that look out onto the street, and through which the street looks in. Perhaps windows are a little like lenses. While we may pass by each other in cities and refuse eye contact, these portraits announce a kind of eye-to-eye recognition, even though the subject looks into the dark void beyond the aperture, as if looking into the retina of the eye itself.

What the *About the Streets Project* also offered was recognition to those who are usually not recognized. Barry's portrait, shown here in Figure 4.3, is a good example. Barry has lived with his mother all his life, in Middlesex Street, close to Petticoat Lane Market. They are part of an east London Jewish community that is diminishing as people move on and out of the area. Gerry explains:

> If [Barry] saw, say, a fashion shoot set up in the street, Barry would just walk by and go back to see his mother – it wouldn't be for him. But he saw me and we got chatting because of the way we were doing it, and the large format camera and all. Barry was drawn into the whole atmosphere of what we were doing. He does his shopping at 11 o'clock every Sunday. It meant a lot to him that we were there.[18]

This kind of acknowledgement or taking notice, through inviting people to the lens, might easily be dismissed. The value of respectful listening, be it through making photographic images or collecting people's stories, is part of what I think sociology is needed for. It is rare, in some ways unique, for someone like Barry to be listened to or noticed. Equally, what is true of this image is that the photograph does not try to make its subject into a heroic figure.

On 12 November 2002 an exhibition of the photography entitled *E2 Portraits* (after the postal district) took place at the Spitz Gallery in the Old

Figure 4.3 Barry (*photograph by Nicola Evans, Antonio Genco and Gerard Mitchell*)

Spitalfields Market. Many of the subjects portrayed in the photographs were there to see themselves in the show. It was a unique event – I could not imagine a similar equivalent in the context of sociological or anthropological proceedings. It is rare that research participants are present at sociology conferences where their lives are being discussed. Somehow the presence of 'the subjects' made it impossible for their representations to be cast in caricature. The people and the images were allowed to be prosaic compounds of vice and virtue, they were allowed to be annoyingly human. There was something precious about this, yet at the same time people like Barry felt that they had been acknowledged and taken seriously, perhaps for the first time. Gerry remembered: 'When he came on the night of the show in Spitalfield Gallery there were tears in Barry's eyes when he saw himself in that show. It's made a difference to his life that he was in that show. It made me feel better about it.'[19] The portraits capture a moment in someone's life that is gone in a fraction of a second, that quarter or eighth of a second in which the aperture is exposed. It is often said that photographs are taken. It is interesting to me that Salgado in the above quotation speaks of pictures being *given*. There are at least two senses in which these pictures are given. The first is in the sense of the verb, to give. Those who look back give them; their look is a gift that is received. The second is in the sense of the adjective, something that is known, bestowed and specified in the look of those who stand before the lens. This is a description of a condition that outlines a sense of being that isn't fully articulated.

Epitaphs to the Living

These photographs are a gift in which existence is performed and presented to the camera's lens. This does not mean such impression management is inauthentic, for all social relations are like this. In a way, part of the conceit of the 'whole truth' version of social analysis is that it claims to know it all.[20] It is an advance to say that these social selves are incomplete and partial as they are presented and dramatized. We can't claim to know it all but it does not follow that we grasp no likeness at all. The portrait of Jackie in Figure 4.4 could not be more self-styled. She addresses the camera and she takes her spot and strikes her pose. Nicola remembered: 'She was just larger than life. It was like "How do you want me?" She was ready to go. She just posed where she was and there was no staging of the image. She was that kind of person. She called everyone "Honey"!'[21] Jackie comes to Brick Lane each Sunday from her home in Peckham to buy cheap cigarettes. For all her confidence and poise there is something else that is opaque beneath the veneer of brashness, perhaps hidden injuries or confidential frailties. Roland Barthes once wrote: 'In front of the lens, I am at the same time: the one I think I am, the one I want others to think I am, the one the photographer thinks I am, and the one he makes use of to exhibit his art.'[22] What is being played out on the surface of the image is both the internal and external world of identity and existence. But it is also an existence that has passed.

The Peruvian poet César Vallejo once asked in a poem: 'Must we die every second?'[23] Of course, the life that is outlined in these images is a phantom life passed in living. The merit in recording a life passed in living might easily be dismissed or scoffed at. Actually, I think this is exactly where the ethical value

Figure 4.4 Jackie (*photograph by Nicola Evans, Antonio Genco and Gerard Mitchell*)

of projects such as this one is to be found. The photographs are like epitaphs to the living – unlike the flesh of the subject they depict, they will not age. Donna's unusual portrait (Figure 4.5) reminds us too that the skin can serve as a canvas for remembrance in a similar way to the examples discussed in the previous chapter. She shows the tattoos inscribed on the inside of her upper arms, tattoos that are usually obscured by her arms, although not completely hidden. The music we have to listen to through looking is the melody of Stevie Wonder's 'Isn't She Lovely?'. Donna lives in West Norwood, South London and she had the tattoos done to commemorate her goddaughter, Lyric, who died of brain cancer at Christmas in 1997. Donna kept a vigil beside Lyric's bed along with the baby's parents. 'Isn't she lovely?' was a lullaby they had sung to Lyric before her illness, but they also comforted her with it in hospital. Donna chose to have the tattoos on the inside of her arms because that is where she held Lyric before she died. 'I guess I hug my tattoos', she said. In the portrait she turns the notes and melody outward and shows them to us. The tattooist's needle perforated inside and out, and the price of these indelible lines was a physical pain that is befitting, given the grief and loss that inspired them. Donna's look contains a strong presence – it is both frail and inviolable.

Nicola, Antonio and Gerry took the idea of the photograph as a gift literally. Each person who gave their presence to their camera was given a print in return. There was, however, one exception. In Figure 4.6, Bill is pictured close to the Bagel Bake. At the time Bill was homeless, or more accurately he was sleeping rough. But this is not a picture of destitution; in fact Bill had made a world for himself in front of the bagel shop. From the beginning of the project he was fascinated by the mechanics of the camera and was insistent about being included. Nicola remembered 'Bill just followed us down the street and said, "Could you take my photograph?" He kept saying to us, "What's that? What's that?"'[24]

Bill became part of the regular cast of Sunday morning characters. As time passed he seemed to be fashioning a place for himself. As we saw in Chapter 2, a sense of 'home' can exist without a postal address; it is the 'centre of the world – not in a geographical, but in an ontological sense'.[25] In this way Bill was 'at home' in front of the Bagel Bake. He would set up a stall of trinkets, mostly rubbish, and became a kind of trader in what others had discarded. He hardly sold anything. Gerry reflected on Bill's portrait: 'You wouldn't think that was a man who was living on the street – there is a life in it, he hadn't given up on life. The bagel shop was the centre of his universe in a way – he was still enjoying himself. In a way he'd found his patch, his place in life.'[26] It is important to say that the Bagel Bake is a place of encounter. It is a twenty-four-hour place. On any given night all stripes of London life come through its

Figure 4.5 Donna (*photograph by Nicola Evans, Antonio Genco and Gerard Mitchell*)

door – clubbers, policemen, vagrants, black-cab drivers, newspaper delivery men, all come to pick up bagels, onion platzels, chollahs, lox and salt beef sandwiches laced with pungent English mustard. The shop is the oldest of its kind and it is owned by an Israeli who wears a big gold 'Chai' symbol (which means 'life') around his neck.

One of Bill's close associates is Nobby, shown here in Figure 4.7. Nobby is one of the Jewish Old Boys who turn up each Sunday in Brick Lane to work their trade. Originally from Bow, in his youth Nobby was a featherweight boxer, and knew the infamous east London gangsters the Kray twins. He has his dog with him – Snoopy – part as companion, part protector. Around his neck are gold chains and rings that are 'for sale'. Nobby is one of the key

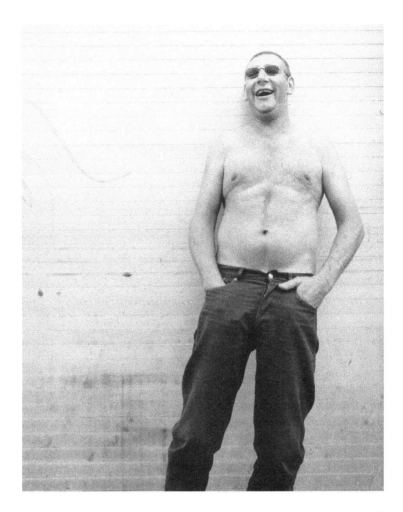

Figure 4.6 Bill (*photograph by Nicola Evans, Antonio Genco and Gerard Mitchell*)

sources of local knowledge – he seemed to know everyone in the area and Antonio developed a special rapport with him. In the lead up to the show at the Spitz Gallery, the photographers tried to contact all the participants. Antonio remembered:

> Bill didn't have an address – we wanted people at the opening – we went looking for him, we couldn't find him. I had a print of his picture and then a few days before the exhibition I spoke to Nobby. He told me that two-and-a half weeks before, Bill was killed on the streets – a car hit him, smacked his head and that was it. He looked so alive in the photograph I'd been carrying around with me and then he was gone.[27]

Figure 4.7 Nobby (*photograph by Nicola Evans, Antonio Genco and Gerard Mitchell*)

Bill's photograph takes on poignancy now – a gift from the dead to the living that can never be reciprocated.

Cities of Time

The E2 portraits are about the city and its citizens. Paradoxically it is through these intimate portraits that we learn about a place or landscape that we usually hardly see. I think at its core the project is also about time – the shutter time, the long exposure. In the two years that the photographers worked in Brick Lane they took a total of 200 negatives. Taken as a whole, the shutter on their ancient camera was exposed for less than a minute. 'We were collecting things from time', commented Gerry: 'We were scraping against the fabric of time and then you would be normal for the rest of the week and you'd think about it and then you would worry the fabric of time again. When you are taking a photograph you are really aware of time.'[28] The photographs are also about engagement and about spending time. But the rhythm of each session couldn't be controlled and the photographs couldn't be staged. Some days they would go looking for particular people and settings but would never find them. They would have to respond to the rhythm of the street. These portraits are cast against the commercial panoramas evident in the publicity material and websites produced by the corporations of the New London. The panorama itself is a form that attempted to represent the 'whole truth' about the natural order, these portraits tell a different story and they won't be cheapened in the same way.[29] Neither are they a complete visual rendering of the people who live in and move through these places, rather they contain just a fraction of life, a deep partiality that is nonetheless vital and, to my mind, precious.

Marshall Berman has written:

> I think it's an occupational hazard for intellectuals, regardless of their politics, to lose touch with the stuff and flow of everyday life. But this is a special problem for intellectuals on the left, because we, among all political movements, take a special pride in noticing people, respecting them, listening to their voices, caring about their needs, bringing them together, fighting for their freedom and happiness ... Unless we know how to recognise people, as they look and feel and experience the world, we'll never be able to help them recognize themselves or change the world. Reading Capital won't help us if we don't also know how to read the signs in the street.[30]

What's refreshing about Berman is how much his work on urban culture stands in contrast to the jaded cynicism produced under the influence of anti-humanism and its various companions. Berman is acutely aware of this:

> The bad news is how sour and bitter most left-wing writing on culture has become. Sometimes it sounds as if culture were just one more Department of Exploitation and Oppression, containing nothing luminous or valuable in itself ... Read, or try to read, a few articles on 'hegemonic/counter hegemonic discourse'. The way these guys write, it's as if the world has passed them by.[31]

Berman challenges us to try to read the signs in the street. This is something that the work here has already anticipated. It avoids the kind of heroic immersion that has also been part of the left's legacy with regard to its writing on culture, from George Orwell to Bea Campbell. At the same time it is driven by a desire to engage with people in their ordinary circumstances of life.

As James Clifford once warned, in order to return to naturalism we first have to leave it.[32] These photographs are not unproblematically realist images; they are produced by many hands. What is compelling about them is precisely the attention to dialogue, their way of reaching out and of trying to read the signs, but always from a particular point of view. The city is ground anew in this lens. It may be labouring the point but the reason why there are no quotations from Bill, Jackie or Shireen here is that they communicate with us through their photographs. They come to the camera as if speaking in a telephone box with a direct line to eternity. Paraphrasing Walter Benjamin's famous phrase, it is not what they *say* it is what they *show* that is important.[33] This is another way to think about the place of photography in accessing and investigating social life. Here images are not 'eye candy' but contain the essence of the message. The photographs also invite a reading that transcends purely visual terms of reference within wider ranges of senses. Of course, photography is a mute form; there is no sound, no smell or touch. But I think there is also an invitation being issued in these photographs. To hear the still voices of the citizens who inhabit these pictures we have to listen as we look at them. We need to project ourselves into them in order to hear the spectral chatter of those who address us directly with their look.

Conclusion: Sociology's Ethical Stage

Returning to the question I started with, I am not claiming that this project is an example of unproblematic dialogue or balanced reciprocity between researchers and participants. Research, like life itself, is unstable and risky. The fact that each participant signed a consent form at the beginning of the process provided no guarantees or protection. The *About the Streets Project* facilitated real exchange and this is captured in the vitality and beauty of the portraits themselves. Bill's portraits provided a poignant reminder of the unreciprocated gift that he gave to the research. However, I think the portrait of him is a powerful defence of the project's moral and political worth. As visual methodologies are used more and more, it may be that they offer us an opportunity to think differently about the technology and equipment of social investigation.[34] There could be nothing surreptitious about the ancient cameras that we set up in the streets. They provided a very specific staging for recording the participant's self-presentation. An attention to this context may also have provided protection against the temptation to make grand claims about portraits as a representation of all the people who pass through Brick Lane.

By contrast, anthropological film-maker Jean Roche once commented: 'For me … the only way to film is to walk with the camera, taking it to wherever it is the most effective, and improvising a ballet in which the camera itself becomes just as much alive as the people it's filming.'[35] Conversely, people had to come to the cameras and wait patiently to address it. As Bourdieu wrote: 'I think it important above all to reflect not only on the limits of thought and of the powers of thought, but also on the conditions in which it is exercised, which lead so many thinkers to overstep the limits of a social experience that is necessarily partial and local, both geographically and socially.'[36] To say that these portraits are partial is not quite the same as claiming they are limited or lack depth. By being honest about their limitations I think it is possible to interpret the rich quality contained within them regardless of whether the person being photographed is aware of what they are communicating or not.

Here we might think of sociological ethics being staged in two related ways. The first is the ethical dimension of research situated in a place or context. This is where the interactions between participants and researchers take place in all their surprising and counter-intuitive complexity. Ethical guidelines are often of limited use when faced with the unstable and fluid nature of the contexts of research. The regulatory approach to ethics adds little to our understanding or appreciation of sociology in action. Secondly, sociological ethics are staged through time. This includes the unfolding relationship with research participants but also the craft of writing and the kinds of audiences we address. In the Introduction to this book I quoted the challenged posed by Nirmal Puwar, namely how can we listen to people and write about them 'amid the risks of enacting symbolic and epistemic violence'? One way to avoid objectifying them is to draw the subjects of sociology into the very spaces where research is shown and discussed. This means inviting research participants to become sociological readers and viewers in much the same way that I described in relation to the exhibition of the *E2 Portraits*. They may simply not be interested in an invitation of this kind and I have been guilty of such mistaken presumption many times. However, this is not a reason to retreat back into the Ivory Tower. Similarly, it is a good rule of thumb to imagine that the people we work with are reading our words as we write them or hearing our arguments as we voice them. The issue of public sociology has been widely debated, particularly in relation to Michael Burawoy's appeal for greater engagement. 'What should we mean by public sociology? Public sociology brings sociology into conversation with publics, understood as people who are themselves involved in conversation', he comments.[37] I will return to this discussion in the final chapter but for now I want to suggest that the participants in our research should be party to and involved in the public conversation about sociology.

In this chapter I have argued for a photography that listens. Moving on from the discussion of urban portraiture, the next chapter examines what we can learn from recording the call of the city and subjecting it to serious sociological attention. In the following chapter I will argue that developing a sense of the city as a soundscape or a sonic panorama offers a way to think about the quality of urban multiculture and the phobias that have followed in the wake of the war on terror. It is with this in mind that I want to take you to where I work and the offices of the Department of Sociology at Goldsmiths at the top of Warmington Tower in New Cross.

CHAPTER 5

London Calling

I think a good place to begin is to listen to the sounds of belonging to time. Listen to the contemporary – or, better, listen to the sounds around you! Listen in order to imagine a non-history of the future. Learn to listen in new ways, ways that open us up to new possibilities. Without the ability to stop the change, one listens to the change itself. Without the ability to distinguish between the important and the trivial, one listens to whatever, or, perhaps, to whatever it is that matters. Sometimes such imaginations can be heard in the speed of change itself.

Lawrence Grossberg[1]

The Department of Sociology at Goldsmiths College is housed at the top of a once-condemned twelve-storey tower block on Lewisham Way in south London. Close to the banks of the River Thames, it looks out on to the city's panorama. 'Love the view' visitors say as they point out familiar London landmarks like the Palace of Westminster or the twenty-first-century glass edifices of the Canary Wharf and HSBC towers. Standing out on the rooftop it is not the look of London that captures my imagination, rather it is the sound of the city. With the aid of my friend and colleague John Drever, we began recording the sounds of London in April 2005. There were many false starts. On one occasion we ascended the tower only to find a seminar full of young intellectuals blocking our way to the roof. West of this high open perch is the beautiful twenty-first-century Ferris wheel, the London Eye. Suspended over the River Thames, the wheel's 'flights' offer an inimitable line of sight by raising its passengers out of the city's grasp. The general public are raised to the status of what de Certeau would call 'voyeur-gods'.[2] When the sun shines on its glass pods the London Eye looks like a jewelled necklace. With the help of John's sophisticated sound recording technology we have attempted something quite different, the creation of a kind of aural panorama fashioning from the once-condemned tower a kind of London Ear.

What is at stake in listening to the call of London? Paying this serious sociological attention, the voices and sounds of the city take on a greater importance in the aftermath of the 7 July 2005 bombings. I will address this question
in two ways: firstly, to use our listening apparatus to make audible that which
is taken for granted in the clamour of urban life; secondly, I want to argue that
contained in London's call are important lessons regarding the co-presence of
multiculture and racism. In *Noise* Jacques Attali writes that 'we must learn to
judge a society by its sounds'.[3] Lewisham Way is noisy. RoadAlert.org.uk
voted it the second noisiest road in Britain.[4] Whatever the deafening truth
might be about this corner of London, our strange little sonic experiment has
taught us that you never hear what you are listening for. On one occasion we
ascended the tower, tuned John's sound equipment and recorded the unthink-
able: New Cross was unnervingly quiet, almost entirely still. I had never heard
the sound of children laughing from twelve storeys up or the arcane clip-clop
of police horses trotting past or even more unsettling complete silence.

The sound of the city has changed dramatically. There have been few still
moments in the London soundtrack since the 7 July bombings, the exception
being the uneasy silence that filled the tube cars underground. After the
second wave of abortive attacks on 21 July, commuters travelled silently to
work, trying not to notice the police men with their machine guns or the eth-
nically profiled stop-and-search policy that targeted people for being 'Asian' or
'Arab' looking. Both attacks occurred on Thursdays and the security level was
heightened every Thursday that followed along with a corresponding atmosphere of fear and dreadful anticipation.

'If you listen, you can hear it', writes John McGregor in the opening passage
of his novel *If Nobody Speaks of Remarkable Things*. 'The city, it sings … so
listen, and there is more to hear.'[5] Camus once commented that some cities
'open to the sky like a mouth or wound'.[6] Our city not only sings, it cries.
Since that summer the wail of police siren has become what Murray Shaffer
would call a keynote sound.[7] The police car approaching from the Old Kent
Road gains in volume as it dodges the traffic along Lewisham Way.[8] There are
other things contained on these recordings if we listen closely – the sound of
movement. The dull metallic moan of a jet aeroplane passing overhead as it
carries some of the 90 million passengers that pass through London's main airports each year. The sound of a motorcycle accelerating, moving cars and the
squeal of their brakes as they come to a temporary halt, a seagull passing overhead are also there to be heard. It is perhaps an obvious point but the targets
of terror are more often than not technologies of movement – the bus, the
underground and the aeroplane. Phobic racists paste hateful graffiti on bus
shelters or roadside walls in a vain attempt to slow down contact and human
traffic.

Sounds are, after all, the sensing of vibrations: our ears pick up the vibrations of movement. Listening to cosmopolitan London is different from looking at it, in part because race and racism operate within ocular grammars of difference. Listening admits presences in such encounters that can be missed in the visual play of skin. Sit on any London bus today and the languages you'll hear are more likely to be Russian, Polish or Portuguese Brazilian, depending on your route. These languages are the registers of new movements and migrations that are not always visually accessible. It is the sound of the police sirens that predominate and I wonder why the police use them so routinely. In Los Angeles the LAPD have cleared whole areas by switching on their police car sirens simultaneously. The sirens contain a desire to control the space they fill. Perhaps the sirens have always been there and it is just that we notice them now – I doubt it, though. It is worth noting that police cars in Britain only started carrying sirens in 1965. The 'twos and blues' (two tones and blue lights) are 'get out of the way signs', they have come to signal what Martin Amis calls a 'nameless dread'.[9]

There is nothing inherent in the tones of the sirens themselves that produces this effect and their frequency can and has been rendered into banal music. A student living on the New Cross Road told me that her infant starts to dance when she hears the police sirens. Rather, the effect has a history that aligns the sound of the siren to a state of emergency and domestic threat. Before the police had sirens and cars they carried rattles, whistles and only a few distinguished police cars – The Wolseleys – had the luxury of bells. The rattle shown in Figure 5.1 is particularly interesting because it was carried during the First World War to warn Londoners of the threat posed by Germen Zeppelin bomber raids. The sounding of an alarm also signals the threat of external attack, be it from a Zeppelin or, later, planes or rockets. Every police station in London was equipped with a siren from the 1940s onwards (see Figure 5.2). They would be sounded during air raids or as flood warnings and were kept in use during the Cold War in case of a nuclear missile attack.

The sirens provide unintended sonic signposts. Regular convoys of high security prisoners pass through New Cross from Her Majesty's Prison at Belmarsh, SE28 en route to the High Courts in central London at Temple Bar. Belmarsh – opened in 1991 – holds more than 900 category A prisoners, including suspects held under the anti-terrorist legislation. As a result, the prison has been dubbed London's Guantanamo Bay. Sometimes the procession of police cars and their high security escorts finds the route through south London hard to navigate. They regularly attempt to drive the *wrong way* around the one-way system in New Cross. The deafening gridlock that results produces a spectacle of panic, alarm and emergency. These scenes of urban pandemonium could be easily avoided. The prison architects who built

Figure 5.1 Rattle used by police during the First World War to warn of Zeppelin air raids, London Metropolitan Police Archive (*photograph by author*)

Figure 5.2 Police station siren, London Metropolitan Police Archive (*photograph by author*)

Belmarsh constructed a magistrate's court opposite the prison. The idea behind the design was that the judicial and the penal elements of the system would be in the same place, and prisoners could move from judgement to incarceration in the space of a few hundred metres. However, judges are reluctant to make the short journey to south-east London and prefer the prisoners be brought to them costing thousands of pounds. An exception was the recent appearance of the men accused of the failed 21 July suicide bomb attacks. This time the judge came to Belmarsh where the four defendants were charged with 'conspiracy to murder and cause explosions'. *The Times* newspaper described the scene at Belmarsh Magistrate's Court on 8 August 2005 as 'the tightest police guard ever seen ... Even plastic cups were screened for harmful substances.'[10] In December that year the suspects appeared in the courtroom of the Old Bailey via video link from the cells in Belmarsh.[11] The sound of the sirens also reveals and betrays London's carceral geography and how the complicities in the war on terror are part of local routines and realities.

The police siren is more often accompanied by the air-chopping sound of the police helicopters that hang in the sky as the motorcade snakes its way through the streets below. 'Living in a street off the New Cross Road, I'm used to the sound of police sirens', writes Jane who works as an administrator at Goldsmiths College.

> The helicopters are harder to become habituated to; in the evenings, the noise obliterates the sound of the TV, and the approaching searchlight inspires a peculiar feeling of guilt, a fear that it will eventually light up the house! When Abu Hamza was remanded in Belmarsh Prison, media coverage of his trial was incessant, but one day I realized that I could follow his progress, not by watching the news, but by listening out for the cacophony produced by the police cars escorting the prison transporter vehicle in which he was being taken from Woolwich to the Old Bailey, up the New Cross Road, with a low-flying helicopter tracking the progress of the convoy.[12]

The soundtrack of the war on terror throws a blanket over the city. The sirens create a sense of imminent threat in which dread and alarm is mutually enhanced.[13] In Greek antiquity, Phobos was the god of fear, terror and alarm from which the word 'phobia' is derived. The sound of the police car and the helicopter is both a cause and an effect of the fear cast over London in the aftermath of the July bombings and part of the damage done as a result is the creation of a climate of misrecognition. The shooting at Stockwell tube station of young Brazilian Jean Charles de Menezes by the police is an example of deadly misrecognition. On 22 July – the day after the second wave of abortive attacks – the policeman saw a 'suicide bomber' in their sights and shot him. Figures 5.3 and 5.4 show the makeshift memorial that has been erected

outside Stockwell station, which provides both a place where news and information relating to the killing can be posted for local people and also where
flowers of remembrance can be laid.

The kind of misrecognition I am trying to describe is to be found in the stare
of passengers who look anxiously at a young Asian man struggling to carry a

Figure 5.3 Memory and News, Jean Charles de Menezes memorial, Stockwell, London
(*photograph by author*)

heavy bag on to the number 36 bus. A London Transport poster campaign warns Londoners, 'Don't Make Your a Bag a Suspect.' It was not bags that identified the suspects, but skin tones and beards. The shooting of Mohammed Abdul Kahar on spurious intelligence is another example. Mohammed Abdul Kahar, twenty-three, and Abul Koyair, twenty, were arrested in the 2 June 2006 raid on their home in Forest Gate, east London, involving 250 officers. After his release Mohammed Abdul Kahar wrote of the ways in which he and his family had been terrorized: 'I feel the only crime I have done, in their eyes, is being an Asian with a long-length beard.'[14] They were released with no charge but at no time were they told why their house was raided so violently. They had been reported because they had grown beards, shaved their heads and attended the local mosque more frequently.

We are all looking at each other differently and this is attested by the ordinary tales of many people moving across a cosmopolitan city in the shadow of the 7 July. London's transport police stopped 6,747 people under antiterrorism laws between July and August 2005. The ethnic profiling of these

Figure 5.4 Jean Charles de Menezes memorial (*photograph by author*)

stops is very stark: 2,390 stops were Asian people (35 per cent of the total) and 2,168 of white people (32 per cent of the total). In London, Asian people comprise 12 per cent of the population, while white people are 63 per cent.[15] Asians were five times more likely to be stopped. The city of fear produces a politics of misrecognition. There has been much discussion and debate about the notion of recognition in discussions of multiculturalism, principally focusing on Charles Taylor's pronouncements on the matter.[16] The sirens don't help us hear each other or to speak against this fear – rather they make our voices inaudible.

Tiggy was stuck on an underground train just outside Stockwell station the day Jean Charles de Menezes was shot. 'I was trying to make my way through town and the tube stopped suddenly my first thought was "damn this is going to make me late."'[17] Tiggy spent many years in South Africa where she was involved in anti-racist politics. 'We were told a suicide bomber was in the train ahead – my first response was "I hope they killed him first."' The police did shoot first; after restraining him, they shot the young Brazilian seven times in the head. 'Isn't that awful', Tiggy reflected later, 'you start to see the world the way the police do'. Part of the work that the sirens do in our time is to maintain the constant sense of war and emergency and amplify fear. The phobocity is not created by the bombers alone, rather it is created by politicians and journalists who are concerned with the thought of them and trade on people's fears.

7 July to 7/7: The Political Longitudes of the War on Terror

Clifford Geertz commented that that the attacks on the World Trade Center on September 11, 2001 or 9/11 marked the beginning of the now.[18] What has been telling since the July bombings in London is the degree of citation that links them to the World Trade Center. Much is revealed in the way that events are named. It might seem trivial, but something very serious is at stake in the calendar shift that has transposed 7 July to 7/7. This kind of naming is more than merely a line through time; it is the temporal alignment of geopolitics. It results in a kind of political longitude that designates a historical moment, yet at the same time comes to occlude historical perspective: Ground Zero has become year zero. It is impossible to speak of the events in London without first situating them relative to the prime meridian of US geopolitical time, which runs through Lower Manhattan.

The attacks on the World Trade Center were experienced in real time as a truly global event. As those domestic aircraft were transformed into incendiary birds of prey, the world watched. Marx's haunting prophecy 'all that is solid melts into air, all that is sacred is profane, and man is at last compelled to face sober senses, his real conditions of life, and his relations with his kind'[19] took on a deadly ring of relevance. Contained in the advancing grey clouds of devastation were millions of pieces of paper, where whole files of documents were scattered across the rooftops of Manhattan perfectly intact. These pages were inscribed by many hands. John Berger has written that 'the opposite of to love is not to hate but to separate'.[20] On the paper, fragile traces of life were held suspended in that envelope of annihilation, as if carried by spectral messengers trying to find their way back. There was no way home, only separation.

In her last book Susan Sontag wrote that the World Trade Center attack highlighted how our encounter with reality is skewed:

> Something becomes real – to those who are elsewhere, following it as 'news' – by being photographed. But a catastrophe that is experienced will often seem eerily like its representation. The attack on the World Trade Center on September 11 2001 was described as 'unreal', 'surreal', 'like a movie', in many of the first accounts of those who escaped from the towers or watched from nearby.[21]

The encounter with these events feels somehow more real through the TV screen, even though the screen itself acts like a sensory prophylactic allowing through only mediated views and filtered sounds. On the other hand, bearing direct witness seemed unreal. New York photographer Frank Schwere felt compelled to visit Ground Zero. He wrote on 13 September 2001: 'Everything was covered with white finger-thick dust. It felt like being on another planet. There were so many little side streets with no colours, no people, no noise. Just broken windows, the extreme smell of burn, dust papers, trashed cars ... The streets felt like a Hollywood set. I had to remind myself that it was real.'[22] One photograph from the time showed an empty bus with the names of lost people written into the thick layer of dust – 'RIP Manny'. A New Yorker wrote with his finger: 'Fuck You Bin Laden.'[23]

One enduring lesson contained in these events is the importance of questioning our relation to reality: what is real and what is unreal? Equally, to whom do these terrible events belong? The fetish for first-person testimony is almost universal – including sociologists like myself – yet at the same time such accounts are from a simple reflection of a stable reality. St Paul's Chapel is literally a few hundred metres from Ground Zero (see Figure 5.5). Miraculously it was not swamped by the debris when the towers fell. It became the headquarters for the emergency services as they attended the wreckage. St Paul's has become an icon of endurance and national mourning. Rector of Trinity Church, in nearby Wall Street, Reverend Dr Daniel P. Matthews spoke in his first sermon on 23 September 2001 of what St Paul's was like immediately after the attack. 'Dust. Dust everywhere, everywhere, everywhere dust. Everything covered with dust. Unbelievable. We couldn't imagine how the whole of South Manhattan Island could be covered with dust. It wasn't long before we began saying: "What should we dust off the first?"'[24] He described how the pews, prayer books and votive candles were cleaned so that people could reflect and pray.

> And we're still dusting. But the dust did not just fall in the southern tip of Manhattan. The dust fell all over the whole world on September 11. Not one inch of this earth is without dust. Little villages all over the world, people, religious groups, faiths of all traditions, nations, people, everybody is covered with the dust of the World Trade Center of September 11. None is without dust.[25]

Michel de Certeau wrote that the Manhattan skyline is a 'wave of verticals' that is arrested by vision.[26] Without the Towers there is a huge hole in the wave. The loss is mourned in the bric-a-brac that the street vendors sell to tourists and pilgrims – pictures of the pre-9/11 skyline and three-dimensional models of Lower Manhattan embalmed in clear plastic. This vanished skyline is like an epitaph (see Figures 5.6 and 5.7). The global resonance of these events has drawn people to make pilgrimages to Lower Manhattan.[27] The huge hole in the ground that is the footprint of the World Trade Center induced in me an intense sense of vertigo. That was my feeling in November 2004. I stood on the Brooklyn Bridge and desperately wanted to return home to London and draw those dear to me near – all that is solid melts into air. The dust fell on the whole world but paradoxically its aftermath has resulted in thicker lines being drawn between its people.

Returning a year later in December 2005 I noticed that the street sellers had been pushed back from the street immediately around Ground Zero (see Figure 5.8). In front of a drugstore on Fourteenth Street I noticed a rack of postcards, one showing the Twin Towers recoloured as the Stars and Stripes. At St Paul's Chapel there was the launch of a children's book by A. B. Curtis called *The Little Chapel That Stood*. At a table an elderly woman wore a badge the size of a dinner plate that read 'I am the Author'. Far from a global event the attacks had been nationalized, here in the chapel that stood, where George Washington prayed and where the firefighters and construction workers slept and rested, amid the flags and NYPD T-shirts, the patriotic claims over the attacks are being choreographed and managed in the daily routines of a wounded and banal nationalism.[28]

On 27 December 2001, Republican Rudolph Giuliani, preparing to leave the mayor's office after eight years, chose St Paul's Chapel to give his farewell address to an invited crowd of approximately 300 people. He stated:

Figure 5.5 St Paul's Chapel, Lower Manhattan, New York (*photograph by author*)

This chapel is thrice-hallowed ground. It is hallowed by the fact that it was consecrated as a house of God in 1766. And then in April of 1789, George Washington came here after he was inaugurated as the first President of our Republic. He prayed right here in this church, which makes it very sacred ground to people who care deeply about America. Then it was consecrated one more time on September 11.[29]

The result is that events and places become politically copyrighted, organized into alignments of them/us in which political commitments and injuries are

Figure 5.6 Manhattan embalmed in plastic, New York (*photograph by author*)

Figure 5.7 Skyline as epitaph, New York (*photograph by author*)

Figure 5.8 Ground Zero, Lower Manhattan, New York (*photograph by author*)

organized and confined to the interests of those who issue them. Such political copyrights are not always expressed so explicitly and a sociological attention to them reveals the norms and ideals that claim them as their exclusive property.

Zebra, a rock musician who lives across the street from the Chelsea Hotel, walks past Ground Zero everyday en route to his day job as a fund-raiser for the Manhattan Synagogue. He took me to Ground Zero for the first time and he was shocked and surprised by my reaction to witnessing the place first hand.

> For me, I just want to try and restore some normality to life. So, I don't make a big deal about it. Some of the other people who come to New York on this big fucking pilgrimage from Kansas or wherever wearing NYPD T-shirts I am not so sure about. Before they probably hated New York and everything New York stands for. They are not showing solidarity with New York, it's about being an American. Right? New York is not all of America, New York is not Kansas.[30]

Zebra wants to restore the ordinary rituals of New York life while citizen tourists make pilgrimages through the same streets to commune with fallen heroes in national mourning.

The impulse to make victims into heroes remains strong in the wake of these events. Many acts of bravery and selflessness were performed in the midst of this carnage. But as Primo Levi warned, abjection does not ennoble its victims and the crown of heroism does nothing for the dead; rather enforced martyrdom gives a warrant for vengeance. Judith Butler points to this precise danger when she writes:

> That we can be injured, that others can be injured, that we are subject to death at the whim of another, are all reasons for both fear and grief. What is less certain, however, is whether the experiences of vulnerability and loss have to lead straightaway to military violence and retribution. There are other passages. If we are interested in arresting cycles of violence to produce less violent outcomes, it is no doubt important to ask what, politically, might be made of grief beside a cry for war.[31]

It does not honour the dead to deify them, rather it offends their memory. It enforces a kind of heroic virtue that they – the lost – were somehow superhuman, not made of the same compound of vice and virtue, of strength and frailty as the rest of us and as a consequence censors the memory of their humanity.

The warrant to vengeance can also be a licence to hate. In December 2005 the makeshift shrines had been more or less removed from the reconstruction site at Ground Zero. A few streets away the fading shrines could still be found. At the corner of Park Place and Greenwich Street was one such improvised cenotaph, red, white and blue wreaths, wilting flowers with dedications, pictures and hundreds of graffiti dedications and memento mori (see Figure 5.9). Like the names that were drawn with fingers in the dust, some graffiti remembered specific individuals. Other messages read: 'So Proud to be an American', 'From Portugal – They Take Our Lives Not Our Hearts, Jose', 'God Bless America – Magda From Poland.' A Stars and Stripes is

Figure 5.9 An improvised shrine at the corner of Park Place and Greenwich Street (*photograph by author*)

nailed to the board and written in the flag's white bands is: 'God Bless USA and all the people who perished here – 906 Trac Teamsters Local 701 NJ' (New Jersey). Next to the flag was scribbled in bold letters: 'FUCK MUSLIMS' (see Figure 5.10). Unlike the street vernacular retort against Osama Bin Laden written in the dust of the deserted bus a few days after September 11, the insult is directed at the second largest world religion, some 1.3 billion people. The graffito is part of the 'thicker lines' being drawn between the people of the world. The dust of the World Trade Center has settled on the world, but the same cannot be said for the wreckage of Baghdad, Kabul or Jerusalem. 'Our capacity to feel hangs in the balance',

Figure 5.10 'Thicker lines' (*photograph by author*)

writes Judith Butler.[32] Some deaths are grieved – like those of September 11 – while others are ungrieveable collateral damage in the war on terror. Equally, some rights are protected while others are sacrificed: internment without trial in Belmarsh Prison under the Terrorism Act being the most obvious example of the surrender of rights in the name of First World self-preservation.

It was not coincidental that the events of 7 July were quickly dubbed 7/7. The clock has literally been reset and it is important to be suspicious of this precisely because it leads to an erasure of the past. Nothing before 9/11 matters in terms of priorities within American foreign policy but also in the domestic discussion of the state of multiculture in Britain. The grim truth is that there is nothing exceptional about bombings in London and I don't mean the much-discussed Blitz unleashed by the Nazi bombers during the Second World War. There is a reason why it is almost impossible to find a rubbish bin in a tube station or why railway station bins have clear plastic liners. There have been many bombs in recent history, including the bombing attacks of the IRA and also of the white supremacist nail bomber David Copeland. In 1999 Copeland subjected London to thirteen days of carnage when three nail bomb explosions in Brixton, Brick Lane and the gay community in Soho where three were killed and 129 people injured. After the

Admiral Duncan pub bombing in Soho a wreath was laid; it read: 'Fascists you are in a minority.' Violent death and flowers of mourning are commonplace on the streets of London rather than exceptional. In the last fifteen years there have been twenty-one 'successful' bombs: eleven by the Irish Republican Army, three by white supremacists and seven by offensive jihadists. The bombs are routine if not predictable. It is often said that London is the world in a city and the place of the bomb in our world cannot be separated from the divisions and thicker lines carved within global society.

An Inventory of Multiculture

The waiting room in Lewisham Hospital's audiology department is full of people waiting to have the wax removed from their ears or more serious problems with their hearing checked out. It's 10 a.m. For those who are looking for a representative snapshot of London multiculture this is as good a place as any. There are probably fifty nationalities represented: their voices hang in the air simultaneously, the sounds of Jamaican patois heard alongside Polish and Urdu. A family sitting next to me is texting a relative news about the hurricane about to hit Jamaica. 'Please, everyone … ' says a nurse trying to gain our attention. 'I have some terrible news to announce. We've just heard that four bombs have exploded in central London. The mobile phone networks have been disabled and the hospital is on full alert. Please remain calm and we will update as far as we can.' This is how I received the news of the 7 July terrorist attacks. The bombs had exploded simultaneously at Edgware Road, King's Cross and Aldgate at 8.50 a.m. A fourth bomber had detonated his device at 9.47 a.m. while travelling on the Number 30 bus through Tavistock Square. We didn't know then that the suicide bombers were 'home-grown', citizens of multicultural Britain, drawn from families like the ones waiting here in the hospital.

Some on the centre right rushed to use the image of the 'home-grown terrorist' to claim that British multiculturalism had been a big mistake, that the bombings were simply a monster of our own making.[33] The portrayal of these events as the end of multiculturalism is a key way in which they have been copyrighted politically. The profiles of the people killed in the blasts were not unlike that hospital waiting room. They represented the ordinary face of cosmopolitan London and one of the most enduring images of these events was a photograph taken by Jonathan Hordle of a dreadlocked black Londoner walking away from a blast site with his arm around a white woman (see Figure 5.11). The expressions on their bloodstained faces spoke to the common human frailty that made their apparent differences only skin deep and ultimately trivial. On 9 July the cover of the populist right-wing newspaper *The*

Sun showed 29-year-old Laura Webb and 20-year-old Shahara Islam with the headline (see Figure 5.12): 'Two beautiful decent women. One Christian, One Muslim. Both missing with dozens more. Pray for them All.'[34] There was a sign of things to come inside this edition of the paper. Columnist Richard Littlejohn wrote, 'Our country has become a safe haven for terrorists. Our capital is not known as Londonistan for nothing.'[35] It is striking too that the bombers themselves have not often been included in the accounting of the dead. Their stories must also be included in the inventory of multiculture.

Figure 5.11 7 July 2005, two survivors walk away from the bomb blast in Tavistock Square, London (*photograph by Jonathan Hordle/Rex Features*)

It is telling that there was no debate about the end of multiculturalism after the nail bomber's hateful campaign in 1999. We might ask, why not? Part of the explanation is a tacit acceptance of the idea that racists are by definition 'home-grown'. The fascism of the majority is taken for granted, albeit with scornful

Figure 5.12 *The Sun* headline, 9 July 2005 *(reproduced courtesy of New International, London Media and Wales News and Pictures)*

embarrassment, while the authoritarianism of the weak is met with a sense of moral cataclysm that detonates the very idea and possibility of a multicultural society. There are similarities between these seemingly opposed forms of violence. A longing for purity and a loathing of the muddle of urban difference is at the heart of both of these otherwise disparate political rhetorics. The official account of the events of 7 July claimed there is 'no firm evidence to corroborate' a link to al-Qaeda.[36] It seems likely that loose connections existed between the people involved in the various plots and key individuals were at least known to each other. There is evidence of a great deal of auto-didacticism – the use of the Internet, the connection with the symbols of offensive jihadism via video, DVD or political and religious materials available via the World Wide Web.[37] The key distinction between the bombers of 7 July and their predecessors is their willingness to sacrifice themselves for their cause. The official parliamentary report into the attacks commented: 'Perhaps the most shocking aspect of the 7 July attacks was the fact that they were suicide attacks.'[38] The naming of these deeds is also a matter of ideological dispute. In an Islamic context, suicide is defined as a sin and for some Islamists sympathetic to violent jihadi movements the notion of a suicide bomber is itself an insult. As a result, sections of the Islamic media and also activists on the anti-racist left favour the term 'human bomb', which tacitly acknowledges – if not accepts – through its avoidance of the notion of suicide the ethics and rhetoric of martyrdom.

Commentators on all sides have taken stock. Bhikhu Parekh wrote: 'Recent terrorist attacks in London show both the progress we have made in fostering a common sense of belonging and the distance we need to travel.' Applauding the 'overwhelming numbers of Muslims' who have remained loyal to Britain, Parekh concluded:

> Suicide bombers are driven by an impotent rage at everything around them, and are easy prey for the peddlers of ill-thought out global causes to give their empty lives a sense of significance. They need among other things, to be given the opportunity to acquire a British identity that is strong and fulfilling enough to moderate and enrich their one-dimensional religious identity.[39]

For politicians and academic commentators the solution has been connected to the fostering of a stronger national identity. Tariq Modood, picking up the same theme, accused multiculturalists, and the left in general, of being: 'too hesitant about embracing our national identity and allying it with progressive politics. The reaffirming of a plural, changing and inclusive British identity, which can be as emotionally and politically meaningful to British Muslims as the appeal of *jihadi* sentiments, is crucial to isolating and defeating extremism.'[40] I want to return to the issue later but suffice to say here that

Parekh and Modood miss the complexities with regard to the cultural politics of the experiences of those who are drawn to such deathly movements.

It is clear from the biographies of the bombers themselves that they possessed an intimate familiarity with British identity. Even a cursory tabloid glance at the social profiles of the people implicated in these attacks demonstrates the point. Jermaine Lindsey – the so-called fourth bomber – a nineteen-year-old, was born in Jamaica and grew up in Yorkshire. He converted to Islam and became Jamal. He met his future wife Samantha Lewthwaite in Luton while she was at university. A white English girl, she had lived in integrated neighbourhoods in Luton. One of her friends described her as having a 'fascination with Asian culture'. She converted to Islam and married Jamal. They lived in Aylesbury in Buckinghamshire. They had a child. Jamal appeared to friends to be a doting father and when he exploded the bomb in Russell Square killing twenty-five people Samantha was expecting their second child. Their life is a story of cross-cultural translation, of reinvention, of becoming other than ascribed social identities.

Then there is Mohammad Sidique Khan, the oldest of the four 7 July bombers. At the beginning of October 2005 al-Jazeera – the Arab news agency based in Doha, Qatar – broadcast his message prior to the bombings. The teaching assistant from Dewsbury, West Yorkshire, told of his anticipation about the way the 'media will paint a suitable picture of me'. Addressing the world through the lens of the video camcorder he said: 'Your democratically elected governments continually perpetuate atrocities against my people all over the world and your support of them makes you directly responsible, just as I am directly responsible for protecting and avenging my Muslim Brothers and Sisters.'[41] The newspaper coverage remarked on his 'broad Yorkshire accent' to point out that the enemy close at hand has a familiar-sounding voice.[42] I want to suggest that something quite different is contained in an attention to the tattoos on his tongue.

What was carried in the sound and grain of Mohammad Sidique Khan's voice was his belonging to the place of his birth, the West Yorkshire accent betrayed his past regardless of his attempts to erase or translate it. 'My people' did not include those who have voices like his or even those who have family drawn from the same regions as his. It is not that Khan lacked opportunities to acquire a British identity, he simply chose not to and more than this he tried actively to expunge his cultural and emotional attachments to Britain. As Paul Gilroy has shown, British identity and nationalism, haunted, as it is, by racism and the relics of a colonial past, may be more part of the problem than the solution.[43] A sudden rise in the number of St George's Cross or Union Jack bumper stickers decorating the automobiles of Britain's Muslim communities is not going to be any kind of solution. A comfortable and safe 'one size fits all' multicultural national costume cannot be fashioned from this discrepant cloth. The kind of Humpty-Dumpty national identity that some commentators yearn for glosses the political incommensurabilities of racism and empire that produced the shattering in the first place. Simply put, the pieces cannot be put together again and this means thinking differently about the history of Britain's present and the cultural and political fragments that are heaped and piled upon each other.

Chetan Bhatt has shown that at the heart of the experience of young Britons who have been drawn into jihadist movements is an extraordinary act of self-reinvention. The people he is aware of have stripped themselves of their everyday culture and remade themselves through an act of will. This is not the 'clash of civilizations' heralded by Samuel Huntingdon but an epic tale of cross-cultural translation and the blurring of social and cultural boundaries. This kind of choice is exceptional. Part of the work of challenging the political copyrights that announce the 'end of multiculturalism' is to insist on situating these lives empirically and contextualizing them socially. The danger of inflating the extent of the threat is that police scrutiny and increased popular racism is felt by whole populations.

One of the paradoxes contained in the cultural politics of these movements is that they are not concerned directly with politics, debate or direct struggle over achievable demands or goals. In fact these groups are actually not about making political claims except at the most diffuse and widespread level. Rather, it is about the pursuit of personal virtue, and the observance of discipline and morals. This is a kind of politics that renounces or rejects values like democracy, argument and, paradoxically, even politics itself. The result is a kind of anti-politics of death. Chetan Bhatt concludes that this is not just a politics of martyrdom or some kind of death cult but about attempts to transcend the distinction between life and death. He writes: 'It is another way of saying that they would go if they believed their earthly death was equivalent to the abolition of death itself.'[44] Well-meant words about multicultural belonging and inclusiveness are meaningless set against the allure of this kind of extreme religious virtue. The result is an absolute line drawn between believers and the worldly or the realm of the unbeliever.

Complicity in the battle lines of the war on terror can take other very different forms. Tiggy's story mentioned earlier is one variety of the damaging sense of emergency and paranoia that seduces the most principled. The challenge is in part how to acknowledge these complicities without giving into phobias produced by the so-called war on terror. During a meeting convened by young Muslims in east London after the bombings, a young man spoke from the platform of his faith and how he had at one time been drawn to jihadist rhetoric. His voice quivering, he said: 'If sacrificing my own life would bring back the people who have been killed I would gladly do it.' This was not a posture; he was not playing to the cameras or the audience. Contained in the grain of his voice was a sense of complicity, he had gone along with some of the rhetoric that had led to the events of that summer which he had witnessed. Others within London's Muslim communities argue that these bombings are nothing to do with their faith and that no justification for violence can be found in the Koran or religious teaching. Consequently, when in the immediate aftermath of the tragedy Tony Blair referred to 'Muslim bombers' many felt that this was offensive and insulting. Is it possible to understand the motivations and world-view of Mohammad Sidique Khan mentioned earlier without his professed faith? His actions have to be situated within the rhetorics of political Islam and to do otherwise is simply denial.

The political landscape has been one dominated by denial and disavowal. In the immediate aftermath, the British government denied any connection between the attacks and the invasion of Iraq two years earlier.[45] Indeed, the geopolitical context is underplayed in the official reports into the events of July 2005.[46] George Galloway, elected as MP for Bethnal Green and Bow in 2005 on an anti-war Respect Party ticket, was quick to connect the bombs in London with the invasion and occupation of Iraq. On the day of the attacks, with the charred bodies underground barely cold, he scolded Parliament:

Does the House not believe that hatred and bitterness have been engendered by the invasion and occupation of Iraq, by the daily destruction of Palestinian homes, by the construction of the great apartheid wall in Palestine and by the occupation of Afghanistan? Does it understand that the bitterness and enmity generated by those great events feed the terrorism of bin Laden and the other Islamists? Is that such a controversial point? Is it not obvious?[47]

Such quick certainties also conceal difficult questions and they in their own way try to own their meaning. How should we understand the attacks on the World Trade Center or the Bali bombings, which pre-date the US/UK military actions in Iraq and Afghanistan? There is little room in the posturing firebrand style of Galloway and others like him to say anything about the allure of offensive jihadism and its anti-politics of death. What of the complicities and culpabilities of people close by – perhaps even among the ranks of Respect voters – who have tacitly legitimized jihadist rhetoric? In October 2005 a piece of graffiti appeared on the Martineau Estate, Cable Street on the edge of Galloway's east London constituency. 'Part 1' of the crude wall drawing showed the Manhattan skyline with planes from 'Bin Laden.co.uk Airlines' crashing into skyscrapers and people jumping from high-rise windows to their deaths. Under the heading 'Part 2' the artists had sketched London's Canary

Wharf and HSBC tower on the banks of the 'Kaffar [sic] river Thames' with missiles and rockets heading towards them. 'BIN LADEN' was etched in block letters.

Suresh Grover, long-time civil rights activist, commented that the left has been guilty of looking upon the life of 'the ghetto from a kind of political sub-urbia'.[48] Academic debates about multiculture have been similarly confined by a lack of willingness to ask searching questions about the authoritarianism of the powerless. Some inside those communities are fearful of speaking publicly against the purveyors of absolutist religious politics. In the current climate the New Labour government created a space for a faith-based politics to flourish. Chetan Bhatt has commented that faced with the complexities of the present the government has reverted to the old colonial strategy of operating through the 'community of faith leaders'. This is particularly manifest in relation to the Muslim Council of Britain – founded in 1997, the same year as Blair's election – which has become the most significant voice with the ear of government. The secretary-general of MCB at the time of the London bombings, Iqbal Sacranie, was knighted in summer 2005.[49] In 1989, Sacranie commented that 'death was perhaps too easy' for the author of *The Satanic Verses* Salman Rushdie. 'If Sir Iqbal Sacranie is the best Mr Blair can offer in the way of a good Muslim, we have a problem' commented Rushdie.[50] Conservative Islamic movements like Jamaat-i-Islami (a radical party in Pakistan and parts of Bangladesh committed to the establishment of an Islamic state ruled by sharia law) have a powerful influence on the forms that community politics take in Britain. Rushdie has argued for the need to create a historical sensibility and a more open interpretation of Islam. Rushdie argued that the refusal to debate a diversity of historical views plays into the hands of 'Islamofascists, allowing them to imprison Islam in their iron certainties and unchanging absolutes'.[51]

The allure of 'iron certainties' is captured by Hanif Kureishi's film *My Son the Fanatic* released in 1997. The film is the fable of an immigrant father whose commitment and enchantment with Britain – even in the face of racism – is cast against his son's rejection of it. Refuting the mores of the world into which he was born and bred, the son has embraced intolerant forms of political Islam and lectures his elder that 'in the end our cultures ... they cannot be mixed'. The father protests that everything is 'mingling already together'. Through gritted teeth the son says: 'Some of us are wanting something more besides muddle.' The embrace of purity and an idealization of the past is a way out of the muddle of modern life. Kureishi's message is that we are living in a time when people suffer not from doubt but from certainty, false certainties that compensate for worldly misgivings and hurts. These are not just relevant to the figures in Kureishi's fable but also to the political caste in the White House and Downing Street.

The mundane, unspectacular ways in which people live with the muddle of cosmopolitan life needs to be defended against those who exaggerate its failure. As I suggested earlier, you can find the qualities of this precious muddle in any hospital waiting room. It was here that the victims of the 7 July bombings were brought for refuge and care. Health care workers from all around the world tended to sick patients. The ultimate triviality of our racial or cultural differences was communicated as the doctors and nurses concentrated on healing and saving lives. These are places of hope where multiculture is ordinary, routine and self-evident. This does not mean that it is simply a matter of asserting that everything is all right, bombs do not detonate every day, celebrate the fact that the dominant experience is that people live with the muddle and mess of multicultural life most of the time. There are hard things to face and Suresh Grover is right to challenge us all to stop speaking – whether politically or academically – from the false comfort of a political suburbia. This means finding a political language that is against racism and terror with equal commitment and vigilance.

Perhaps an awareness of the fragility and preciousness of life itself is the lasting resource left in the wake of these terrible events (Figure 5.13). Any Londoner could have been unlucky, the blast didn't discriminate and no one is immune. Faced with the chaos on the underground that July morning, Shahara Islam decided to give up on trying to get to work. She caught the Number 30 bus en route to the shops in London's West End. On the bus was nineteen-year-old Hasib Hussein, the youngest of the four suicide bombers. Hasib, born in Leeds and of Pakistani parentage, had tried to join the Northern line at King's Cross but it was closed. At 9.47 a.m. he detonated his bomb, ripping the roof off the bus and killing Shahara Islam and twelve other people. She grew up in Whitechapel, east London and was the oldest of three children. Her father Shamsul moved to the capital in the 1960s and is a supervisor with Transport for London. Her Bangladeshi family suffered a longer wait for confirmation than the other victims' loved ones. Some believe this was because the police suspected her of being the bomber. Forensic analysis soon ruled her out. She was just a young Muslim woman who chose to do the most ordinary thing for an East End girl: presented with an opportunity to skive off work she went shopping. 'She was an Eastender, a Londoner and British, but above all a true Muslim and proud to be so', wrote her family in a statement issued after the bombings.[52] The suicide bombers killed themselves and also people like themselves, striking not against some far off enemy but at their own cultural and historical mirror image. The ordinariness of multiculture needs to be apprehended alongside the bombers' apparent disregard for the traces they carried in themselves (Figures 5.14, 5.15).

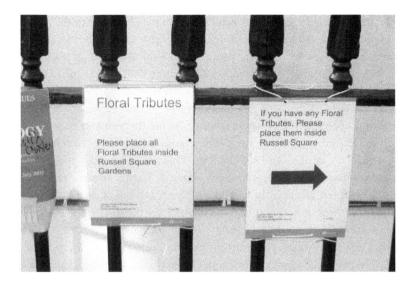

Figure 5.13 Woburn Place, London, 13 July 2005 (*photograph by author*)

Tony Blair and the British government have used the threat of terrorism to gain popularity for limiting the rights of suspects and extending the powers of the police force. On 28 February 2005 the Prime Minister told the audience of BBC Radio 4's *Women's Hour* programme that 'there are several hundred of them [terrorists] in this country who we believe are engaged in plotting or trying to commit terrorist acts'. In the summer of 2005, responding to pressure from the tabloid press, Blair launched his hastily conceived 'twelve-point plan' for tackling terror, including the ill-fated amendment of the 2000 Terrorism Bill that proposed giving police the power to detain suspects for up to ninety days without charge, which was defeated in the Commons on 9 November 2005. Prior to the May 2006 release of the official account of the London bombings, a newspaper quoted a security source saying that the number suspected of involvement in 'terror networks' had increased threefold to 700 and then in the run-up to the anniversary of the 7 July estimates were put at at least 1,200.[53] In November 2006 the head of MI5 Dame Eliza Manningham-Buller said that they were tracking 30 high-priority terrorist plots involving 200 networks and 1,600 suspects. It is very difficult to assess these claims. For example, what does it mean to be a 'suspect' in this context? Additionally, information is often being garnered from prisoners in detention held under duress or from the US secret service or the Pakistani police. The figures released by the Home Office showed that up to 30 September 2005, 895 people were arrested under the Terrorism Act, 2000. Only twenty-three of the people arrested were convicted of terrorism offences.[54] In the midst of

Figure 5.14 Flowers of remembrance, Russell Square, London, 13 July 2005 (*photograph by author*)

these inflated figures the actual number of people subjected to Control Orders is fewer than twenty.[55] Fear of the enemy next door has become a key weapon in statecraft, placating the populism of the tabloid press and garnering political support and public opinion. This strategy is as ancient as the art of politics itself. Niccolò Machiavelli wrote over 400 years ago that 'a prince ought to inspire fear in such a way that, if he does not win love, he avoids hatred'.[56] Whether or not the modern Princes are reviled is a moot point but there is a cost in winning consent through fear: it unleashes and reinvigorates racism, spoiling the ground of multicultural encounter. As Benjamin Barber

Figure 5.15 Patriotism in fragments, Russell Square, London, 13 July 2005 (*photograph by author*)

commented: 'it is not terrorism but fear that is the enemy, and in the end, fear will not defeat fear'.[57]

Conclusion: Patriotism in Fragments

In his first inaugural address in 1933 Franklin D. Roosevelt said famously that 'we have nothing to fear but fear itself'. He could have been addressing our times when he dissected this sense of trepidation: 'nameless, unreasoning, unjustified terror which paralyses needed efforts to convert retreat into advance'.[58] Induced by the great economic depression he comforted his fellow citizens that such 'common difficulties' concerned 'only material things'.[59] This is a stark contrast to the rhetoric of today's political leaders who miss no opportunity to exaggerate the threat of terror as a means to justify the war against it. Far from material, this war seems permanent and metaphysical. Less a struggle against the conditions of life, it is a more a matter of selfhood, re-instituted national identity and the maintenance of a boundary between 'us' and 'them' in an irreversibly connected world society.

The day before the first anniversary of the London attacks, a video of Shehzad Tanweer – the Aldgate East bomber – was released and broadcast on the Arab news agency al-Jazeera. It bore all the hallmarks of the recording by Mohammad Sidique Khan, combining a hectoring address and denunciation of the war in Iraq in an all too familiar sounding voice.[60] It was an immediate reminder of the events of the previous year. Anxious silences fell on many trains and underground carriages. My friend and colleague Michael Keith, professor of sociology and local politician, commented:

On the day before the anniversary of the bomb I went to Aldgate East station, as I do several times a week. I was travelling in rush hour but the station was noticeably less busy than it would be normally at that time. In the terms of that cliché, you could feel the tension. How? Most times when you stand waiting for the tube, the pavement ballet of the station signals the 'busyness' of London but also the informalities of the city as people move quickly through, rapidly moving to one side and another, recognizing a shared space and separate destinations. This time it was like people had lost their choreography, stepping carefully through the platform, a polite concentration on who they stood next to, who they made way for, belying the sixth sense of everyday commuter rush. But the biggest giveaway was when we got on to the train. Most of the people at the station were not white, they were predominantly Bangladeshi but also African, Chinese and the usual east end ethnic admixture. But most were dressed western. And on the train a bearded man sat alone dressed in traditionally Islamic style. We looked at each other as the rest of the full carriage studiously avoided sitting in the vacant chair next to him. A phrase kept coming back to me that somebody had told me – suicide bombers shave before their final hour to make themselves ready for death. The safest man on the tube is the one with the beard.[61]

The politics of misrecognition and fear damages the choreography of life. It undermines not just our ability to coexist and share the public space of the bus or underground carriage; it also inhibits the ability to identify risk and danger. The politics of misrecognition licenses racism; the anxieties produced do not observe the binaries of the colour line and no one is completely free of them.

The maintenance of these boundaries results in comic as well as tragic effects, moments of almost pure absurdity. Anti-terrorist police escorted a man from a plane London-bound from Durham because he had been listening to the Clash's 1979 punk rock anthem 'London Calling'. The story was reported widely in the popular press.[62] During the taxi ride from Hartlepool in northeast England to Teesside Airport 25-year-old Harraj 'Rab' Mann listened to his MP3 player through a portable stereo packed full of rock classics from a pantheon of British music including Procul Harem, Led Zeppelin, Ocean Colour Scene, the Beatles and The Clash. It was Clash lyrics that raised suspicion in the police's mind: 'London calling to the faraway towns. Now war is declared – and battle comes down. London calling to the underworld. Come out of the cupboards, you boys and girls.' The clarion call was interpreted not as a retro incitement to youth cultural rebellion but as suspiciously jihadist in nature.

The story bears closer scrutiny. Harraj documented his experience through a weblog and this is how I got in touch with him.[63] Speaking on the telephone he told me he preferred to be called 'Rab' and that Harraj was his 'Sunday name'.

> You have to laugh about it but it's been my friends – who are mostly white – that have been most angry. I know incidents like this occur regularly around London because my relatives tell me about it. In Hartlepool, I genuinely forget that I am Asian, I have a few Asian or black friends but there's not a lot of Asian people at Durham Airport. When I go out drinking it's always me that is stopped. I just laugh about it but I realize it's not really funny.[64]

Contrary to the press reports, it later unfolded that he had not been reported to the police by the taxi driver who heard his seditious music. On entering the airport he had a minor altercation with the airport security staff, who had been hostile and rude to him. It was these 'toy cops' who notified the anti-terrorist police who subsequently questioned the taxi driver about what had happened during the taxi journey.[65]

The reason Rab was bound for London that day was to meet up with some of his family who live in Southall and Ilford. Part of the intention behind his journey to London was to find out more about Sikhism – his family's faith – and his background: 'You need faith but religion is a double edged sword when politics and religion get involved it all goes to pot. I am agnostic.'[66] Rab has an A level in sociology and he has his own theories about how things have changed since the London bombings.

> The world's gone mad – it really has. You know you've only got to look at music, it is mix and blurred and people are mixed too. I mean like food, I love Italian food, Chinese food and I love Indian food. But there is just this stereotype and people make assumptions. I get little nine-year-olds calling me 'Paki' with such venom. I turn round to them and say 'are you Irish, or Welsh or Scottish?' They look confused and then I explain that 'there is this place called *Pakistan* and another placed called *India* and my parents come from India. I was born in Yorkshire and I have lived in England longer than you have been alive.' Sometimes you can see the shock in their face when I speak with a British accent. It saddens me.

Rab is not planning to take his case against the airport security any further, preferring to concentrate on his future and his plans to do a degree in graphic design and later to study philosophy at postgraduate level.

Rab's everyday life is a story of heterogeneous British multiculture, in which cultural and religious fragments and ideologies coexist as a simple fact of life, albeit reflected upon and questioned with openness. The irony is that the Clash's 'London Calling' could have been viewed as an indicator of his integration, a link with the history that is encoded in post-war British youth cultures. Rab's story is far from the only example of this syndrome. On 19 April 2004 the police announced that they had seized a terrorist gang just as it prepared to launch a suicide bombing attack on Manchester United's Old Trafford Stadium. The police arrested eight men, one woman and a sixteen-year-old youth. No charges were ever laid. Peter Oborne interviewed one of the suspects, a Kurdish asylum seeker, who said that in the context of the police interrogation the young man had revealed that he was a Manchester United fan. The police search of his flat revealed football paraphernalia including a poster of Old Trafford, ticket stubs that the suspect had kept as a souvenir when he had visited the ground to see his team play Arsenal the year before. Oborne concluded: 'The Kurds I spoke to had come to Britain in order to escape the brutality of Saddam Hussein's regime. Perhaps their most meaningful emotional connection with Britain was a love for Manchester United, which was why they kept the souvenirs in their flat ... Nevertheless the police probably viewed the Manchester United souvenirs as potential evidence of a bomb plot.'[67] The results were that, branded as criminals, the falsely accused lost their homes, jobs and friends.[68] A Clash song or a Manchester United programme in the 'wrong hands' is terrorism incognito rather than evidence of British attachments or multiculture. This is resonant with Paul Gilroy's observation that racism's ire is now 'turned toward the greater menace of the half different and the partially familiar'.[69] They are manifestations of the abuses that the war on terror has made routine.

Such complexities cast doubt on the view that a stronger sense of national identity is the answer. Tariq Modood is scornful of writers who characterize Britishness as a 'hollowed out, meaningless project whose time has come to an end'.[70] The solution, he suggests, 'has to be a multiculturalism that is allied to, indeed is the other side of the coin of, a renewed and reinvigorated Britishness'.[71] The problem, as Paul Gilroy has shown trenchantly, is that Britishness remains haunted by its imperial past, which it will neither confront nor let go. A reinvigoration of Britishness, in Gilroy's diagnosis, also enlivens an imperial psychopathology of manic elation postcolonial melancholia.[72] As George Orwell pointed out: 'every nationalist is haunted by the belief that the past can be altered'.[73] The past cannot be altered; it can either be faced up to or denied. Accordingly I want to argue for something that might be referred to as a *patriotism in fragments*.

The much-maligned Millennium Dome included an exhibit entitled the 'Self-Portrait Zone' sponsored by Marks and Spencer. A spiralling ramp contained 400 photographic images with captions nominated by people living in Britain. Subtitled 'Britain by the British' it reflected a complex past and present in what might appear trite or commonplace. Alongside images of garden sheds and pots of Marmite spread and digestive biscuits were photographs of musician Talvin Singh and the memorial plaque to murdered black teenager Stephen Lawrence that is set in the pavement of Well Hall Road in Eltham, south-east London. The debate on multiculturalism is dominated by material metaphors. Commentators often invoke the idea of a 'mosaic' with hard, discrete edges and multicultural society is the likeness assembled from these discrete pieces. Here culture is like a casino chip, which can be traded, gambled and risked. Alternatively, the notion of the 'melting pot' draws on the legacy of an American racial nomology in which the heated encounters liquefy difference and produce fusion. What all these metaphors share is some sense that culture has an inherent material property that is either fixed, as in the pieces of a mosaic, or has changed its properties as a result of the heat of some transformation.[74] Perhaps, the notion of a fragment that refuses to represent some inherent difference – like those 400 photographs – offers another kind of metaphor.

Orwell, in the much-cited passage from 'The Lion and the Unicorn', lists what he considers the 'characteristic fragments' the 'dozens of small things that conspire' to give a feeling of place.[75] Orwell did as much as anyone to confer the trivial pleasures of life – be it a 'nice cup of tea' or the enjoyment of English cooking – to serious cultural study.[76] There can be no assemblage of these fragments into some stable coherent national identity. Rather nationalism remains shattered regardless of the efforts of all the king's horses and all the king's men to put it back together. What endure are pieces that can be shared and combined, which conduct identification without requiring a stable identity at its core. This patriotism of fragments breaks with the longing for stable or whole identities and foregrounds that such grand national identities are forever in pieces. The affinities that result are loose, changing and open, yet powerful like the photographs collected in the Millennium Dome exhibit. The patriotism of fragments contains incommensurable political energies and forces where imperial nostalgia can resonate alongside a future-oriented inclusive worldly diversity. I think it is here that we should look to both describe and valorize what others like Paul Gilroy refer to as a convivial culture in which 'a degree of differentiation can be combined with a large measure of overlapping'.[77]

I want to end by returning to Grossberg's notion of listening to time and change. My argument is at core very simple. The empire of fear is damaging evident multiculture and there is a need to find a language to speak of the unspectacular ways in which people live with and across the cultural complexities of sameness and difference. We have to listen and look more carefully to find them and this is what sociology might be needed for and where it is of use.

'What speaks to us, seemingly, is always the big event, the untoward, the extraordinary: the front page splash, the banner headline' writes Georg Perec.

'Railway trains only begin to exist when they are derailed, and the more passengers that are killed, the more the train exists. The daily papers talk of everything except the daily'.[78] I think this is also true of the debate about multiculturalism in Britain and Perec's observation is chillingly relevant. To my mind at least, we have yet to find a way of describing the daily ways in which people live in and across the histories and futures that they both carry and make on a daily basis. At the same time, a global sociological perspective needs to speak against terrorism and racism simultaneously and with equal vigilance and be able to identify and judge the local complicities in both authoritarian religious movements and the geopolitics of the war on terror.

Conclusion: Live Sociology

We live in a dark time of bombs and war where acts of violence are met by flowers of commemoration and mourning.[1] Geopolitical insecurity, political violence and deepening social and economic divisions provide the context and the need for the development of a global sociological imagination. The task of sociology is to cast doubt on the public understandings that prevail – be they about the 'war on terror' or the nature of 'immigration policy' – and invite other voices to be heard and reckoned with. Edward Said once commented: 'The intellectual can be perhaps a kind of counter-memory, putting forth its own counter-discourse that will not allow conscience to look away or fall asleep. The best corrective is, as Dr Johnson said, to imagine the person whom you are discussing – in this case the person on whom the bombs will fall – reading you in your presence.'[2]

Said speaks here to the issue of how to avoid symbolic violence in the act of listening. Thinking of our interlocutors next to us as we write offers a corrective to the liberties we sociologists are prone to take with their lives. In the course of this book I have written about my own loved ones. This has certainly made me more cautious about the kinds of claims I make about them 'as sociological objects' and I am reminded every weekend that their complex lives move beyond my attempts to portray them in writing. The other point that I want to draw out here is the importance of challenging provincialism. C. Wright Mills commented:

> To the world's range of enormous problems, liberalism responds with its verbal fetish of 'freedom' plus shifting series of opportunistic reactions. The world is hungry; the liberal cries: 'Let us make it free!' The world is tired of war; the liberal cries: 'Let us arm for peace!' The peoples of the world are without land; the liberal cries: 'Let us beg the landed oligarchs to parcel some out!' In sum: the most grievous charge today against liberalism and its conservative varieties is that they are so utterly *provincial*, and thus so irrelevant to the major problems that must now be confronted in so many areas of the world.3

Writing in the middle of the twentieth century, Mills predicted the conservative revolution that would tighten the grasp of liberalism. Free-market methods that aim to limit restrictions on business operations and property rights have been adopted on a global scale and implemented across the polit- ical spectrum. A global sociological imagination seeks to challenge provin- cialism, be it intellectual or political.

It is also necessary to be alert to the complex movements of imagination and cultural interconnection that manifest in the daily life of a world city like London. As a place of refuge and asylum, the city can be prized for the isola- tion and silent reflection it can afford. As Fran Tonkiss has pointed out, it is not always a matter of 'shared community' but the reverse.[4] It is for this reason that people are impelled to find a haven free from scrutiny. It is more often than not that people move in their minds first, seeking space to breathe and freedoms to think. This is something that comes through in the accounts of today's exiles. Javad travelled across Europe in the back of a smuggler's truck from Iran. He spends his days wrapped in the luxurious anonymity of London's crowd. 'It is for me something special to be with people and not seen, not recognized. It is something that is not possible for me in Iran.' This lack of recognition outside the prying eyes of the state can be precarious and double edged, as I tried to show in relation to the killing of Jean Charles de Menezes discussed in Chapter 5. Through a mobile phone Javad contacts his friends, providing a link to fellow Iranian asylum seekers and supportive polit- ical organizations. This flow of imagination moves in many directions. From her bedroom in North London, Azam – an Iranian political refugee – broad- casts treatises on feminism and women's rights over the Internet to listeners in Iran. The coordinates of sociological understanding have to be global in scale in order to make sense of lives that not only move across the borders of nation states but also through time and contrasting political and cultural settings. This means navigating complex political and historical sensibilities. For example, Azam, who is actively involved in anti-racism and asylum seeker rights, refused to attend some of the 'Stop the Iraq War' meetings because in some cases separate meetings were held for men and women. Her secular left gender politics collided with the strategy within the anti-war movement to indulge Islamic concerns regarding mixed political meetings.

Provincialism clouds critical judgement. Chetan Bhatt makes this point when he characterizes a 'methodological narcissism' in much of the debate about identity and alterity in Europe and North America. He writes: 'It seems puzzling that the overwhelming academic obsession with diaspora, racial, ethnic, mixed, hybrid, syncretic, passing self and all its variegated possibilities is occurring during a period of impersonal, brutalizing geopolitics and the greatest relative and absolute impoverishment of large sections of the non- Western world.'[5] The overdeveloped world's grievances and inequalities need to be set in the context of the larger social cleavages that manifest on a global scale. This also involves a critical judgement that is supple enough to cope with the complexity of the relationships between the local and global. For example, unthinking liberals or sociologists might herald a community organization in Britain as an example of multicultural or religious diversity. Yet, the same organization might also be implicated in religiously motivated violence and extremism elsewhere.

In 2004 a report identified the ways in which British-based registered charities, including Hindu Swayamsevak Sangh UK, Vishwa Hindu Parishad UK and Kalyan Ashram Trust UK, were connected to the Rashtriya Swayamsevak Sangh (RSS), a paramilitary political organization implicated in large-scale sectarian violence and violations of human rights in India.[6] It is so easy to fall foul of what might be called the 'local trap'. Avoiding it requires the constant attempt to situate one's own concerns beyond the immediate setting from which they emerge. It is for this reason that sociological thinking needs to address the issue of scale and how to develop a worldly mode of investigation and thought. I want to turn now to another theme addressed in this book, namely the relationship between sociology and time.

Writing in and Against Time

Renato Rosaldo in his book *Culture and Truth* demolishes the idea that we can write about societies as if they hold still while we sketch them.[7] What anthropologists call the ethnographic present (that is, the idea that eternal assertions can be made like Nuer religion is … or middle-class culture is …) simply seems absurd when you think about it. The idea that we are writing in time, at a particular moment, which is partial and positioned and in place is a major advance. I think we are also writing against time, trying to capture an outline of an existence that is fleeting. We cannot know the soul of a person we have listened to, but we can know the traces that they leave 'on top of life' to use César Vallejo's phrase.

I've come to think that this is what I am trying to do as I sit down at the computer with interview transcripts or ethnographic descriptions at my side. The fact that those traces of life are opaque and that the person who made them is always to an extent unknowable doesn't mean that all is lost. In fact, I have become tired of reading elegant pronouncements on the unknowability of culture and social life; there is no compensation in these bold statements of defeat for me any more. The task, it seems to me, is to pay truth the courtesy of serious effort without reducing the enigmatic and shifting nature of social existence to caricature and stereotype. Part of the aftershock of the poststructuralist critiques of social science is a turning away from the kinds of

encounters that I want to argue for. This critique is centred on the meaning
and status of writing.

Roland Barthes argued that writing is not a means to reflect the world.
Rather, 'to write' is an intransitive verb with the result that writing is reified as
a thing in itself, almost regardless of content.[8] Writing here is an act of language rather than a means of recording a sense of a reality beyond it. In short,
when we write we are drawn into a series of already available patterned com-
municative formulae. This web of discourses or representations means that
our message is already subverted by The Word and the structure of language
itself. These arguments have a long historical lineage and go back to Plato and
Socrates, who both argued against the adequacy of written speech as a poor
transcription of 'spoken truths'. Jacques Derrida is critical too of the way
Western philosophy makes speech and, by extension, writing the original site
of truth. The notion of logocentrism here attempts to name this dependence
on language. It is derived from the Greek 'logos', meaning the original structure that orders the nature of truth. Derrida's notion of deconstruction is
aimed at a critique of logocentrism and language, both written and spoken.

Part of Derrida's critique is an argument for a broader notion of inscription,
which would include photography, music, embodiment and sculpture as forms
of writing. While one might accept aspects of this line of argument, the effect
of deconstruction on the research agenda of the last decade has been a turning
away from the project of empirical enquiry. In Britain at least, the impact of
the critique of 'writing culture' associated with the work of anthropologist
James Clifford has led to an anxiety with regard to the epistemological
mooring of ethnographic engagement.[9] In a sense these concerns about the
relationship between power and knowledge have come to eclipse a long-
standing critique – albeit from a different angle – of the abuses of sociological
knowledge. Here the epistemological challenge to sociological authority was
based on the political consequences of the work of white sociologists for
minority communities. Information gathering and the scrutiny of racialized
migrant communities becomes synonymous with a note-taking hand that is
little more than an extension of the political arm of a racist state.[10] Sociological
writing is complicit in producing, circulating and legitimizing cultural patholo-
gies about minority communities. Bluntly put, sociology needs to avoid being
racism's accomplice. On a more mundane level, as Errol Lawrence pointed
out, white sociological accounts of the cultural life of black and minority communities were boring travesties in which the sociologist was analogous to a dry
mouthed fool who remained thirsty in the midst of an abundance of water.[11]

At least two, perhaps unintended, consequences follow from the lines of critique outlined above. The first is a turning away from empirical research,
which is in part a refusal to be placed in the position of a 'data collection agent'

for oppressive forces. The second consequence is that the empirical accounts that are written have the quality of 'good news stories' in which anything that is difficult or potentially damaging is filtered out. I want to return later to the consequences this may have. In an overview of the field of racism and ethnicity research, Martin Bulmer and John Solomos point to the emergence of: 'a type of research agenda that is overtly textual and theory-driven in focus. If anything, we have seen the denigration of the role of ethnographic and fieldwork styles of research.'[12] There may be another way to respond to both the epistemological and political critiques particularly in the field of race, ethnicity and racism research, and this involves embracing the idea that our writing always falls short. The acceptance that the best we can hope for in writing about the social world is degrees of failure (that is, part truths) need not result in a turning away from a commitment to dialogue. Partiality and failure do not suggest that the lines in our portraits have no semblance of likeness.

Some might conclude that proximity to research participants and empirical dialogue always runs the risk of the researcher's judgement being clouded and duped through overfamiliarity. Part of the politics of doing the work I've done – particularly with people who are avowed or common-sense racists – is to subject odious and pernicious views to critical evaluation, deconstruction and analysis: it is not merely a matter of reproducing them. I would suggest that familiarity, rather than militating against criticism, involves the deepening of critical judgement. But, I want also to say that this process is precarious and more complex than it seems and cannot be glossed or compensated through political postures. I want to explore this issue through looking at the work of George Orwell and the recent controversies surrounding his legacy.

Critical Insight and the Uses of Autobiography

The diaries of Malcolm Muggeridge provide a tragic commentary on George Orwell's last few days and weeks. Muggeridge was his friend and discussant and they shared many lunchtime debates on politics and culture in the heart of London. Orwell was just forty-six when he died. The entry in Muggeridge's diaries for 26 January 1950 described the scene at Orwell's funeral. He wrote of his surprise that so many of the mourners were Jewish. 'Interesting, I thought, that George should have so attracted Jews because he was at heart strongly anti-semitic. Felt a pang as the coffin was removed, particularly because of its length, somehow this circumstance, reflecting George's tallness, was poignant.'[13] Orwell wrote extensively and critically about anti-Semitism, as well as against the colour bar, British racism and colonialism. Yet, the idea that Orwell was at core anti-Semitic has lingered and been reinvigorated during the discussion of the centenary of his birth. It is worth remembering that Orwell never wanted a biographer. He must have turned in his grave as three biographies appeared in a single year. [14] In 2002, prior to the publication of his Orwell biography, D. J. Taylor wrote that anti-Semitism was Orwell's 'dirty secret'.[15] I am not going to discuss these biographies in depth. While these books – in my view – fill a gap in the published record of literary Orwellia, they do provide a spur – joking aside – to re-examine Orwell's writing and particularly his treatment of anti-Semitism. In them we can find interesting and important questions about the relationship between cultures of racism and personal culpability in thinking and criticism.

To characterize Orwell as a bigot misses the complex way in which he took his own cultural legacy as the starting point for critical reflection. In this sense, the world Orwell was born into – aspirant, imperial and petty bourgeois – was riddled with anti-Semitism. Yet, at the same time he sought to develop a political critique of anti-Semitism from the inside. He wrote in 1941: 'What vitiates nearly all that is written about anti-semitism is the assumption in the writer's mind that he himself is immune to it. "Since I know that anti-semitism is irrational," he argues, "it follows that I do not share it." He thus fails to start his investigation in the one place where he could get hold of some reliable evidence – that is, in his own mind.'[16] Orwell complicated any simple or comfortable separation between racism and anti-racism and he made a case for understanding racism in terms of its warped rationalities and equally what its believers need it for. These essays point towards developing interpretative tools that engage with racism's pernicious and enduring power.

Central to the process of grappling with the power of racist rhetoric is to try to establish why people find its erroneous answers appealing. For Orwell that also begins with an impulse to situate the understanding of hate within oneself. He wrote at the conclusion of his essay on anti-Semitism:

> It will be seen, therefore that the starting point for any investigation of anti-semitism should not be 'Why does this obviously irrational belief appeal to people?' but 'Why does anti-semitism appeal to me? What is there about it that I feel to be true?' If one asks this question one at least discovers one's own rationalizations, and it may be possible to find out what lies beneath them. Anti-semitism should be investigated – and I will not say by anti-semites, but at any rate by people who know that they are not immune to that kind of emotion.[17]

Is this an admission of a 'dirty secret'? Of course not. Does it mean that he recognized the power of anti-Semitism in himself and his work? I think the answer must be an unequivocal 'yes'. Yet at the same time he is consciously trying to identify, interpret and transcend the culture of racism of which he is himself a part. Is this transcendence total and complete? I think not, but this is true of the power of racism in our time and the contingencies in reckoning with its efficacy in the lives of white people both personally and professionally.

George Orwell wrote in 1944 that:

> the weakness of the left-wing attitude towards anti-semitism is to approach it from a rationalistic angle. Obviously the charges made against the Jews are not true. They cannot be true, partly because they cancel out, partly because no one people could have a monopoly of wickedness. But simply by pointing this out one gets no further … If a man has the slightest disposition towards anti-semitism, such things bounce off his consciousness like peas off a steel helmet.[18]

The same can be said of what might be referred to as moral anti-racism today. Orwell's suggestion is that, rather than pointing out why racism is bad or wrong, we start from the point of view of trying to understand why racism appeals to people and what they need it for. The police cling to the stereotypes of violent black youths and what they see as 'the truth' about the policing of black communities, because it helps them make sense of a world that confounds and shuns them. Orwell's challenge is how to get inside or proximate to the appeal and commitment to racism.

In an essay on 'H. G. Wells, Hitler and Totalitarianism' published in 1941, he concluded: 'The people who have shown the best understanding of Fascism are either those who have suffered under it or those who have a Fascist streak in themselves.'[19] This is perhaps a confession of sorts. One might easily supplant Fascism here with anti-Semitism or racism and the sense of Orwell's approach would be the same. I think there is something in this that also destabilizes our categories of thinking and the places where we might find understanding, or tools for interpretation. In this sense, the 'racist feeling' that is deposited in dominant social groups can provide a tool or a resource for interpretation and critical reckoning that is both sociological and political.

I think, too, we have to allow the people about whom we write to be complex, frail, ethically ambiguous, contradictory and damaged. The tendency to write society as if it were populated by Manichaean camps of either good or bad people, angels or devils, is a strong temptation. When one is writing about stigmatized and excluded social groups, this temptation is particularly keen. I know for example that this is most acute in the situation of asylum seekers and refugees. To accept that desperate people do entirely human reckless things like lie or falsify their documents is unspeakable because it plays into the hands of the forces of law who seek to expunge them. What right do we have to outline their weakness or failings? The danger here in creating heroic portrayals is that we make the very people whose humanity one may want to defend less than human. We do not allow them to be as complicated as we are, namely com-pounds of pride and shame, weakness and strength. This kind of self-censoring can also lead to a turning away from difficult political complexities, as illus-trated by the involvement of members of British ethnic minorities in salafi-jihadi and irhabi politics or Hindutva groups (Hindu nationalistis) implicated in human rights abuses in India. Equally, when we make white racists into monsters there is a danger of organizing racism in to some bodies (often very predictable ones like the white working classes) and away from other bodies (genteel educated liberals). I think sociology can play a role in opening up the false comforts achieved in such absolute moral categories.

Perhaps I am mindful of this precisely because people I have loved have also given popular racism a voice, including my own father who I mentioned earlier. One of the paradoxes of this – and I am always compelled by the par-adoxical effects of racism on our culture – is that towards the end of his life the only person who could reach through the morphine haze was a black nurse called Thelma. I remember visiting him in Mayday Hospital in Croydon in April 1999, just a few weeks before he died. As I walked onto the ward Thelma was fussing at the end of his bed. They were talking about her son who was at that time studying for his 'A levels' at Stanley Technical College. I asked him how he was feeling. 'See that girl there?' he said, ignoring my question and pointing at Thelma. 'She's a diamond.' He called her over. 'This is my son, he's one of the top lecturers in the University.'

He had a way of talking about 'The University' as if only one existed in the whole world. It was true for him perhaps because the University of London, and Goldsmiths College specifically, was the only one he had set foot inside. She smiled and we laughed and talked about her son.

It was just a week later that he started to slip in and out of consciousness. A massive tumour in his groin cut off the circulation of blood. The doctors could do no more than ease the pain. We surrounded his room with photographs of his grandchildren and decorated it with the paintings they'd made for their granddad. Through the morphine mist he reached out to each photograph, it was as if an invisible wallet was resting on his chest and he handed out phantom pocket money to each in turn. He would lie looking at the photographs, taking a drag on an imaginary cigarette and waving the smoke away as if trying to conceal the secret pleasure. It was Thelma who held his hand as he passed the brink of life. After that awful night my brother and I went to register his death and decided to go for a drink in a local pub. I described to him what had hap-pened at his bedside and the Old Man's struggle to hold on to life.

After a long medicinal gulp from his pint, Ken said: 'It's funny knowing how Dad felt about coloured people that Thelma should have been the one to be with him. That she should be there with you.'

'Perhaps it's a kind of coming to terms, Ken. Making things right?' I replied.

He was not defined by racism as a man; he did not live his life that way. He was capable of saying those all too common hateful things, but in his later years less so. I want to believe that the care and connection in those last moments was some kind of atonement or making peace. It makes me think again of the common human frailty captured in Jonathan Hordle's photograph taken on 7 July 2005 of the dreadlocked black Londoner walking away from a blast site with his arm around a white woman. Perhaps, contained in the touch, or embrace, is a reminder of the triviality of our differences.[20]

The hand has been iconic in the thinking of philosophers in relation to what it means to be human. For both Kant and Heidegger the hand was emblematic of human distinction. 'The hand reaches and extends, receives and welcomes – and not just things: the hand extends itself, and receives its own welcome in the hands of others.'[21] But the hand too is the symbol of exclusive power: the straight fingers of the Nazi salute,[22] the open hand halt of the racial segregationists[23] or the gendered exchange in the hand that is taken in patriarchal marriage.[24] What I want to foreground here is the hand that touches or the tight and sometimes desperate material surfaces of connection. Touch may be a useful metaphor for sociological ethics, namely to take care of what we touch. Returning to Kierkegaard's notion of thinking as a dance the embrace of the experience of others necessitates also the recognition that what we touch moves irreducibly and remains a mystery that we only partially solve.

Centring the act of writing on the positioned and reflective sociologist is something that I want to argue for, yet there are real risks in this as well as rewards. In short, autobiography or what might be called *compulsory reflexivity* has its misuses. Self-reflection can inhibit or pre-empt the need for dialogue and deep listening to others. I have felt this several times when working or talking with people who are writing about worlds that they are part of in a direct sense. I recognize traces of this in my own work. The danger here is that autobiographical experience becomes the only necessary resource needed to think or write with. Listening to others becomes irrelevant because s/he already knows the culture from the inside and paradoxically the accounts of the people being listened to become muted. The role of autobiographical or experiential knowledge is in my view an interpretative device. In this sense, subjectivity becomes a means to try to shuttle across the boundary between the writer and those about whom s/he is writing. It is not about narcissism and self-absorption but common likenesses and, by extension, contrasts. It is those likenesses and contrasts that enable the sociologist to hold accounts of social life in place without folding the person one is listening to back into one's self – 'Oh, OK. You are just like me, after all!' Otherness doesn't begin at the boundaries between class or 'racial' groupings or differences of gender and sexuality but at the surface of our touch. There can be no simple appeal by the sociologist to be part of the inside that does not also acknowledge the variegations within those social groups.

If a writer's experience and subjectivity is useful we need to think why? Here I am suggesting that these experiences are of little use if they are not put to work in service of reaching out to others. In her beautiful book *Remembered Rapture*, bell hooks comments: 'A distinction must be made between that writing which enables us to hold to life even as we are clinging to old hurts and wounds and that writing which offers to us a space where we are able to confront reality in such a way that we live more fully.'[25] Although she is not talking about sociological research, such a distinction might be applied to the misuses of autobiography outlined here. The acid test is the degree to which it enables the writer to 'confront reality' in a way that enhances insight.

Reflective Engagement and Life Passed in Living

Theodor W. Adorno warned that 'Every debate about the ideals of education is trivial and inconsequential compared to this single ideal: never again Auschwitz. It was the barbarism all education strives against.'[26] The politics of understanding the features of contemporary racism and the imitators and apologists of Nazism is dedicated to this aim. Critical thinking, that is the commitment to think at the intersection of horizons and contrasting values, can play a modest part here. It involves critical judgement while remaining open to counter-intuitive possibilities that challenge both our interpretations and our political beliefs. Michael Burawoy's spirited call for 'public sociology' has reinvigorated the debate about the relationship between sociology and the public realm.[27] In his 2004 Presidential Address to the American Sociological Association, Burawoy argued: 'Public sociology brings sociology into a conversation with publics, understood as people who are themselves involved in conversation.'[28] In Burawoy's scheme this includes students as our first or prime public and beyond campus it extends to 'labor movements, neighborhood organizations, communities of faith, immigrant rights groups, human rights organizations'.[29] Here public sociology – previously dismissed as something we do in our 'spare time' – is viewed as having an organic and mutually enhancing relationship to professional sociology, critical sociology and policy sociology, which are the other forms defined in his model. 'The interest in a public sociology is, in part, a reaction and a response to the privatization of everything' writes Burawoy.[30] This resonates with the ways in which the audit culture in universities has made academic writers much more individualistic and concerned to place their work in the high-prestige secret realm of specialized journals. Burawoy's call for greater public involvement is appealing, but he has little to say about the messiness of entering into public life as a sociologist. In Burawoy's account, the reader might be forgiven for thinking that the public realm is only populated with emergent radical forces. As well as providing an opportunity to reach a wider audience, stepping out in public as a sociologist can also involve vulnerability and political compromise.

I will come to the issue of vulnerability later, but first I want to illustrate how public interventions also involve compromises that affect the quality of writing and criticism. In Chapter 1 I described the South London Citizens Enquiry into the British immigration service based in Croydon which opened up a public debate about the experience of users.[31] The citizens' enquiry provides a good example of the kind of public sociology Michael Burawoy calls for. The enquiry's hearings provided an unprecedented public opportunity to voice the concerns of people subjected to the immigration system. The commissioners who heard all the evidence included an array of bishops and senior members of the legal profession. When the enquiry was completed, three people – myself included – took responsibility for the task of drafting the report. It was agreed from the very beginning that this would have to be the commissioners' report and that they would need to take ownership of it. It had to be their report and not ours. Achieving this was not an easy task, akin to a kind of ventriloquism in reverse. The first question was, what kind of tone should we strike in the writing? Should the enquiry read like a political tract, a judicial document or a sociological treatise?

The first draft was openly partisan, angry and damning of the immigration service. The commissioners were unhappy with its tone and they asked us to moderate it. Their view was that presented in this way the report would be easily dismissed by politicians and civil servants. As a result the report was revised and conveyed the user's truly horrible experiences in a very flat and factual fashion. Our aim now was to make the report read as if set in a tenor of almost contemptuous fairness. Whether this was intellectually or politically the right thing to do is debatable. I am still not sure if this was the right strategy. The report did get an airing in the most senior levels both in the Home Office and also amongst government ministers. It contributed to a growing public pressure for reform. On 19 July 2006 the Home Secretary John Reid announced in the House of Commons that the Home Office would be transformed through 'ambitious reform' including separating the Immigration and Nationality Directorate from the rest of the Home Office.[32] A few days later Reid announced that a uniformed border control force would be set up, which would be responsible for policing immigration, and he promised to double the investment in immigration enforcement to £280 million by the end of 2010.[33]

Some of the worst abuses of the power of immigration officers are addressed in the proposed reforms. However, their overriding emphasis is to militarize the policing and enforcement of border control. Future critics may well accuse the enquiry and its authors of pulling its political punches. This criticism may be justified, but the compromise was necessary in order to achieve the consent of the commissioners. My point here is that, like any form of activism, the outcome of public sociology is very uncertain and hard to measure confidently.

Hyper-political posturing is not necessarily politics. More than a few self-professed 'political intellectuals' – of all ages – indulge in pieties of this sort on the conference circuit. Such histrionics mask difficult matters of substance. As political tools books are fairly weak instruments of change, regardless of the current talk about the relationship between knowledge and power. Primo Levi once wrote: 'It is a matter of practical observation that a book or a story, whether its intentions be good or bad, are essentially inert and innocuous objects ... Their intrinsic weakness is aggravated by the fact that today all writing is smothered in a few months by a mob of other writings which push up behind it.'[34] Perhaps the desperate academic invocations of 'political intent' are a response to the inherent weakness identified so eloquently here. Academic 'prophets' and 'demagogues' – to cite Max Weber's telling phrase – may take comfort from playing to the colloquium gallery.[35] I want to suggest, in contrast, that the political value of sociological work lies in being open to unsettling dialogues with humility. This is not a good way to produce a stirring manifesto, but it perhaps has the merit of greater honesty with regard to the truths that are touched, if not wholly grasped, through sociological endeavour.

It does not, however, follow that this means a retreat from political issues and toward detachment and neutrality. In this sense, Rojek and Turner's notion of 'engaged detachment' is not only a literal contradiction but also confused and obfuscating.[36] The kind of orientation I want to propose with regard to the relationship between understanding and public activism might be described as reflective engagement, that is a political intervention that realizes the limits of writing and the complexities of dialogue and listening. The urgency and speed of politics mean that the window of opportunity for making an intervention will not wait for a beautifully crafted monograph three years after the fact. As I argued at the beginning of this book, the value of sociological attention and writing may be in the length of time that considered analysis takes. There is a tension between the political necessity for intervention and the sociological value in taking time to think carefully and critically. Making public interventions and aspiring to be a public intellectual involves embracing a wide range of writing genres alongside academic forms. It includes writing letters to newspapers, journalism and essays for popular and political journals.

These forms are not without their problems and constraints. For example, how much analysis can be crammed into an 800-word op-ed piece of journalism? The public sociologist has to be mindful of the values and limitations of both academic and non-academic forms of writing.

What is Sociology Needed for?

In the globalized world, the relationships between centre and margin are becoming more complex, patterns of suffering and uncertainty ever more terrifying. The kind of engaged listening I want to argue for may turn out to be less dispensable than it might on first sight seem. John Berger once wrote that writers, storytellers and by extension sociologists, are 'death's secretaries'.[37] He suggests that writing is about keeping a record and producing a kind of register of life. Regardless of the epistemological melancholy and self-mutilating doubt abroad in today's social science faculties, the tradition of drawing and transcribing life passed in living is a noble one to be cherished. Ruth Behar concludes: 'One thing remains constant about our humanity – that we must never stop trying to tell stories of who we think we are. Equally, we must never stop wanting to listen to each other's stories. If we ever stopped, it would all be over.'[38] It is far from over. If sociological literature is to have a future it must hold to the project of listening and speaking to people who live the consequence of the globalized world with respect and humility while maintaining critical judgement.

Some are suspicious of this sociological desire to eavesdrop on life as it passes before us. As one colleague put it 'What do we actually learn from talking to people?' The paradox is that we academic scribes are not always very sociable. We cling to the library like bookish limpets that, like Kierkegaard, find real human beings too heavy to embrace. We speak a lot about society but all too often listen to the world within limited frequencies. I am proposing an approach to listening that goes beyond this, where listening is not assumed to be a self-evident faculty that needs no training. Somehow the grey books written on sociological method do not help much with this kind of fine tuning. The lacklustre prose of methodological textbooks often turns the life in the research encounter into a corpse fit only for autopsy. I want to end by returning to C. Wright Mills, who famously referred to sociology and scholarship as a craft. I have been searching for a better metaphor to describe the quality of sociological practice but have failed to find one.

For Mills there is nothing workaday in this notion of sociological craft because integral to it is creative thinking and expression. In Mills' view sociology at its best is a compound of craft and imagination that is concerned with the patterns that are evident in 'reality' yet at the same time trying to envisage something important that lies beneath or beyond life's surface. Sociological craft involves choosing the right tools of investigation and honing them in a way that is appropriate to the task. This also means thinking carefully about the analytical status of the research data that the tool makes or creates. At its simplest, what quality of truth do we take the sociological data to reflect? Many people have questioned the validity of data produced in interviews precisely on the grounds that it cannot be assumed that the account corresponds to a truth outside of the telling. A way around this problem is simply to treat interview accounts as moral tales that are interesting regardless of whether they are lies or simply wrong. The shape of a lie reveals something interesting about the teller's moral universe. Therefore in our craft as sociologists we need to know not only if we have the correct tool but also whether we are holding it the right way up.

Mills was also clear that sociological imagination meant being self-consciously committed to affecting argument and writing creatively for a variety of what he called 'reading publics'.[39] The danger he foresaw was that the sociological work might develop a technical language that turns inward on itself. Jean Améry once observed that specialist language 'in sounding learned, strives to prove its own significance more than the value of its knowledge'.[40] To avoid this we have to aspire to make sociology more literary. Others are sceptical of such a move, David Silverman wrote: 'Risking the scorn of modern-day deconstructionists, let me suggest that the craft of writing fiction or verse is quite different from the craft of social science. In any event, if I want to read a good poem, why on earth should I turn to a social science journal?'[41] Silverman is a very good writer committed to a minimalist aesthetic for social science that celebrates clarity and rigour. However, minimalism can result in what I referred to as *thin description* or *flat sociology* bereft of vitalism or life or – and I hesitate to write this – any beauty. I am advocating a literary sociology that aims to document and understand social life without assassinating it.

John Law and John Urry argue that social research creates or enacts the society it claims to actually reflect. They suggest that because the 'globalising world is complex, elusive, ephemeral and unpredictable' conventional research methods with its origins in nineteenth-century thought are of little use.[42] In order to engage this capriciousness and volatility in social life, the sociological toolkit needs to be expanded to meet the complexity of the task at hand. Law and Urry conclude:

> if social science is to interfere in the realities of that world, to make a difference, to engage in an ontological politics, and to shape new realities, then it needs tools for understanding and practising the complex and elusive. This will be uncomfortable.

Novelty is always uncomfortable. We need to alter academic habits and develop sensibilities appropriate to a methodological decentering.[43]

Reassessing the appropriateness of our tools need not lead to epistemological defeat or a turning away from vital life. Rather, I want to suggest that it might invite an opportunity to bring sociology alive. Here I am using 'live' as an adjective to describe a sociology that is imbued with vitality. It always strikes me as odd to read sociological treatises that present not a single human voice or portrait. They result in accounts of society that do not breathe or feel. It seems that theoretically at least we are more attuned than ever to the embodied nature of social experience.[44] Representing that embodied experience is quite something else.

A reassessment of sociological craft invites an opportunity to reinvent the nature of observation and measurement. The scope of this opportunity is increased thorough the availability to social researchers of multimedia techniques and new informational technologies. By introducing interactivity and exploiting the possibilities of new media for iterative analysis we might think of sociological texts having a life beyond the final full stop of a research manuscript. Michael Wesch at the University of Virginia has for example launched an innovative digital environment that focuses on an anthropological representation of the Nekalimin people of Papua New Guinea. The site harnesses the potential of new media 'without sacrificing solid scholarly argument and analysis. Though there are currently over 300 pages of information on this site.'[45] A new literature is emerging precisely addressing these themes.[46] This is not simply a matter of thinking through the relationship between on-line and off-line research but also the emergence of new kinds of sociological writing be it in the form of CD-ROMs, unfolding interactive websites, or interacting combinations of written arguments, still and moving image and recorded sound.

Sociology is a way of living and something that is practised as a vocation, a way of holding to the world and paying critical attention it. So, 'live' is being used here as a sociological verb. The price of insight may well be discomfort, be it in the puncturing of soothing illusions or the questioning of our most basic assumptions about progress or hope. Paul Rabinow observed for modern intellectuals like sociologist Max Weber: 'The calling of science must include a sense of passionate commitment, combined with methodical labour and a kind of almost mystical passivity or openness.'[47] Such a posture remains relevant to the kind of sociological disposition that I am arguing for. Finally, I want to end by returning to the question that I posed at the very beginning of this book, namely what is sociology needed for today?

The answer provided in the *Art of Listening* is sixfold. Firstly, the service that sociology can perform in our time is to point to those things that cannot be

said.[48] 'The preconstructed is everywhere. The sociologist is literally beleaguered by it, as everybody else is', Bourdieu observes.[49] It is in silence that
inequitable relations and gross political complicities are hidden. Here the sociologist is a guide to those things that are muted. Secondly, sociological
thinking is required to provide a sensitivity to and respect for the uncelebrated.
This is not simply a matter of giving ordinariness a voice, but rather a critical
reflection that makes the familiar strange and investigates the self-evident.
Thirdly, sociology is needed in order to create an ethical and critical imagination that transcends provincialism and operates on a worldly scale. This is the
task of offering an alternative story to the glossed and bowdlerized official
account, pointing to the implications of what happens close-by with events
elsewhere. Fourthly, the world we live in is blighted by a blinding certainty:
sociological doubt is needed precisely as a kind of counterbalance. The value
of the kind of scholarship I am arguing for is that it dwells in productive uncertainty – a kind of critical openness to the other view. However, living with
doubt is not always productive or comfortable. It can lead to a paralysis in
thought and the challenge of scholarship is to be open-minded and sceptical,
while remaining committed to social criticism. Fifthly, and not least, the kind
of sociology I am arguing for is needed because it *hears*. The art of listening to
the world, where we take the people we listen to as seriously as we take ourselves, is perhaps the most important quality that sociology can offer today.
The desire to listen opens up the sociologists' preconceptions and offers a new
kind of understanding, even when the sociological encounter involves their
political enemies.[50] Lastly, sociology is needed in order to act as a historical
witness. The sociological listener is, to my mind at least, a kind of equivalent
to *Clio*, one of the nine muses who personify the highest aspiration of art and
intellect in Greek mythology. She attends not only to the implication of the
past in the present, but she is also concerned with the relationship between the
close-at-hand and the remote. Dedicated to a history of the anonymous, as
Walter Benjamin put it, her song celebrates the uncelebrated and aims to
'brush history against the grain – even if [she] needs a barge pole to do it'.[51]

Hannah Arendt noted: 'History knows many dark times in which the public
realm has been obscured and the world becomes so dubious that people have
ceased to ask any more of politics than that it show due consideration for their
vital interests and personal liberty.'[52] People living in such times come to
despise the workings of the public realm. As a way of coping they 'reach
behind them – as if the world were on a façade behind which people could
conceal themselves – in order to arrive at mutual understanding with their
fellow men'.[53] The task of sociology is to provide a diagnosis of the social
world and how it is organized; but, also it involves listening to what goes on

behind the public façade, attending to the ways that people achieve a 'bit of humanness in a world become inhuman'.[54] The empire of fear and the 'war on terror' correspond with Arendt's portrayal of a dubious and obscured public world. Here the words that politicians speak make no sense at all to the people who live on the planet now. 'Democracy' is championed to justify military invasion in Iraq and bombing its people is said to be part of a 'humanitarian' effort. The maxims of political life demand repair from such debasement, and sociological thinking can play a part in the development of a worldly political conscience that, as Edward Said put it, 'will not allow us to look away or fall asleep'.[55] This regeneration must critically reflect on those core principles – freedom in need of freedom, democracy in need of democracy, and public life in need of the public.

This leads me to the final and most important reason why sociology is needed, namely as a resource of hope. Twentieth-century intellectuals had very contrasting views of hope and its political connotations. To live in hope, for Albert Camus, is to surrender to inertia, fatalism and defeat. He pointed out that, for the Greeks, hope is the last, and most dreadful, of the ills left inside Pandora's Box. Camus concluded: 'I know no more stirring symbol; for, contrary to the general belief, hope equals resignation. And to live is not to resign oneself.'[56] Others like Raymond Williams argued that hope can be found in the infinite resilience of people to endure damaged life: 'That is why I say we must speak of hope, as long as it doesn't mean suppressing the nature of the danger.'[57] This kind of hope is established in the accumulation of small acts that defy division, hatred and mutual misunderstanding, where the counter-intuitive (that is, that people refuse to be defined by the differences that are socially ascribed to them) is intuitive. We live in dark times but sociology – as a listening art – can provide resources to help us live through them, while pointing to the possibility of a different kind of future.

Epilogue: The Craft

A few years ago I was invited to talk to a group of PhD students who had set up a kind of support group, a place to share ideas but also to invite speakers to come and talk about their research. On this occasion I was the invited guest speaker. I had finished my PhD over ten years before, but the anxiety in the room was all too familiar. We took our seats around a large circle of desks. The young scholars fished out pens and notebooks from their bags and readied themselves for the session. Looking at each other furtively, we exchanged smiles like wordless greetings. The chair of the session asked everyone to introduce themselves and say, in one sentence, what their PhD was about. I watched the contorted expressions on their faces as each graduate student struggled with this deceptively innocent form of torture. I racked my brains. What should I say? My heart started to palpitate in the way that it does at moments like this. Then it was my turn. 'My name is Les Back and I am a recovering PhD student.'

In this final part of the book I focus on the craft of scholarship and its challenges, perils and rewards. These reflections are aimed particularly at young scholars who are facing up to the prospect of doctoral research. Practising scholarship means having to cope with awkward questions. These are sometimes focused on your research, but they can come in a variety of forms. On the one hand, there is the presumption that study and the 'life of the mind' is akin to one long vacation. Here the university library is viewed as equivalent to a beachside holiday camp where students lay about all day reading books and drinking cocktails. PhD students in particular have to endure endless jokes about watching day-time TV and comments like: 'It must be nice not to work' or 'What do you do in the afternoons?' On the other hand, a PhD can seem to the outsider like a jail sentence. 'How long have you got to go?' they ask sadly as if referring to the days until release. The intention here is also to discuss the quality of sociological life and outline some controversies about scholarship, including those relating to academic language and the ethics and nature of criticism. Before moving on to these important topics I have a confession to make.

One of the reasons why I finished my own PhD was because it became something of an addiction: it was going to finish me, or I was going to finish it! It took me much longer than it should have to complete my thesis. Graduate research students in my generation who studied during the 1970s and 1980s simply didn't finish. In fact, while many had been registered, no one had ever 'completed' a doctoral thesis in the Department of Social Anthropology at Goldsmiths College where I studied. Then one day my PhD supervisor, to whom this book is dedicated, said to me: 'Someone has got to finish and you are the closest!' So, it's a bit rich really that I am reflecting here on the things to do and the things to avoid in doctoral research. My conscience tells me I am not quite the right person to offer advice. I guess I did, in the end, finish but certainly not in an exemplary fashion.

I have, however, supervised many students to the successful completion of their doctorates and I read a lot of theses, having acted as an examiner for over seventy. At any given moment there are at least two bound volumes peering at me from across my desk. As I write this now four blue tomes are there in my peripheral vision pricking my conscience. I am not sure why I get asked so often to act as a reader and examiner. Sometimes I flatter myself with the idea that this is a reflection of respect and academic standing. Although I suspect I have a bit of a reputation for being a bit of a 'soft touch' academically and this is perhaps a more accurate explanation for the frequency of such requests. Regardless, each invitation is a compliment.

The first criterion for a student choosing or nominating a potential reader is that the examiner should *not* be a self-absorbed egoist. An academic whose first impulse is to gut a thesis for references to themselves in the bibliography would be automatically ruled out on this count. The second criterion is to avoid mercurial personalities and 'academic psychopaths'. This can seriously limit the field of potential candidates, but the last thing any students needs is to catch such a personality structure on a bad day. The ideal reader of a thesis is – to my mind – someone who will be critical but fair. So, whatever way you look at it, being asked to be an examiner is a compliment. It is one of the most pleasurable things in academic life to say at the end of a sometimes long and tense viva, 'Congratulations Dr ... we are recommending that your thesis be passed subject to minor typographical changes.'

Reading theses can also be an education beyond the specific content. Contained in each – positively or negatively – are insights into the form of the thesis itself as a particular kind of writing. Every time I read a thesis or have a PhD supervision meeting or attend a seminar with a group of postgraduates I add something else to this list of tips. So, what I have to offer you is a compendium of insights gathered as a bystander who has watched other people complete their PhDs with more grace and efficiency than I did my own.

Your PhD is a Career

I want to begin by quoting an extended passage from John Berger, which I mentioned very briefly in the previous chapter. It is taken from his book *And Our Faces, My Heart, Brief as Photos*:

> What separates us from the characters about whom we write is not knowledge, either objective or subjective, but their experience of time in the story we are telling. This separation allows us, the storytellers, the power of knowing the whole. Yet, equally, this separation renders us powerless: we cannot control our characters, after the narration has begun. We are obliged to follow them, and this following is through and across the time, which they are living and which we oversee.
>
> The time, and therefore the story, belongs to them. Yet the meaning of the story, what makes it worthy of being told, is what we can see and what inspires us because we are beyond its time.
>
> Those who read or listen to our stories see everything as through a lens. This lens is the secret of narration, and it is ground anew in every story, ground between the temporal and the timeless.
>
> If we storytellers are Death's Secretaries, we are so because, in our brief mortal lives, we are grinders of these lenses.[1]

Berger is an art critic, a novelist and storyteller, a poet and writer of stunning proto-ethnographic documentary books. There are a number of things that I want to draw out with regard to sociological craft from this beautiful piece of prose.

Writing a PhD has a relationship to time in the way that Berger describes it. A thesis is also an exercise in storytelling. The people we listen to – what we call 'informants' in the trade – are like Berger's characters: we are the narrators who are outside of their time. This is a useful way of thinking about authorial responsibility: we are the authors and the lens grinders. In part the challenge of a PhD or any sociological study is: (a) to set up the framework for what we know, the structure of knowledge, usually referred to as epistemology; and (b) to establish a claim to what we see and hear through this epistemological lens or sensor. So the first thing I want to invite is an examination of the relationship between thinking, listening, writing and time.

Doing a PhD is about beginning a career, but not in the usual sense of the word. I don't mean the shallow vocationalism that government bodies like to encourage in the form of research training schemes and transferable skills. The notion of career that I want to focus on is not as a noun, that is to have a career, as a possession. Rather, I want to use career as a verb to describe intellectual movement, a kind of passage or pathway in thought. Each year of study is a particular type of journey: it has a departure and a destination.

In a crude sense the timetable for a full-time student looks something like this:

Year 1. Qualifying courses in 'research training' often involving advanced quantitative and qualitative method, specialist course that coincide with the student's research topic and a pilot study in which research techniques are applied.

Year 2. Read and review literature relevant to the proposed research, writing short papers and planning and refining your research strategy.

Year 3. Conduct research, draft thesis chapters and other materials for the MPhil/PhD upgrade viva vocé sit the upgrading viva exam.

Year 4. 'Writing up', finalizing the thesis draft, nominating external examiners, entering your exam entry form, sitting the viva.

So there are stages and particular sets of issues that relate to each part of the PhD career. The sociological path can be frustrating. The extensive range of qualifying courses in research methods can seem like a futile distraction. Michael Burawoy comments:

> A typical graduate student, perhaps inspired by an undergraduate teacher or burnt out from a draining social movement – enters graduate school with a critical disposition, wanting to learn more about the possibilities of social change ... There she confronts a succession of required courses, each with its own abstruse texts to be mastered or abstract techniques to be acquired ... It is as if graduate school is organized to winnow away at the moral commitments that inspired the interest in sociology in the first place.[2]

Maybe so, but the situation described here by Burawoy is the effect of the globalization of an American model of graduate education. In the face of this, graduate students do retain their moral and political commitment despite everything that may threaten to diminish them. Sometimes the sheer scale of challenge of PhD research and writing can seem overwhelming and daunting. If you feel overwhelmed, I think the best way to stay on the path is to concentrate only on the next step.

What I want to suggest now is that there are things you can do to keep your project moving forward. I've tried to formulate these ideas as a series of aphorisms. They are just things that I've found myself saying and thinking over and over again, they are things that seem to make sense to me and that I've tried to use as the basis of my own craft. So, read them as offerings of consolation from a fellow traveller who is still recovering from the malaise that scholarship inflicts upon us.

Ten Aphorisms

These are not commandments, I am not Moses and neither is anyone else. There is no formula; there is no equivalent to an 'intellectual colouring' book where you just fill in the blank pages of the thesis according to some pre-given palette of elements. There are lessons, there are common pitfalls, there are some things to be wary of, but, like scholarship itself, creative thinking does not involve any simple technocratic set of rules. The first thing I want to say is trust the blind energy that makes you keep working on your project.

1. Trust Your Own Interest

I am thinking here of the mysterious desire that keeps your attention focused, that keeps you looking up the next reference or wanting to do another interview. This interest is often opaque. Don't be thrown by the obscure or diffuse nature of what keeps you passionate about what you are doing. The indulgence of individual inquisitiveness is part of what is precious about doing sociological research. Also, the feeling that 'something isn't quite right' in the world, or, as Rachel Dunkley Jones put it recently, 'a sense of uncertainty about the things that everyone is so certain about' provides one kind of warrant for sociological investigation.[3] For the best and most interesting research questions are there to be identified in these uncomfortable and edgy curiosities.

My doctoral research took me over seven years to complete, albeit as a part-time student. There were long periods when I was pretty sure that I didn't know what I was doing. It wasn't until I got to the end that I realized I knew all along what I was doing, it was just that I wasn't always aware of it. Your curiosity and intuition is a good guide and part of the challenge of scholarship is to train it so as to accumulate insight and understanding along the way.

2. Keep a Ledger of Your Thinking

The thing about ideas is that you can't will them to come. I am reminded of the great Dustin Hoffman movie *The Little Big Man*. The film adapted by Arthur Penn from Thomas Berger's novel of the same name stars Hoffman as Jack Crabb, the only white survivor of the Battle of Little Big Horn. Hoffman's character is taken in by an Indian band and schooled in their ancient tribal philosophy and culture. His adopted grandfather is very old and tired of life. He asks his grandson to accompany him to the ancestral burial grounds. There he summons death and calls the spirits to take him. At the climax of an elaborate funereal soliloquy he lies down, closes his eyes and waits for death. After about five minutes he opens one eye, looks around startled and disappointed. He dusts himself off, gets up and says to his confused and relieved grandson: 'Am I still in this world?'

'Yes, Grandfather', says Jack Crabb.

The grandfather groans: 'I was afraid of that. Well, sometimes the magic works, sometimes it does not.' [4]

Academic work is like this. Sometimes the 'magic works', the ideas flow and then a few days later you can be pulling your hair out. Then in the middle of a creative drought you will be doing something else – shopping, being out on the town, or in the middle of a completely unrelated conversation when you should be paying attention to the person in front of you – and an idea will arrive. My advice is to be ready for this unexpected visitor. Carry a notebook all the time and keep a record of these ideas. You need to devise a system to record how your thinking evolves over time. C. Wright Mills referred to this as the practice of 'opening a file'. This is a place to arrest 'fringe thoughts', be they the by-product of an overheard conversation or stimulated by reading a novel or an idea that comes while daydreaming. Mills wrote: 'By keeping an adequate file and thus developing self-reflexive habits, you learn how to keep your inner world awake.'[5]

The other thing that I do which I think is a good habit – although it is not something I have advertised until now – is keep a notebook of new words or phrases. Don't just pass over words whose exact meaning you don't understand. Make a note, look them up later and expand your vocabulary. The temptation is just to pass over words you half know, but greater precision will improve both your understanding and expression.

3. Read Promiscuously with an Open Mind

I've never understood academics who claim to have stopped reading, or who say they 'don't have time to read'. I always think secretly when I hear this: 'if that's true, you're in the wrong business'. Reading is essential and I think it is important to be reading all the time. Read everything, read promiscuously, you never know where you'll find good ideas. Read inside your discipline and outside it. Read popular articles, novels, poetry – you can find a good turn of phase in unexpected places.

Reading is the basic tool of sociological craft and I think we are always reading in at least two ways. The first is reading for ideas, leads – this is reading for the content of what is being communicated. The second is reading for style of argumentation and rhetoric. Here I am thinking of rhetoric as the art of persuasion, not hollow sloganeering. The point is to read for tone and the aesthetic quality of the writing. One thing that I think is a really important and difficult problem is how to combine empirical and analytical elements in written argument. Learn from the ways other people resolve this dilemma.

Part of the challenge of a PhD is learning a new genre of writing. A PhD thesis has a different quality to an essay, a conference paper or journal article. It is not just a matter of expressing the content of your ideas or the things you have encountered but to become the author of book-length arguments. You have to learn to carry a coherent argument over 75,000–100,000 words. This involves learning the form as well as discovering the content and I want to return to this and the issue of form shortly.

4. Don't Become Addicted to the Library

Some pieces of theoretical or archival work can be entirely library-based. More often than not, your PhD will involve the generation of new primary research material. While I want to recommend you read widely, be suspicious of the false comforts of The Library. I want to call this the *perils of bibliophilia*. There is a wonderful short story by Jorge Luis Borges called 'The Library of Babel' in which he tells of a hellish search to find the one book that will unlock the secrets of an immense library.[6] The curse in the story is that the search is eternal and doomed. The lesson in terms of sociological craft is that you won't find a book that will solve the problem that your thesis is concerned with because such a book remains to be written ... by you.

Bibliophilia also carries the danger of being dazzled by the aura of the latest explosively brilliant text you've read. This can sometimes result in inertia. 'I can never write anything as good as that, so I won't bother writing anything at all.' As much as I love the library and books, I have to tell you that you won't find the answers to the questions you want to pose there. What you will find on those musty shelves, and on pages that are yellowed by time, are other people's answers. This is an important distinction to make. One student told me recently that she found this observation profoundly depressing. Looked at another way it is also an opportunity and a calling.

Often a sociological thesis involves some level of empirical research in the form of interviewing people, surveys or participant observation. I often find myself saying to students at the end of their research: 'You won't find your thesis in the next book you read, you'll find it in your interview transcripts and your field note books.' There is a temptation when writing the initial chapters of a thesis to foreground the work that is already there in the library. This results in the deferral of argument or what might be called a *back loading syndrome*. You can look at the table of contents of a thesis and spot this right away. Doctoral students often feel that they have to rehearse the arguments of everyone they have ever read before they say anything themselves. As a result a thesis can contain two or sometimes three literature review chapters. You simply don't need to do this. The result is that the contribution that you are making gets squeezed into the last few chapters and original insights do not have enough space to breathe. Your review of the literature needs to be purposeful in that it should show where the concerns of the thesis are placed within the intellectual landscape. It also needs to direct the reader to the gap in the existing literature that you aim to fill. It doesn't have to be exhaustive but it does have to define the intellectual agenda of the thesis. Otherwise the words of others fill your mouth like a kind of academic gag, making it very hard to find your own voice. Bibliophilia can stop you clearing your throat. I always think that you need to begin writing from your own individual concerns from the very first sentence of the thesis.

5. Don't be Afraid to get Close to the Thing You're Trying to Understand

Open yourself to the issues at the heart of your work and also to the people you work with. Raymond Williams wrote that: 'a writer's job is with individual meanings, and with making these meanings common'.[7] This process of shuttling between the individual and the common is reminiscent of C. Wright Mills' sociological appeal to make 'personal troubles public issues'.[8] It involves getting close, sometimes closer than is comfortable.

All researchers can feel a real sense of trepidation when it comes to beginning their research, particularly if this involves having to contact 'live people' who talk back. Just making a phone call can feel like moving a giant inert rock. If you suffer from this – and I certainly still do – I think it is important just to push yourself. Contact people without worrying too much, no commitment is necessarily binding and every choice can be changed. But you have to make a start in order to find out what is interesting and which leads are blind alleys.

Getting close to something also carries dangers, so be mindful of the specific risks involved in your project. Several years ago I was involved in a project on football and racism and received a concerted campaign of hate mail and harassment. If those pieces of hate mail had come in my mid twenties I wouldn't have been worried about them. I would have brushed it off as the twisted activities of a crazy right-wing maniac. But I had a six-year-old daughter at the time and my biggest fear was that she would pick up the phone one day and hear a tirade of racist bile. Get close, but also think about the risks of being open and getting close.

6. Don't Become a Fieldwork Junkie

The paradox of field research is that once you've made the sometimes terrifying leap into the messy daily realities of people's lives, it can seem almost impossible to give them up. There is always something else to do, another lead to follow up. This is the 'one more interview' syndrome. Remember it is not the quantity but the quality of what you write about that matters. One of the frightening things about doing a PhD, or a book, is that only a fraction of the empirical material you collect can be included. So, don't stay in the research phase longer than is necessary. Trust your supervisor's advice when s/he says 'You've done enough.'

This leads us to the next and perhaps biggest challenge, namely the writing of the thesis itself. We often talk about writing up research as if it is some kind of automatic process. PhD students are said to be in the 'writing-up stage' as if it were some natural phase in the postgraduate circle of life. There is nothing natural or automatic about writing a PhD thesis. In fact, it is – dare I say – profoundly unnatural to subject oneself to such forms of tortured isolation. I would like to propose you start writing from the very beginning and get into the habit of writing. Now, no one can bash out 2,500 words day after day. However, it is possible to make yourself write a little all the time. It is as much about a sense of being constantly engaged with the challenge of writing, as it is the production of useable or enduring prose.

7. Embrace the Challenge of Becoming a Writer

Academic writers are often little more than figures of fun. Derided for the opacity of our jargon-filled books, we swim often unnoticed at the shallow end of the literary pond. To some degree it is our own fault because it seems that, to be a serious academic, you need to be a seriously bad writer. Anthropologist Brian Morris commented in his inaugural lecture in 1999: 'I try to write in a way that is lucid and readable ... I am continually rebuked for this and told to write in an academic style, that is with pretension and in scholastic jargon, for in academia, obscurantism is equated with intellectual profundity. This I refuse to do.'[9] Russell Jacoby takes this a step further when he suggests that: 'academics invariably note that clarity is repressive, which becomes the standard alibi for half-written and sometimes unwritten prose.'[10] Jacoby and Morris are absolutely right to admonish academic authors who often confuse 'being clear' with 'simplistic thinking'. Or, conversely, conflate 'being opaque and obtuse' with 'sophistication and insight'. However, there is also a case to be made for the importance and usefulness of complex writing and – dare I say – a literary value in academic style.

Sometimes difficult and abstract language serves a purpose. I think it is important to defend the necessity of this kind of writing. The two figures that loom in my mind around this issue are Theodor W. Adorno and George Orwell. In *Minima Moralia* Adorno makes a strong case for the necessity of difficult abstract language. 'The logic of the day, which makes so much of its clarity, has naively adopted this perverted notion of everyday speech ... Those who would escape it must recognize the advocates of communicability as traitors to what they communicate.'[11] The insistence on communicability results in the betrayal of critical thinking. Common sense does little more than conserve the status quo. Feminist philosopher and critic Judith Butler, who has been pilloried for her difficult prose style, cites Adorno in her defence. She argues that the utility of 'unlovely' academic words is in the challenge they pose to common sense and in helping to 'make our way toward the politically new'.[12] So, there is a point to difficult language as the medium through which to express difficult and challenging ideas.

In contrast, George Orwell's extraordinary essay 'Politics and the English Language' offers a powerful critique of the corruption of language.[13] I try to read it at least once a year. Orwell takes to pieces the language of totalitarian propagandists alongside a critical assessment of the writing of academics of his day like Professor Harold Laski who worked at the London School of Economics. 'If thought corrupts language, language can also corrupt thought. A bad usage can spread by tradition and imitation, even among people who should know better' wrote Orwell in 1947. My feeling is that we have to insist on having both Adorno and Orwell at our elbow as we write. Complex writing is necessary but so is clarity and the virtues contained in each can be debased. Pristine clarity or abstract complexity is no protection from writing truly awful things. James Miller points out that there is a further paradox in Adorno and Butler's defence of subversive difficulty. 'Does this mean that Adorno's and Butler's most challenging ideas, precisely because of their relative popularity among a not-insignificant number of left leaning intellectuals, have lost their antithetical use value and, by the infernal logic of exchange, been alienated and perhaps even dialectically transformed – turned into something hackneyed and predictable?'[14] Miller argues that if we accept Adorno's logic then this conclusion is inevitable.

Writing a PhD is a literary event. The next question is: what kind of literary event is it? Russell Jacoby writes in his book *The Last Intellectuals* that the planning and execution of a doctoral thesis for young intellectuals is:

the cultural event and context of their lives. When completed it could not be ignored; the dissertation became part of them. The research style, the idiom, the sense of 'the discipline', and one's place within it: these branded their intellectual souls. And more:

the prolonged, often humiliating effort to write a thesis to be judged by one's doctoral advisory and a 'committee' of experts gave rise to a network of dense relations – and deference – that clung to their lives and future careers. Even if they wished, and frequently they did not, the younger intellectuals could not free themselves from this past.[15]

The PhD thesis, for Jacoby, is the equivalent of a 90,000-word literary suicide note. I do not share the view of this doomsayer. Neither do I accept that the acknowledgement of a great mentor or the intellectual craft of other academic writers necessarily condemns one to compliance or uncritical quietism. Writing a thesis marks the birth of a writer of book-length arguments. It does not necessarily determine the quality of that writer's work forever in the manner suggested by Jacoby. It is a place to try out ideas and experiment with thinking.

Crafting a thesis or a book involves finding an aesthetic or a style that you feel comfortable with. I study the style of the writers I admire the most, adapt and assimilate some of the 'tricks of their trade'. A successful PhD candidate, who is now a commissioning editor of a large academic press, wrote this advice in an email: 'The only piece of advice I'd give is write 500 words a day. Make yourself do it from day one.' The written word is our most basic tool and we need to be using it all the time as part of our routine. The novelist Stephen King makes a similar proposal in his book *On Writing*. An aspiring writer, King suggests, should set an achievable word target each day.[16] Set a target and when you have met the target get up and do something else. Before leaving your computer always have the next thing that you want to write prepared, so as to make starting the following day easier. If you can do this on a routine basis the word count soon mounts up. If you do not start now the whole business of 'writing up' will loom like a large dark cloud on the horizon.

The best book I've come across that addresses these issues is Howard Becker's wonderful *Writing for Social Scientists*.[17] There are hundreds of excellent tips alongside humorous reflections contained within its pages. I also find author memoirs good places to find inspiration as well as insight into the nature of their craft.[18] Before ending I want to list a few observations or suggestions that relate to a thesis or sociological monograph. The first of these is start with questions and do not end with new ones. As a reader it can be very irritating to arrive at the concluding passages of a thesis only to be confronted with a new series of questions. A thesis requires answers, proposals, arguments this is why it is called – a thesis! So don't fudge the issue of taking a position by importing a new series of questions at the end. Equally, do not introduce key concepts at the end of the thesis. The place to define the conceptual toolbox of a thesis is in the literature review. If you introduce a major new theoretical problematic or conceptual framework in the last few chapters a thesis can start to implode and crumble from the inside.

Don't rely on the reader to write your thesis for you. A related tendency in thesis writing is to defer the argument or to make it implicit. Remember the average examiner is overstretched, overcommitted and reading on the run. You don't want to alienate them or make them work hard to connect the elements within the overall thesis. Also, don't assume that the reader knows the literatures and key concepts you are working with. Sometimes PhD candidates are anxious about spelling out things that appear basic. Rather than insult their examiner's intelligence, they simply assume that the august reader will know about whatever detail is in question. I think it is better to run the risk of overstating your argument than leaving your point of view implicit or underwritten.

You need to keep directing your reader and it is useful to write into the text intellectual signposts that stop the reader from getting lost, or feeling that they cannot see the point of what they are reading. The thesis needs to have clear threads that unify and connect the chapters, and your argument needs to accumulate with each chapter. The temptation – particularly writing the early chapters – is to make all your big arguments at once. Sometimes the first chapter you write contains all the elements of the entire thesis. The trick is to pace the argument and this is very difficult to achieve. At best a thesis, or indeed a book, has the meter of a drum roll that builds and builds, getting louder and louder, until it reaches the intellectual equivalent of a final crash of cymbals.

I'd like to end this discussion with a comment made by one of my favourite writers, Primo Levi, who wrote: 'He who does not know how to communicate or communicates badly, in a code that belongs only to him and a few others, is unhappy, and spreads unhappiness around him. If he communicates badly deliberately, he is wicked or at least a discourteous person, because he imposes labour, anguish, or boredom on his readers.'[19] Whether we can avoid boring our readers is a moot point, but as a first principle we should try to avoid alienating them.

8. Don't Carry the Burden of Originality

Much is made about PhDs being an original piece of research. This expectation can be a real burden. In truth there are very few – if any – theses that are completely original. Like musical figures, ideas are borrowed and recombined. The novelty is in the combination, the particular insights and the counterintuitive nature of the things that people say when we listen to them. So, don't carry the burden of originality, follow your curiosity and your intuition: it will lead you to uncharted forms of thinking.

9. Don't Try to Judge Your Own Work

The sense of trying to establish the worth of what you've done can lead to intellectual paralysis. Let others decide. That's what your PhD supervisor is for, and ultimately, this is the function of your examiners. Just try to do your work to the best of your ability and let the reader be the judge. Do as much as you can and move on. Don't get mired in self-doubt because we can never really judge the quality of our own work because we are simply too close to it.

Scholarship necessitates responding to criticism and comments from our readers. In order to get the best out of ourselves we need to be open to constructive criticism. This is not always easy. I still recall the terrible sense of dread I felt studying the comments made by my supervisor on early drafts of my PhD. Looking at the pages slashed with red ink was almost physically painful and analogous to a kind of bloodletting. As my supervisor corrected the grammar and sentence structure she scribbled slogans of protests – 'jargon', 'unclear', 'turgid', 'meaning?' On one occasion she took her red pen to a passage that was in fact a quotation – almost page length – from a famous Marxist sociologist without realizing it. This was not an oversight on her part. She was a brilliant supervisor and a careful and thoughtful reader. She alerted me to the fact that in attempting to emulate a convoluted academic style I had lost sight of what I aimed to communicate. Scholarship requires responsible criticism but often we are confronted with rash dismissive remarks or clever jibes made in bad faith.

In a seminar academic allies can turn up like a visiting athletic team ready for a match. A kind of 'sports intellectualism' ensues where dialogue and argument is sidelined and discussion degenerates in an intellectual fixture. The most undermining question is celebrated among intellectual teammates with a series of metaphorical 'high fives'. In the end, this isn't about struggling to think about complex ideas or arguments, it is rather a matter of scoring points and deciding the contest's outcome. This raises broader issues about the nature and ethics of criticism. Criticism can serve as a means to bolster or enhance the critic's moral or political position. Criticism of this kind does not necessarily involve dialogue; all it needs is an opponent. The effect can be devastating to the person being criticized in this way.

After the publication of *White Collar*, C. Wright Mills received a particularly nasty review by Dwight Macdonald. In the early 1950s Macdonald was trying to distance himself from his left-wing friends. The review was damning but contained hardly any reference to the content of the book itself. In a letter to his editor – William Miller – Mills wrote: 'I can't conceal that it hurts … Doubtless I'll get over it, but the thing temporarily incapacitates me. There's only one question that seems important to me, and I'd be very grateful if you'd answer it: Can I learn anything from this review?'[20]

The expectation behind Mills' comment is that criticism is connected to learning and intellectual growth. Mills is so troubled by the review that he writes to Macdonald. 'I don't mind criticism if I can learn from it … The only thing you left me to do is: close up shop.'[21] Mills asks his former friend to prepare a constructive and practical critique and invites him to visit for dinner. The letter continues with a careful list of directions for Macdonald to follow for his journey from New York City to Mills' country home in Pomona, New York State. The care taken over the detailed directions is warm, inviting and oddly hospitable for an author who has been so bruised by the guest he is inviting. The prelude of civility comes to an end with sharp words: 'You'll enjoy the country air, you ignorant, irresponsible bastard!'[22] Needless to say Macdonald did not take up his invitation.

Jonathan Swift wrote in 1704 that he who 'sets up to read only for an occasion of censure and reproof is a creature as barbarous as a judge who should take up a resolution to hang all men that came before him upon a trial'.[23] There is plenty of 'censure' and 'reproof' in academic life. The wide use of anonymous peer-review by publishers and journal editorial boards seems to encourage this kind of thing. Academics can indulge in intellectual sectarianism and snobbery hidden safely behind the curtain of anonymity. Brian Morris concludes in his brilliant critique of the abuses of anonymous academic reviewing that referees' comments are often arbitrary, contradictory and rather inane.[24] So, a young scholar cannot take for granted that s/he will receive fair and consistent criticism. Faced with academic criticism the question posed by C. Wright Mills seems to me to be the right one, namely: 'can I learn anything from it?' Criticism is integral to scholarship and being open to criticism challenges us to think harder. Unthinking approval or uncritical applause is of little use, as Pierre Bourdieu commented: 'truth isn't measured in clapometers'.[25] You need to find an open-minded but critical reader whose judgement you can trust. Ideally your supervisor should fulfil this role, but most sociological writers rely on the critical view of at least one loyal critic who isn't afraid to give an honest appraisal.

10. Have Faith in the Value of What You are Doing

Be comforted by the fact that there is real but elusive value in what you are doing. It is easy to lose sight of this. There is real value in completing a thesis or a book, a value that is beyond financial or professional calculation. It is to be found in the moment when each writer finds his or her own voice, enriching the stories that we tell about ourselves and the world in which we live. To me there is something miraculous in this. Too often our own projects and literary endeavours feel useless or worthless. While one's critics make their presence felt all too keenly, it is much harder to measure the silent approval of the readers who find value in our writing.

A graduate student who completed her thesis in 2004 told me a very moving story that illustrates the point I want to make here about the value of intellectual work. Her name is Emma Nugent. Her research is an ethnographic study of a magazine company and focuses on the ways workers are expected to be 'creative' all the damn time. Here some workers are described as 'The Creatives' to signal this emphasis. Before beginning her research, Emma had been a graphic designer but she left the company because she found the workplace suffocating. 'Put downs' and professional gaming had become integral to the culture of work. Emma returned to the company as an ethnographer to try to make sense of this place sociologically.[26] At the end of the project she gave her thesis to a friend to read, a professional proofreader, who had also worked at the company that formed the basis of the study. She wanted her friend's help to try to make the thesis as readable as possible. When the corrected draft was returned, the proofreader said: 'reading this has helped me forgive myself for that episode in my life'. That one unexpected comment vindicated Emma's whole project and showed the value of what she had achieved. The fact that her thesis passed without any corrections is a minor detail by comparison. Emma's story reminded me of Pierre Bourdieu's claim that sociology is a martial art: 'Like all martial arts it is to be used in self-defense and foul play is strictly forbidden.'[27]

Dancing and Wrestling

When your research is going well it is a good dancing partner. When it is going badly it feels like you are being thrown around in some terrible intellectual equivalent of a wrestling match. You can't see your opponent but you feel the force of their presence. The thing is you can never quite know when you are going to be dancing, or when you will be wrestling with your work. So, I think, it is best to be prepared for both, all the time.

Also, be prepared for a crisis of nerve, the sense that what you are doing is worthless or adds nothing to the existing literature. The thing is books lie, and so do theses. It is always a good idea at the beginning of your project to go and get half a dozen theses out of the library, a random sample. Truth is their quality is really variable: there are stunning ones, competent ones and also quite a lot of mediocre ones. Between the words and pages are hidden torments and moments when the writer's spirits were low. Be comforted by the knowledge that the hidden ruins of confidence are there regardless of whether or not the author is willing to acknowledge them. George Orwell commented that: 'Writing a book is a horrible, exhausting struggle, like a long bout of some painful illness.'[28]

You will move on to other things and new interests but the problem with scholarship is that the completion of a project always lags behind the horizon of our interest. As a result we are usually thoroughly sick of what we are doing by the time we have to share it with anyone else. This is not an individual failing but part of scholarship itself. So do not worry if you get sick to death of your thesis because it is almost certainly a sign that you are moving closer to completing it. When you have polished and honed it, until you cannot read it any more, it is time to let it go and submit it to the glare of your examiner's attention.

Your PhD is the end of your formal induction into scholarship. I think it is really important to remember that it is your first piece of work and not your last. You do have to finish it and the thing that can be overwhelming is the sense that what you are doing is inconsequential. In contrast to the elegant pronouncements of other people, our own work can seem like a banal footnote. As I have already argued I think it is important to suspend personal judgement. Nikolas Rose pointed out, quite rightly, that there is a paradox at the heart of scholarship. A PhD, or for that matter a professorship, is judged to be an individual achievement. Yet, scholarship is a collective endeavour produced through the exchange of many tips, leads and hunches. Also, academic work is always conducted through reading the ideas of others, dialoguing with scholars both living and dead and sometimes contesting the veracity of their ideas.[29] I think one way to respond to a crisis of nerve is to be comforted by the knowledge that one is not doing sociology alone. We have the companionship of thinkers and writers who have struggled with similar problems. This larger project is summed up by Zygmunt Bauman: 'Doing sociology and writing sociology is aimed at disclosing the possibility of living together differently, with less misery or no misery: the possibility daily withheld, overlooked or unbelieved. Not-seeing, not-seeking and thereby suppressing this possibility is itself part of human misery and a major factor in its perpetuation.'[30] Do your work to the very best of your ability and then let it go to take its place within that greater sociological conversation about the possibility of living otherwise.

Notes

Prologue: Kierkegaard's Ruse

1. John Urry, *Global Complexity* (Cambridge: Polity Press, 2003), p. 38.
2. Paul Rabinow, *Anthropos Today: Reflections on Modern Equipment* (Princeton, New Jersey: Princeton University Press, 2003), p. 103.
3. Dave Harper, 'Psychology and the "War on Terror"', *Journal of Critical Psychology, Counselling and Psychotherapy*, 4 (2004): 1–10.
4. Following Zygmunt Bauman, *Legislators and Interpreters* (Cambridge: Polity, 1987).
5. C. Wright Mills, *The Sociological Imagination* (London: Oxford University Press, 1959), p. 219.
6. C. Wright Mills, *White Collar* (New York and Oxford: Oxford University Press, 1956).
7. Kathryn Mills and Pamela Mills (eds), *C. Wright Mills: Letters and Autobiographical Writings* (Berkeley, Los Angeles and London: University of California Press, 2000), p. 136.
8. Vron Ware and Les Back, *Out of Whiteness: Color, Politics and Culture* (Chicago: University of Chicago Press, 2002). I don't mean to imply that this book is itself an example of ponderous prose and it was written out of a similar aspiration to the one being described here.
9. George Orwell, 'How the poor die' in Sonia Orwell and Ian Angus (eds), *George Orwell: The Collected Essays, Journalism and Letters: Volume 4* (London: Penguin Books, 1970 [1941]), pp. 261–72.
10. Søren Kierkegaard, *Philosophical Fragments* (Princeton, NJ: Princeton University Press, 1936), p. 7; see also Adam Phillips, *Darwin's Worms* (London: Faber and Faber, 1999), p. 65.
11. See also discussion of Kierkegaard's formulation in Phillips, *Darwin's Worms*, p.65.
12. César Vallejo, *The Complete Posthumous Poetry* (Berkeley, Los Angeles and London: University of California Press, 1978), p. 15.
13. Michael Young and Lesley Cullen, *A Good Death: Conversations with East Enders* (London: Routledge, 1996), p. 198.
14. Jacques Derrida, 'Circumfession', in Geoffrey Bennington and Jacques Derrida, *Jacques Derrida*, trans. Geoffrey Bennington (Chicago: University of Chicago Press, 1993), p. 36.
15. Derrida, 'Circumfession', p. 37.
16. See also Jacques Derrida, *The Work of Mourning*, eds Pascale-Anne Brault and Michael Naas (Chicago: University of Chicago Press, 2001). Phillip Roth's memoir *Patrimony: A True Story* (London: Vintage, 1999) is haunted by a similar double bind. Roth admits that this beautiful elegy is compromised by the fact that he had turned his father's illness into a literary muse even before his death from a

brain tumour: 'in keeping with the unseemliness of my profession, I had been writing all the while he way ill and dying' (Roth, *Patrimony*, p. 237).

17. Terry Eagleton, *After Theory* (London: Penguin Books, 2004), p. 210.
18. Bellow's comment forms the *leit-motif* of Martin Amis's book, *Experience* (London: Vintage, 2001), p. 202. Amis never cites the source of the quotation. When he visited Goldsmiths in 2003 I asked him where Bellow had made the remark. Ever the name-dropper, he replied dismissively: 'Oh, I think it was in conversation.'
19. Elizabeth Ford Pitorak, 'Care at the Time of Death', *American Journal of Nursing* 103, no. 7 (July 2003): 42–52.

Introduction: Sociology as a Listener's Art

1. Theodor W. Adorno 'On the Fetish Character in Music and the Regression in Listening', in J. M. Bernstein (ed.), *The Culture Industry: Selected Essays on Mass Culture* (London: Routledge, 1991), p. 49.
2. Eudora Welty, *One Writer's Beginnings* (Cambridge, MA: Harvard University Press, 1984).
3. See Alvin Gouldner, 'The Sociologist as Partisan: Sociology and the Welfare State', *American Sociologist* 3, no. 2 (May 1968): 103–16 or more recently Michael Burawoy, 'For Public Sociology', *American Sociological Review*, 70, no. 1 (February 2005): 4–28.
4. Eric Fromm, *The Art of Listening* (New York: Continuum, 1994), p. 169.
5. Emmanuel Levinas, *Totality and Infinity: Essays in Exteriority* (Boston: M. Nijhoff Publishers, 1979), p. 29.
6. Following Joachim-Ernst Berendt, *The Third Ear: On Listening to the World* (New York: Henry Holt, 1985), p. 32.
7. Jon McGregor, *If Nobody Speaks of Remarkable Things* (London: Bloomsbury, 2003), p. 239.
8. Walter Benjamin, 'Surrealism: The Last Snapshot of the European Intelligentsia', in Michael W. Jennings (ed.), *Walter Benjamin Selected Writings: Volume 2 (1927–1934)* (Cambridge, MA and London: Belknap Press, 1999), pp. 207–21.
9. Marc Auge, *Non-Places: Introduction to an Anthropology of Supermodernity* (London: Verso, 1995).
10. C. Wright Mills, *The Sociological Imagination* (New York: Oxford University Press, 1959), p. 3.
11. Mills, *The Sociological Imagination*, p. 8.
12. Since the time of this portrait – May 2005 – Jonathan has been deported.
13. Ulrich Beck, *The Risk Society: Towards a New Modernity* (London: Sage Publications, 1992), p. 60.
14. Beck, *The Risk Society*, p. 60.
15. For more details: http://viaproject.org/
16. Jennifer Patashnick 'Understanding Illness from the Patient's Perspective: Video Intervention/Prevention Assessment (VIA)', Redesigning the Observer: Live Sociology Seminar, University of Manchester, 30 April 2006.
17. Following Hans-Georg Gadamer, *Truth and Method* (London: Sheed Ward, 1975).
18. Monica Greco, 'On the Vitality of Vitalism', *Theory, Culture and Society* 22, no. 1 (2005): 15–27.
19. Michel Foucault, *Discipline and Punish: The Birth of the Prison* (Harmondsworth: Penguin, 1991).

20. Thomas Mathiesen, 'The Viewer Society: Michel Foucault's "Panopticon" Revisited', *Theoretical Criminology*, 1–2 (1997): 231.
21. See http://www.beonscreen.com/uk/user/all-reality-tv-shows-documentaries.asp
22. 'Galloway gives his reasons for taking on Big Brother', *Respect: The Unity Coalition*, http://www.respectcoalition.org/?ite=960
23. Laurie Taylor 'Culture's Revenge: interview with Stuart Hall', *New Humanist*, March/April (2006): 16.
24. Martin Amis, 'Reading from "Yellow Dog"', Richard Hoggart Lecture, Goldsmiths College, University of London, 9 December 2003.
25. Barry Smart, 'Sociology, Ethics and The Present', *Thesis Eleven*, Number 30 (1991): 143.
26. Zygmunt Bauman, *Liquid Modernity* (London: Polity Press, 2000).
27. William Hazlitt, 'On the Pleasure of Hating', in Geoffrey Keynes (ed.), *Selected Essay of William Hazlitt* (London: The Nonesuch Press, 1944), p. 244.
28. 'Guantanamo suicides as "PR move"', BBC News On-Line http://news.bbc.co.uk/2/hi/americas/5069230.stm
29. 'Guantanamo suicides as "PR move"'.
30. Mills, *The Sociological Imagination*, p. 75.
31. Anthony Giddens, *The Consequences of Modernity* (Palo Alto, CA: Stanford University Press, 1990), p. 43.
32. Pierre Bourdieu, *Pascalian Meditations* (Cambridge: Polity Press, 2000), p. 2.
33. Les Back and Mitch Duneier, 'Voices from the Sidewalk: Ethnography and Writing Race', *Ethnic and Racial Studies* 29, no. 3 (2006): 543–65.
34. See Sara Lawrence-Lightfoot and Jessica Hoffman Davis, *The Art and Science of Portraiture* (San Francisco, CA: Jossey-Bass, 1997).
35. See Mitch Duneier, *Sidewalk* (New York: Farrar Strauss and Giroux, 1999) and in particular his collaborations with photographer Ovie Carter and participant author Hakim Hasan.
36. Clifford Geertz, *Available Light: Anthropological Reflections on Philosophical Topics* (Princeton, NJ: Princeton University Press, 2000), p. 30.
37. Edward Said, *Humanism and Democratic Criticism* (Houndsmills, Basingstoke: Palgrave Macmillan, 2004), p. 72.
38. Walter Benjamin, 'Goethe's Elective Affinities', in Marcus Bullock and Michael W. Jennings (eds), *Walter Benjamin: Selected Writings Volume 1 1913–1926* (Cambridge, MA: Harvard University Press, 1996), p. 298.
39. See Clive Seale, Giampietro Gobo, Jaber Gubrium and David Silverman (eds), *Qualitative Research Practice* (London: Sage, 2004), part 1.
40. Hannah Arendt, 'Introduction: Walter Benjamin: 1892–1940' in Hannah Arendt (ed.), *Illuminations* (London: Fontana Press, 1992), p. 54.
41. Clifford Geertz, *The Interpretation of Cultures: Selected Essays* (New York: Basic Books, 1973), p. 6.
42. Geertz, *The Interpretation of Cultures*, p. 20.
43. W. G. Runciman, *A Treatise on Social Theory Volume 1: The Methodology of Social Theory* (Cambridge: Cambridge University Press, 1983), p. 265.
44. Donna J. Haraway, *Modest_Witness@Second_Millennium. FemaleMan© _Meets_ OncoMouseª: Feminism and Technoscience* (New York and London: Routledge, 1997), p. 24.
45. Mills, *The Sociological Imagination*, p. 8.
46. Michael Keith, *After the Cosmopolitan: Multicultural Cities and the Future of Racism* (London: Routledge, 2005), p. 187.

47. Anthony Giddens, *Runaway World: How Globalisation is Shaping Our Lives* (London: Vintage, 1999).
48. Michael Hardt and Antonio Negri, *Empire* (Cambridge, MA: Harvard University Press, 2000) and Paul Gilroy, *After Empire: Melancholia or Convivial Culture* (Abingdon: Routledge, 2004).
49. John Berger, 'What the Hand is Holding: Writing Now', *Here is Here We Meet* season, Queen Elizabeth Hall, South Bank Centre, London, 11 April 2005.
50. Walter Benjamin, *The Arcades Project* (Cambridge, MA: Belknap Press of Harvard University, 1999), p. 463.
51. Georg Simmel, 'The Stranger' [1908] in Charles Lemert (ed.), *Social Theory: The Multicultural and Classic Readings* (Boulder, San Francisco and Oxford: Westview Press, 1993), p. 200.
52. Hannah Arendt, *Essays in Understanding 1930–1954* (New York and London: Harcourt Brace and Company, 1994), p. 323.
53. Nirmal Puwar, 'What is an Inaugural', *Goldsmiths Sociology Research Newsletter*, Issue 21 (2006): 10.
54. Jean Améry, *Radical Humanism: Selected Essays* (Bloomington: Indiana University Press, 1984), p. 141.
55. Améry, *Radical Humanism*, p. 141.
56. Paul Rabinow, *Anthropos Today: Reflections on Modern Equipment* (Princeton, NJ: Princeton University Press, 2003), p. 94.
57. Jonathan Crary, *Suspension of Perception: Attention, Spectacle, and Modern Culture* (Cambridge, MA: MIT Press, 1999), p. 10.
58. Margaret Mead, 'Visual anthropology in a discipline of words', in Paul Hocking (ed.), *Principles of Visual Anthropology*, 2nd ed. (Berlin and New York: Mouton de Gruyter, 1995), pp. 3–10.
59. Joachim-Ernst Berendt, *The Third Ear: On Listening to the World* (New York: Henry Holt, 1985), p. 32.
60. Saul Bellow, *The Adventures of Augie March* (London: Penguin Books, 2001), p. 536.

1 Falling from the Sky

1. An earlier version of this chapter was originally published in *Patterns of Prejudice*, Vol. 37 (1993) although the argument has been revised here and substantially expanded.
2. George Orwell, *Homage to Catalonia* (Harmondsworth: Penguin Books, 1980), p. 220.
3. Orwell, *Homage to Catalonia*, p. 221.
4. Jamie Reid and Jon Savage, *Up They Rise: The Incomplete Work of Jamie Reid* (London: Faber, 1987), p. 5.
5. Michael Walzer, 'Pleasures and Costs of Urbanity', *Dissent* (Fall 1986): 470–475.
6. *Suburban Press*, Number 5, p. 2.
7. Father Ian Knowles, Interview, 30 June 2005
8. William Edward Burghardt Du Bois, *The Souls of Black Folk*. (New York: Bantam Books, 1989), p. 29.
9. Stuart Hall, 'Culture, Community, Nation', *Cultural Studies* 7 (1993): 361
10. Robert Wohl, *The Spectacle of Flight: Aviation in the Western Imagination, 1920–1950* (New Haven and London: Yale University Press, 2005).

11. Slavoj Žižek, *The Ticklish Subject: The Absent Centre of Political Ontology* (London and New York: Verso, 1999), p. 230.
12. Žižek, *The Ticklish Subject*, p. 229.
13. David Blunkett, 'Integration with Diversity: Globalisation and the Renewal of Democracy and Civil Society', in Foreign Policy Centre (ed.), *Reclaiming Britishness: Living together after 11 September and the Rise of the Right* (London: Foreign Policy Centre, 2002), p. 77.
14. George Orwell, 'The Art of Donald McGill', in Sonia Orwell and Ian Angus (eds), *George Orwell: The Collected Essays, Journalism and Letters: Volume 2* (London: Penguin Books, 1970 [1941]), pp. 183–94.
15. British Broadcasting Corporation News, 'Cockling Death Toll 24', Sunday 15 February 2004, http://news.bbc.co.uk/1/hi/england/lancashire/3488109.stm
16. Home Office, *Secure Borders, Safe Heaven: Integration with Diversity in Modern Britain* (London: The Stationery Office, 20022001), p. 1.
17. Giorgio Agamben, *Homo Sacer: Sovereign Power and Bare Life* (StamfordStanford, CA: Stamford Stanford University Press, 1998), p. 1.
18. Agamben, *Homo Sacer*, p. 8.
19. Walter Benjamin, 'Paralipomena to "On the Concept of History"', in Howard Eiland and Michael W. Jennings (eds), *Walter Benjamin Selected Writings Volume 4: 1938–1940* (Cambridge, MA and London: Belknap Press, 2003), p. 406.
20. Paul Lewis 'Stowaway suspect found dead by road', *The Guardian*, Tuesday 13 June 2006, http://www.guardian.co.uk/immigration/story/0,,1796252,00.html
21. 'Immigration: the facts', *The Independent*, 30 August 2006, p. 2.
22. Organization for Economic Co-operation and Development *International Mobility of the Highly Skilled: Policy Brief* (2002), http://www.oecd.org/dataoecd/9/20/1950028.pdf
23. Greater London Authority, *The London Plan: Spatial Development Strategy for Greater London* (London: Greater London Authority, 2004), p. 25.
24. 'The Longest Journey: A Survey of Migration', *The Economist*, 2 November 2002: 3.
25. Philip Thornton, 'British leaders seek "unlimited immigration" from new EU states', *The Independent*, 30 August 2006, p. 2.
26. Philip Thornton, 'British leaders seek "unlimited immigration" from new EU states', p. 15.
27. Janet Dobson and Gail McLaughlan, 'International migration to and from the United Kingdom, 1975–1999: consistency, change and implications for the labour market', in *Population Trends 106 Winter* (London: National Statistics, 2001), http://www.statistics.gov.uk/downloads/theme_population/PT106_v1.pdf
28. Refugee Council, *The Truth About Asylum* (London: The Refugee Council, 2005).
29. Maeve Sherlock, 'Closing the door: the UK's erosion of the right to asylum', speech given at British Institute of Human Rights, Courtauld Institute, London, 8 December 2005, p. 6.
30. Quoted in David Goodhart, 'Too Diverse', *Prospect* 95 (2004): 30.
31. Goodhart, 'Too Diverse', p. 30.
32. Goodhart, 'Too Diverse', pp. 30–1.
33. Paul Gilroy, *After Empire: Melancholia or Convivial Culture* (London: Routledge, 2004), pp. 165–6.
34. Zygmunt Bauman, *Globalisation: The Human Consequences* (Cambridge: Polity, 1998), p. 74.
35. Robert Hunter Wade, 'Inequality of world incomes: what should be done?'

Opendemocracy (2001), http://www.opendemocracy.net/themes/article.jsp?id= 7&articleId=257

36. Wade, 'Inequality of world incomes', p. 2.
37. The World Bank Committee on the Payment and Settlement Systems, *General principles for International Remittance Service* (Basel, Switzerland: Bank of International Settlements, 2006), p. 1.
38. 'The Longest Journey', p. 3.
39. Paul Gilroy, 'Raise Your Eyes', *Opendemocracy*, 11 September 2002, http://www. opendemocracy.net/conflict-911/article_249.jsp
40. Wystan Hugh Auden, *Selected Poems* (London: Faber and Faber, 2000), p. 29.
41. William Carlos Williams, *Selected Poems* (London: Penguin Books, 1972), p. 212.
42. Translation taken from http://en.wikipedia.org/wiki/Yaguine_Koita_and_Fode_ Tounkara
43. Richard Sennett, *Respect: The Formation of Character in an Age of Inequality* (London: Allen Lane and Penguin, 2003).
44. Hannah Arendt, *On Revolution* (London: Faber and Faber, 1963), p. 82.
45. Gilroy, *After Empire*, p. 165.
46. 'The Longest Journey', p. 14.
47. C. Wright Mills, *The Sociological Imagination* (Oxford and New York: Oxford University Press, 1959).
48. Edward Said, *Humanism and Democratic Criticism* (London: Palgrave Macmillan, 2004), p. 80.
49. Les Back, Bernadette Farrell and Erin Vandermaas, *A Humane Service for Global Citizens: Enquiry into Service Provision by the Immigration and Nationality Directorate at Lunar House* (London: South London Citizens, 2006), p. 130.
50. Jamie Doward and Mark Townsend, 'Revealed: "sex-for-asylum" scandal at immigration HQ', *Observer*, Sunday 21 May 2006, http://www.guardian.co.uk/ immigration/story/0,,1779854,00.html
51. Back et al., *A Humane Service for Global Citizens*, p. 21.
52. 'Illegal Immigrants Working at the Home Office', *Daily Mail*, Friday 19 May 2006, pp. 1 and 6.
53. Hélène Mulholland and Matthew Tempest, 'System "not fit for purpose", says Reid', *The Guardian*, Tuesday 23 May 2006, http://www.guardian.co.uk/ immigration/story/0,,1781315,00.html
54. Zygmunt Bauman, *Liquid Love* (Cambridge: Polity Press, 2003), p. 148.
55. Paul Gilroy, *Between Camps: Nations, Cultures and the Allure of Race* (London: Allen Lane The Penguin Press, 2000).
56. Jean Améry, *On Aging: Revolt and Resignation* (Bloomington Indianapolis: Indiana University Press, 1994), p. 11.
57. Primo Levi, 'News From the Sky', in *Other People's Trades* (London: Abacus Press, 1991), p. 12.

2 Home from Home

1. An earlier version of this chapter was originally published in Claire Alexander and Caroline Knowles (eds), *Making Race Matter* (Basinstoke: Palgrave Macmillan, 2005).
2. Gail Lewis, 'From Deepest Kilburn', in Liz Heron (ed.), *Truth, Dare or Promise: Girls Growing Up in the Fifties* (London: Virago, 1985), p. 219.

3. Lewis, 'From Deepest Kilburn', p. 220.
4. Michael Keith, 'Postcolonial London and the Allure of the Cosmopolitan City' *AA files – London: Postcolonial City*, 49 (2003): 57–67; Michael Keith, *Race, Riots and Policing: Lore and Disorder in a Multi-racist Society* (London: UCL Press, 1993).
5. Franco Moretti, *Atlas of the European Novel 1800–1900* (London: Verso, 1998), p. 100.
6. Italo Calvino, *Invisible Cities* (London: Vintage, 1997), p. 165.
7. Colin MacCabe and Hanif Kureishi, 'Hanif Kureishi and London', *AA files – London: Postcolonial City*, 49 (2003): 40.
8. Anne Phoenix, '"Multicultures", "Multiracisms" and Young People', *Soundings* 10 (1998): 96.
9. James Clifford and George Marcus (eds), *Writing Culture: The Poetics and Politics of Ethnography* (Berkeley: University of California Press, 1986).
10. George Marcus, 'After the Critique of Ethnography', in Robert Borofsky (ed.), *Assessing Cultural Anthropology* (New York, McGraw-Hill, 1994), p. 46.
11. Deptford City Challenge Evaluation Project, *City Challenge in Deptford* (London: Centre for Urban and Community Research, Goldsmiths College, 1997).
12. Phil Cohen, 'All White on the Night', in Michael Rustin (ed.), *Rising East* (London: Lawrence and Wishart, 1996).
13. Chris T. Husbands, *Racial Exclusion and the City: the Urban Support for the National Front* (London and Boston: Allen and Unwin, 1983).
14. See Stanley Cohen, *Folk Devils and Moral Panics* (London: MacGibbon & Kee, 1972); Stuart Hall, Charles Critcher, Tony Jefferson, John Clark and Brian Roberts, *Policing the Crisis: Mugging, the State, and Law and Order* (London: Macmillan, 1978); Tony Jefferson, 'Race, Crime and Policing', *International Journal of the Sociology of Law* 16, no. 4 (1988): 521–39.
15. Labour Party Conference Speech, Blackpool, 29 September 1998.
16. Iris Marion Young, 'The Ideal of Community and the Politics of Difference', in Gary Bridge and Sophie Watson (eds), *The Blackwell City Reader* (Oxford: Blackwell Publishing, 2002), p. 432.
17. Young, 'The Ideal of Community and the Politics of Difference', p. 437.
18. Richard Sennett and Jonathan Cobb, *The Hidden Injuries of Class* (Cambridge: Cambridge University Press, 1977).
19. Claire Alexander, '(Dis)Entangling the "Asian Gang": Ethnicity, Identity, Masculinity', in Barnor Hesse (ed.), *Un/settled Multiculturalisms: Diasporas, Entanglements, Transruptions* (London & New York: Zed Books, 2000), p. 127.
20. See Garry Robson, *'No One Likes Us We Don't Care': The Myth and Reality of Millwall Fandom* (Oxford: Berg, 2000); Philly Desai, 'Spaces of Identity, Cultures of Conflict: The Development of New British Asian Masculinities', PhD Thesis, Goldsmiths College, University of London, 1999.
21. See Roger Hewitt's, *Routes of Racism* (London: Trentham, 1997) and *White Backlash and the Politics of Multiculturalism* (Cambridge: Cambridge University Press, 2005).
22. Anthony Giddens, *The Third Way: The Renewal of Social Democracy* (Cambridge: Polity Press, 1998).
23. Neil Leach, 'Belonging', *AA files – London: Postcolonial City* 49 (2003): 76–82.
24. Vikki Bell (ed.), *Performativity and Belonging* (London: Sage, 1999).
25. Caroline Knowles, *Race and Social Analysis* (London: Sage, 2003), p. 105.
26. Parminder Bhachu, 'Culture, ethnicity and class among Punjabi Sikh women in 1990s Britain', *New Community* 17, 3 (1991): 401–12.

27. Avtar Brah, *The Cartography of Diaspora* (London: Rourledge, 1996), p. 208.
28. Nigel Thrift, *Spatial Formations* (London: Sage, 1996).
29. Gillian Rose, *Feminism and Geography* (London: Polity, 1993).
30. Tracey Skelton and Gill Valentine (eds), *Cool Places* (London: Routledge, 1998).
31. Jean-Paul Sartre, *Sketch for a Theory of the Emotions* (London, Methuen, 1962), p. 62. Emphasis added.
32. John Berger, *And Our Faces, My Heart, Brief as Photos* (New York: Vintage International, 1991), p. 55.
33. Berger, *And Our Faces*, pp. 55–6.
34. Sartre, *Sketch for a Theory of the Emotions* p. 62.
35. Fran Tonkiss, *Space, The City and Social Theory* (Cambridge: Polity, 2005), p. 130.

3 Inscriptions of Love

1. An earlier version of this chapter was originally published in Helen Thomas and Jamilah Ahmed (eds), *Cultural Bodies: Ethnography and Theory* (Oxford: Blackwell, 2003).
2. Debbie Back treated this patient in the winter of 2000 and I am grateful to her for sharing his story.
3. C. P. Jones, 'Stigma and Tattoo', in Jane Caplan (ed.), *Written on the Body: the Tattoo in European and American History* (London: Reaktion Books, 2000), p. 1.
4. Jane Caplan, 'Introduction', in Jane Caplan (ed.), *Written on the Body: the Tattoo in European and American History* (London: Reaktion Books, 2000).
5. Harriet Guest, 'Curiously Marked: Tattooing and Gender Difference in Eighteenth-century British Perceptions of the South Pacific', in Jane Caplan (ed.), *Written on the Body: the Tattoo in European and American History* (London: Reaktion Books, 2000).
6. Mark Gustafson, 'The Tattoo in the Later Roman Empire and Beyond', in Jane Caplan (ed.), *Written on the Body: the Tattoo in European and American History* (London: Reaktion Books, 2000).
7. Charles W. MacQuarrie, 'Insular Celtic Tattooing: History, Myth and Metaphor', in Jane Caplan (ed.), *Written on the Body: the Tattoo in European and American History* (London: Reaktion Books, 2000).
8. Alfred Gell, *Wrapping in Images: Tattooing in Polynesia* (Oxford: Clarendon Press, 1993), p. 10.
9. Marcus Rediker, *Between the Devil and the Deep Blue Sea: Merchant Seamen, Pirates, and the Anglo-American Maritime World* (Cambridge: Cambridge University Press, 1987).
10. Patrick Modiano, *The Search Warrant* (London: The Harvill Press, 2000), p. 23.
11. Hamish Maxwell-Stewart and Ian Duffield, 'Skin deep devotions: religious tattoos and convict transportation to Australia', in Jane Caplan (ed.), *Written on the Body: the Tattoo in European and American History* (London: Reaktion Books, 2000), p. 133.
12. Mick Harris, Personal Communication, 15 December 2000.
13. Gell, *Wrapping in Images*, p. 37.
14. Michel Foucault, *Discipline and Punish: The Birth of the Prison* (London: Allen Lane, 1977), p. 25.
15. Michel Foucault, *Aesthetics, Method, and Epistemology* (London: Allen Lane, 1994), p. 375.

16. Foucault, *Aesthetics, Method, and Epistemology*, p. 376.
17. Nahum Norbet Glatzer (ed.), *The Collected Stories of Franz Kafka* (London: Penguin Books, 1988), p. 144.
18. *The Collected Stories of Franz Kafka*, p. 145.
19. Primo Levi, *If This is a Man/The Truce* (London: Abacus, 1987), p. 76.
20. Susan A. Phillips, 'Gallo's Body: decoration and Damnation in the Life of a Chicano Gang Member', *Ethnography* 2, no. 3 (2001): 369–70.
21. Phillips, 'Gallo's Body', p. 384.
22. BBC Radio 4, *The Sunday Papers*, Sunday 4 August 2001.
23. 'True Hair to the Chav Throne', *The Croydon Guardian*, Wednesday 26 January 2005, http://www.croydonguardian.co.uk/misc/print.php?artid=564189
24. Julie Burchill, 'Yeah but, No But, Why I am Proud to Be A Chav', *The Times*, 15 February 2005, http://www.timesonline.co.uk/article/0,,7–1488120,00.html.
25. See http://www.chavscum.co.uk/ and http://www.chavtowns.co.uk/
26. Mia Wallace and Clint Spanner, *Chav!: A User's Guide to Briattain's New Ruling Class* (London: Bantam Books, 2004), p. 211.
27. See Basil Bernstein, 'Social Class, Language and Socialisation', in Jerome Karabel and A. H. Halsey (eds), *Power and Ideology in Education* (New York: Oxford University Press, 1979) and Bernstein, *The Structuring of Pedagogic Discourse* (London: Routledge, 1990).
28. Simone Weil, 'Human Personality', in George A. Panichas (ed.), *The Simone Weil Reader* (New York: David McKay Company, Inc, 1977), pp. 332–3.
29. Zygmunt Bauman, *Liquid Love: On the Frailty of Human Bonds* (Cambridge: Polity, 2003), p. 2.
30. John Tagg, *The Burden of Representation* (Basingstoke: Macmillan, 1987).
31. John Berger and Simon McBurney, *The Vertical Line* (London: Artangel, 1999).
32. Maurice Merleau-Ponty, *The Phenomenology of Perception* (London: Routledge & Kegan Paul, 1962), p. 206.
33. Maurice Merleau-Ponty, *The Visible and the Invisible* (Evanston, USA: Northwestern University Press, 1968), p. 146.
34. Garry Robson, *'No One Likes Us, We Don't Care'*, p. 19.
35. Interview with author, 11 April 1996.
36. Interview with author, 11 April 1996.
37. Interview with author, 11 April 1996.
38. Interview with author, 11 April 1996.
39. Jane Caplan, 'Introduction' in *Written on the Body*.
40. John Bale, *Landscapes of Modern Sport* (Leicester: Leicester University Press, 1994).
41. Yi-Fu Tuan, 'Geopiety', in David Lowenthal and Martyn Bowden (eds), *Geographies of the Mind: Essays in Historical Geosophy in Honor of John Kirtland Wright* (New York: Oxford University Press, 1975).
42. *The Sun*, 8 November 2001, p. 27.
43. Housk Randall and Ted Polhemus, *The Customized Body* (London: Serpent's Tail, 1996).
44. bell hooks, *All About Loving: New Visions* (London: The Women's Press, 2000), p. 3.
45. hooks, *All About Loving*, p. 5.
46. *Nil By Mouth*, 1997, Twentieth Century Fox Film Corporation, written and directed by Gary Oldman.
47. Julie Burchill, *The Guardian Columns 1998–2000* (London: Orion Publishing Group, 2001).

48. See Michael Collins, *The Like of Us: A Biography of the White Working Class* (London: Granta Boooks, 2004).

49. Toby Young, 'Action Man', *The Guardian*, G2, 16 January 2002, p. 3.

50. Michael Young, 'Christmas Day Remembrance', *The Independent*, Tuesday 27 December 1988, p. 15.

51. Beverley Skeggs, *Formations of Class and Gender* (London: Sage Publications, 1997), p. 83.

52. Skeggs, *Formations of Class and Gender*, p. 83.

53. Skeggs, *Formations of Class and Gender*, p. 83.

54. 'The Ugliness of New Addington', *Croydon Advertiser*, 22 June 1956, p. 1.

55. 'The Politics of Housing', *The Suburban Press* 4 (1972): 2.

56. Fieldnote, 22 July 2001.

57. Pierre Bourdieu, *Distinction: A Social Critique of the Judgment of Taste* (London: Routledge, 1986).

58. James Bradley, 'Body Commodification? Class and Tattoos in Victorian Britain', in Jane Caplan (ed.), *Written on the Body: the Tattoo in European and American History* (London: Reaktion Books, 2000).

59. Raymond Williams, *Marxism and Literature* (Oxford: Oxford University Press, 1977).

60. Jacque Lacan, *Écrits: A Selection* (London: Tavistock Publications, 1977).

61. Les Back, 'Out of the Shadows', in Daryl Bravenboer (ed.), *Contagious* (London: Croindene Press, 2001).

62. Paul Connerton, *How Societies Remember* (Cambridge: Cambridge University Press, 1989).

63. London Development Agency, *Production Industries in London: Strategy and Action Plan 2005–2008* (London: London Development Agency, 2006), p. 4.

64. See Fran Tonkiss, 'Between Markets, Forms and Networks: Constituting the Cultural Economy', in Alan Warde and Stan Metcalfe (eds), *Market Relations and the Competitive Process* (Manchester: Manchester University Press, 2002) and Andy Pratt, 'New Media, the New Economy and New Spaces', *Geoforum* 31 (2000): 425–36.

65. Prime Minister's Strategy Unit, *London Project Report* (London: Cabinet Office, 2004), p. 7.

66. Bourdieu, *Distinction*, p. 474.

67. Daniel R Schwarz (ed.), *James Joyce's 'The Dead': A Case Study of Contemporary Criticism* (New York: Bedford Division of St. Martin's Press, 1994), p. 94.

68. Clifford Geertz, 'From the Native's Point of View: On the Nature of Anthropological Understanding', in Paul Rabinow and William M. Sullivan (eds), *Interpretive Social Science: A Reader* (Berkeley, Los Angeles: University of California Press, 1979).

69. Kirsten Campbell, 'The Slide in the Sign: Lacan's Glissement and the Registers of Meaning', *Angelaki: Journal of the Theoretical Humanities* 4, no. 3 (1999): 135.

70. Williams, *Marxism and Literature*, pp. 129–130.

71. Clifford Geertz, *Available Light: Anthropological Reflections on Philosophical Topics* (Princeton, NJ: Princeton University Press, 2001), p. 21.

72. Pierre Bourdieu, 'Understanding', in Pierre Bourdieu et al. (eds), *The Weight of the World: Social Suffering in Contemporary Society* (Cambridge: Polity Press, 1999), p. 614.

73. Sue Benson, 'Inscriptions of the Self: Reflections on Tattooing and Piercing in Contemporary Euro-America', in Jane Caplan (ed.), *Written on the Body: the Tattoo in European and American History* (London: Reaktion Books, 2000), p. 25.

74. Jacques Derrida, *Specters of Marx: the state of the debt, the work of mourning, and the New International* (London: Routledge, 1994), p. 175.

4 Listening with the Eye

1. An earlier version of this chapter originally appeared in Caroline Knowles and Paul Sweetman (eds), *Picturing the Social Landscape: Visual Methods and the Sociological Imagination* (London: Routledge, 2004).
2. The British Sociological Association ethical guidelines can be read in full at http://www.britsoc.org.uk/about.htm
3. Charles Lemert, 'Can the Worlds be Changed? On Ethics and the Multicultural Dream', *Thesis Eleven* 78 (2004): 46.
4. Paul Rabinow, *Anthropos Today: Reflections on Modern Equipment* (Princeton, NJ: Princeton University Press, 2003), p. 115.
5. Walter Benjamin, 'Theses on the Philosophy of History', in *Illuminations* (London: Fontana, 1992).
6. Interview, 15 April 2003.
7. John Berger, *The Shape of a Pocket* (London: Bloomsbury, 2001), p. 248.
8. Interview, 9 April 2003.
9. Interview, 9 April 2003.
10. See particularly John Tagg, *The Burden of Representation* (Basinstoke: Macmillan 1987).
11. Anastassios Kavassos, plenary contribution to the *Street Signs Conference*, Parfitt Gallery, Croydon College, Croydon, 20 November 2001.
12. Monica Ali, *Brick Lane* (London: Doubleday, 2003).
13. Interview, 9 April 2003.
14. Halima Begum, 'Commodifying Multicultures: Urban Regeneration and the Politics of Space in Spitalfields', PhD dissertation, Queen Mary College, University of London, 2004, p. 179.
15. Begum, 'Commodifying Multicultures', p. 187.
16. Fran Tonkiss, *Space, the City and Social Theory* (Cambridge: Polity, 2005), p. 111.
17. Quoted from 'Salgado: The Spectre of Hope', *Arena*, BBC2, 30 May 2001.
18. Interview, 15 April 2003.
19. Interview, 15 April 2003.
20. Erving Goffman, *The Presentation of Self in Everyday Life* (London: Allen Lane, 1960).
21. Interview, 9 April 2003.
22. Roland Barthes, *Camera Lucida* (London: Verso, 2000), p. 13.
23. César Vallejo, *The Complete Posthumous Poetry*, translated by Clayton Eshleman and José Rubia Barcia (Berkeley, Los Angeles and London: University of California Press, 1978), p. 219.
24. Interview, 9 April 2003.
25. John Berger, *And Our Faces, My Heart, Brief As Photos* (New York: Vintage International, 1991), p. 55.
26. Interview, 15 April 2003.
27. Interview, 9 April 2003.
28. Interview, 15 April 2003.
29. See Walter Benjamin, *The Arcades Project* (Cambridge, MA: Belknap Press, 1999), p. 6.

30. Marshall Berman, *Adventures in Marxism* (London: Verso, 1999), pp. 168–9.
31. Berman, *Adventures in Marxism*, p. 260.
32. James Clifford, 'Introduction: Part Truths', in James Clifford and George Marcus (eds), *Writing Culture: The Poetics and Politics of Ethnography* (Berkeley, Los Angeles and London: University of California Press, 1986), p. 25.
33. Benjamin commented of his own work and his use of montage in particular that 'I have nothing to say, only to show.' Quoted in Susan Buck-Morss, *The Dialectic of Seeing: Walter Benjamin and the Arcades Project* (Cambridge, MA: MIT Press, 1991), p. 73.
34. Sarah Pink, *Doing Visual Ethnography* (London: Sage Publications, 2001).
35. Jean Rouch, 'The Camera and Man', in Paul Hocking (ed.), *Principles of Visual Anthropology*, 2nd ed. (Berlin & New York: Mouton de Gruyter, 2003), p. 89.
36. Pierre Bourdieu, *Pascalian Meditations* (Cambridge: Polity Press, 2000), p. 2.
37. Michael Burawoy, 'For Public Sociology', *American Sociological Review*, 70 (2005): 7.

5 London Calling

1. Lawrence Grossberg, 'History, Imagination and the Politics of Belonging', in Paul Gilroy, Lawrence Grossberg and Angela McRobbie (eds), *Without Guarantees: In Honour of Stuart Hall* (London and New York: Verso, 2000), p. 160.
2. Michel de Certeau, *The Practice of Everyday Life* (Berkeley: University of California Press, 1984), p. 93.
3. Jacques Attali, *Noise: The Political Economy of Music* (Minnesota: University of Minnesota Press, 1985), p. 3.
4. http://www.roadalert.org.uk/index.php
5. Jon McGregor, *If Nobody Speaks of Remarkable Things* (London: Bloomsbury, 2002), pp. 1–2.
6. Albert Camus, *Summer in Algiers* (London: Penguin, 2005), p. 1.
7. Murray Shaffer, *The Soundscape: Our Sonic Environment and Tuning the World* (Richmond, Vermont: Destiny Books, 1994), p. 58.
8. The recording made on 28 September 2005 can be heard at http://www.goldsmiths.ac.uk/csisp/
9. Martin Amis, *Visiting Mrs Nabokov and Other Essays* (London: Vintage, 2005), p. 146.
10. Simon Freeman, 'Maximum Security as London Bomb Suspects Appear in Court', http://www.timesonline.co.uk/article/0,,22989-1726498_1,00.html
11. Associated Press, 'London Bombing Suspects Appear in Court, via Video', http://www.msnbc.msn.com/id/6448213/did/10384766
12. Jane Offerman, personal communication, email, Monday 15 May 2006.
13. Sound has been put to work by the torturers and interrogators who subject prisoners in solitary confinement to high volume music often accompanied by flashing lights. The music played is a bizarre range from heavy metal rock like Metallica's 'Enter Sandman' to songs from children's television including the 'I Love You Song' from *Barney & Friends*, a purple dinosaur puppet show. See Jon Ronson, *The Men Who Stare at Goats* (Basingstoke and Oxford: Picador, 2004), pp. 130–1. More chillingly Moazzam Begg – a British detainee in Guantanamo Bay, Cuba – wrote in his memoir of how he was subjected to the continuous sound of a woman screaming. See Moazzam Begg, *Enemy Combatant: A British Muslim's Journey to Guantanamo and Back* (London: The Free Press, 2006), p. 161.

14. Mohammed Abdul Kahar, 'I Just Thought: One by One They are Going to Kill Us', *The Independent*, 14 June 2006. p. 2.

15. Vikram Dodd, 'Asian Men Targeted in Stop and Search', *The Guardian*, 17 August 2005.

16. Amy Gutmann (ed.), *Multiculturalism and the Politics of Recognition* (Princeton, NJ: Princeton University Press, 1994).

17. Field notebook, 27 July 2005.

18. Clifford Geertz, 'An Inconsistent Profession: The Anthropological Life in Interesting Times', *Annual Review of Anthropology*, 31 (2002): 13.

19. Karl Marx and Frederick Engels, *The Communist Manifesto: A Modern Edition* (London: Verso, 1998), pp. 38–9.

20. John Berger, *And Our Faces, My Heart, Brief as Photos* (New York: Vintage International, 1991), p. 89.

21. Susan Sontag, *Regarding the Pain of Others* (London: Hamish Hamilton, 2003), p. 19.

22. Frank Schwere, 'New York Sept 13th 2001', *Baby* 6 (2002): 89.

23. Schwere, 'New York Sept 13th 2001', p. 91.

24. This extract is transcribed from the St Paul's website time line http://www.saint-paulschapel.org/pyv/

25. http://www.saintpaulschapel.org/pyv/

26. de Certeau, *The Practice of Everyday Life*, p. 91.

27. See Kevin Bubriski, *Pilgrimage: Looking at Ground Zero* (New York: Powerhouse Books, 2002).

28. Michael Billig, *Banal Nationalism* (London: Sage, 1995).

29. The abridged speech can be viewed at the St Paul's Chapel website, http://www.saintpaulschapel.org/in_depth/videos.shtml

30. Field notebook, 19 December 2004.

31. Judith Butler, *Precarious Life: The Powers of Mourning and Violence* (London and New York: Verso, 2004), p. xii.

32. Butler, *Precarious Life*, p. xxi.

33. William Pfaff, 'A Monster of Our Own Making', *The Observer*, 21 August 2005, http://observer.guardian.co.uk/comment/story/0,6903,1553394,00.html; see also Martin Wolf, 'When Multiculturalism is a Nonsense', *Financial Times*, 31 August 2005, http://www.ft.com/cms/s/4c751acc-19bc-11da-804e-00000e2511c8.html. See also Melanie Phillips, *Londonistan: How Britain is Creating a Terror State Within* (London: Gibson Square, 2006).

34. *The Sun*, 9 July 2005.

35. *The Sun*, 9 July 2005, p. 8.

36. *Report of the Official Account of the Bombings in London on 7 July, 2005*, London: The Stationary Office, 11 May 2006, p. 21.

37. See Milan Rai, *7/7: The London Bombings, Islam and The Iraq War* (London and Ann Arbor, MI: Pluto Press, 2006), pp. 51–56.

38. Intelligence and Security Committee, *Report on the London Terrorist Attacks on 7 July 2005*, London: Houses of Parliament, May 2006, p. 26.

39. Bhikhu Parekh, 'British Commitments', *Prospect*, September 2005, p. 40.

40. Tariq Modood, 'Rethinking Multiculturalism after 7/7', *Opendemocracy*, 29 September 2005, http://www.opendemocracy.net/debates/article.jsp?id=2&debateId=124&articleId=2879, p. 7.

41. *Daily Mail*, 2 September 2005, p. 3.

42. *Daily Mail*, 2 September 2005, p. 2.

43. Paul Gilroy, *After Empire: Melancholia or Convivial Culture* (Abingdon, Oxfordshire: Routledge, 2004).

44. Chetan Bhatt, 'Fundamentalism and the Seductions of Virtue: Politics, Absolutism and South Asia', Centre of South Asian Studies Annual Lecture, School of African and Oriental Studies, London, 14 March 2005.

45. Peter Oborne, *The Uses and Abuses of Terror: the construction of a false narrative on the domestic terror threat* (London: Centre for Policy Studies, 2006).

46. Intelligence and Security Committee, *Report on the London Terrorist Attacks on 7 July 2005*, London, Houses of Parliament, May 2006.

47. The United Kingdom Parliament, *Hansard*, see http://www.publications.parliament.uk/pa/cm200506/cmhansrd/cm050707/debtext/50707-26.htm

48. Suresh Grover, 'After 7/7', Xenos Conference, Goldsmiths College, 15 February 2006.

49. After two years in the position Sir Iqbal Sacranie stepped down as secretary-general of the MCB in June 2006.

50. Salman Rushdie, 'Muslims unite! A New Reformation will Bring Your Faith into the Modern Era', *The Times*, 11 August 2005, http://www.timesonline.co.uk/article/0,,1072-1729998,00.html

51. Rushdie, 'Muslims unite!'

52. 'Obituary: Shahara Islam', *BBC News On-Line*, http://news.bbc.co.uk/1/hi/england/london/4738141.stm

53. See 'Security Services Identify 700 Potential al-Qa'ida Terrorists at Large in Britain', *The Independent*, 10 May 2006, http://news.independent.co.uk/uk/crime/article363121.ece and Frank Gardner, 'One Year on: Is Britain Any Safer', *BBC News*, http://news.bbc.co.uk/1/hi/uk/5140958.stm

54. Audrey Gillan, Richard Norton-Taylor and Vikram Dodd, 'Raided, Arrested, Released: The Price of Wrong Intelligence', *The Guardian*, Monday 12 June 2006, http://www.guardian.co.uk/terrorism/story/0,,1795482,00.html

55. Oborne, *The Uses and Abuses of Terror*, p. 17.

56. Niccolò Machiavelli, *The Prince* (London: M. Dent and Sons, 1958), p. 93.

57. Benjamin Barber, *Fear's Empire: War, Terrorism, and Democracy* (New York: W. W. Norton and Company Inc, 2003), p. 32

58. Franklin D. Roosevelt, 'Inaugural Address, 4th March, 1933', in Samuel Roseman (ed.), *The Public Papers of Franklin D. Roosevelt, Volume Two: The Year of Crisis, 1933* (New York: Random House, 1938), pp. 11–16.

59. Roosevelt, 'Inaugural Address', p. 11.

60. Sarah O'Neill and Daniel McGrory, 'I Blame War in Iraq and Afghanistan, 7/7 Bomber says in Video', *The Times*, 7 July 2006, p. 4.

61. Personal communication, email, 12 July 2006.

62. 'Man Taken off Plane', *Hartlepool Mail*, 3 April 2006; 'Man Held as Terrorism Suspect Over Punk Song', *Reuters,* Wednesday 5 April 2006; 'Clash Fan Taken Off Plane', *The Sun*, 5 April 2006; 'Air Terror Alert Over Clash Hit', *The Mirror*, 5 April 2006.

63. This can be found on 'myspace' at http://blog.myspace.com/index.cfm?fuseaction=blog.ListAll&friendID=63403172&MyToken=c898b5c2-cf25-41a8-9e7a-c56062822c78ML

64. Interview, 9 May 2006.

65. In the aftermath of a wave of airport terror alerts in the summer of 2006, two students from the University of Manchester – Sohail Ashraf and Khurram Zeb – were forced off a Monarch flight from Malaga, Spain. The mental atmosphere of paranoia

and misrecognition among the white passengers was so intense that they were asked
to leave the aeroplane: two Asian students enjoying the 'quintessentially English tradition' of living it up in the sun were viewed as dangerous potential terrorists.

66. Interview, 9 May 2006.
67. Oborne, *The Uses and Abuses of Terror*, p. 28.
68. Oborne, *The Uses and Abuses of Terror*, p. 26.
69. Gilroy, *After Empire*, p. 137.
70. Modood, 'Rethinking Multiculturalism after 7/7', p. 7.
71. Modood, 'Rethinking Multiculturalism after 7/7', p. 7.
72. Paul Gilroy, *After Empire*; 'Multiculture in Times of War', Inaugural Lecture,
    London School of Economics, Wednesday 10 May 2006.
73. George Orwell, 'Notes on Nationalism', in Sonia Orwell and Ian Angus (eds),
    George Orwell: The Collected Essays, Journalism and Letters: Volume 3 (London:
    Penguin Books, 1970 [1945]), p. 420.
74. For a full genealogy of the notion of the 'melting pot', see Werner Sollors, *Beyond
    Ethnicity: Consent and Descent in American Culture* (New York and Oxford: Oxford
    University Press, 1986), pp. 66–101.
75. George Orwell, 'The Lion and the Unicorn: Socialism and the English Genius', in
    Sonia Orwell and Ian Angus (eds), *George Orwell: The Collected Essays, Journalism
    and Letters: Volume 2* (London: Penguin Books, 1970 [1941]), p. 75.
76. George Orwell, 'In Defence of English cooking' and 'A Nice Cup of Tea', Sonia
    Orwell and Ian Angus (eds), *George Orwell: The Collected Essays, Journalism and
    Letters: Volume 3* (London: Penguin Books, 1970), pp. 56–8 and pp. 58–61.
77. Gilroy, 'Multiculture in Times of War', p. 28.
78. Georges Perec, *Species of Spaces and Other Pieces* (London: Penguin Books, 1997),
    p. 209.

Conclusion: Live Sociology

1. See also Michael Taussig, *Walter Benjamin's Grave* (Chicago and London:
   University of Chicago Press, 2006), p. 199.
2. Edward Said, 'The Public Role of Writers and Intellectuals', *The Nation*, 17
   September 2001, p. 35.
3. C. Wright Mills, *The Marxists* (Harmondsworth, Pelican bookshop, 1963), pp.
   30–1.
4. Fran Tonkiss, *Space, the City and Social Theory* (Cambridge: Polity, 2005), pp.
   10–14.
5. Chetan Bhatt, 'Geopolitics and "Alterity" Research', in Martin Bulmer and John
   Solomos (eds), *Researching Race and Racism* (London and New York: Routledge,
   2004), p. 34.
6. Awaaz, *In Bad Faith?: British Charity and Hindu Extremism* (London: Awaaz South
   Asia Watch Ltd, 2004).
7. Renato Rosaldo, *Culture and Truth: The Remaking of Social Analysis* (London:
   Routledge, 1989).
8. Roland Barthes, 'To Write – an Intransitive Verb', in Richard Macksey and
   Eugenio Donato (eds), *The Languages of Criticism and the Sciences of Man*
   (Baltimore and London: Johns Hopkins Press, 1966), p. 142.
9. James Clifford and George E. Marcus (eds), *Writing Culture: The Poetics and Politics
   of Ethnography* (Berkeley and London: University of California Press, 1986).

10. Joyce J. Ladner (ed.), *The Death of White Sociology* (Baltimore: Black Classics Press, 1998 [1973]).
11. Errol Lawrence, 'In the Abundance of Water the Fool is Thirsty: Sociology and "Black" Pathology', in Centre for Contemporary Cultural Studies (ed.), *The Empire Strikes Back: Race and Racism in 1970s Britain* (London: Hutchinson, 1982).
12. Martin Bulmer and John Solomos, 'Introduction: Researching Race and Racism', in Bulmer and Solomos (eds), *Researching Race and Racism* (London and New York: Routledge, 2004), p. 10.
13. John Bright-Holmes (ed.), *Like it Was: The Diaries of Malcolm Muggeridge* (Collins: London, 1981), p. 374.
14. See D. J. Taylor, *Orwell: The Life* (London: Chatto and Windus, 2003); Gordon Bowker, *George Orwell* (London: Little, Brown and Company, 2003); Scott Lucas, *Orwell: Life and Times* (London: Haus, 2003).
15. D. J. Taylor, 'Orwell's Dirty Secret', *The Guardian G2*, 13 August 2002, pp. 4–5.
16. George Orwell, 'Anti-Semitism in Britain', in Sonia Orwell and Ian Angus (eds), *George Orwell: The Collected Essays, Journalism and Letters: Volume 3* (London: Penguin Books, 1970 [1941]), p. 387.
17. Orwell, 'Anti-Semitism in Britain', p. 388.
18. George Orwell, 'As I Please – 11th February, 1944', in Sonia Orwell and Ian Angus (eds), *George Orwell: The Collected Essays, Journalism and Letters: Volume 3* (London: Penguin Books, 1970 [1941]), pp. 112–13.
19. George Orwell, 'Wells, Hitler and the World State', in Sonia Orwell and Ian Angus (eds), *George Orwell: The Collected Essays, Journalism and Letters: Volume 2* (London: Penguin Books, 1970 [1941]), p. 172.
20. In the 'Death Row Appreciation Seminar' held in the Louisiana State Penitentiary, Angola, Louisiana an ethics of touch and of holding is part of the prisoner's struggle to maintain a sense of dignity and worth. The prisoners embrace each other as a reminder that 'I am somebody', that they are still alive. Sister Prejean, a nun and author of *Dead Man Walking*, said at a seminar in 1994: 'We're touching here today. That's what human being do with one another. The touching is what makes us human.' Douglas Dennis, 'Religion in Prison', *The Angolite: The Prisoner Magazine*, May/June 1994. p. 69.
21. Martin Heidegger, *What is Called Thinking?* (New York: Harper Torchbooks, 1968), p. 16.
22. Jacques Derrida, 'Geschlecht II: Heidegger's Hand', in John Sallis (ed.), *Deconstruction and Philosophy* (Chicago: University of Chicago Press, 1987).
23. Avery F. Gordon, *Ghostly Matters: Haunting and the Sociological Imagination* (London and Minneapolis: University of Minnesota Press, 1996).
24. Vikki Bell, 'Taking Her Hand: Becoming, Time and the Cultural Politics of the White Wedding', *Cultural Values* 2, no. 4 (1998): 463–84.
25. bell hooks, *Remembered Rapture: The Writer at Work* (London: The Women's Press, 1999), p. 11.
26. Theodor W. Adorno, *Critical Models: Interventions and Catch Worlds* (New York: Columbia University Press, 1998), p. 191.
27. Michael Burawoy, 'For Public Sociology', *American Sociological Review*, 70 (2005): 4–28.
28. Burawoy, 'For Public Sociology', p. 7.
29. Burawoy, 'For Public Sociology', p. 8.
30. Burawoy, 'For Public Sociology', p. 7.

31. Les Back, Bernadette Farrell and Erin Vandermaas, *A Humane Service for Global Citizens: Enquiry into Service Provision by the Immigration and Nationality Directorate at Lunar House* (London: South London Citizens, 2006).
32. 'Reid Reveals Home Office Shake-up', BBC News, 19 July 2006, http://news.bbc.co.uk/1/hi/uk_politics/5193340.stm
33. 'Reid plans Border-Control Force', BBC News, 23 July 2006, http://news.bbc.co.uk/1/hi/uk_politics/5207112.stm
34. Primo Levi, *Other People's Trades* (London: Abacus, 1991), p. 157.
35. Max Weber, 'Science as a Vocation', in Hans H. Gerth and C. W. Mills (eds), *From Max Weber: Essays in Sociology* (London: Routledge and Kegan Paul, 1948), pp. 129–56.
36. Chris Rojek and Brian Turner, 'Decorative Sociology: Towards A Critique of the Cultural Turn', *Sociological Review*, 48, no. 4 (2000): 629–47.
37. John Berger, *and Our Faces, My Heart, Brief as Photos* (New York: Vintage Books, 1991), p. 31
38. Ruth Behar, 'Ethnography and the Book that was Lost', *Ethnography* 4, no. 1 (2003): 37.
39. Kathryn Mills and Pamela Mills (eds), *C. Wright Mills: Letters and Autobiographical Writings* (Berkeley, Los Angeles and London: University of California Press, 2000), p. 276. See also the thoughtful assessment of Mills' career in Graham Crow, *The Art of Sociological Argument* (Houndmills and New York: Palgrave Macmillan, 2005), chapter 6.
40. Jean Améry, *On Aging: Revolt and Resignation* (Bloomington and Indianapolis: Indiana University Press, 1994), pp. 4–5.
41. David Silverman, 'Towards an Aesthetic of Research', in *Qualitative Research: Theory, Method and Practice*, ed. David Silverman (London: Sage, 1997), p. 240.
42. John Law and John Urry, 'Enacting the Social', published by the Department of Sociology and the Centre for Science Studies, Lancaster University, 2003 at http://www.comp.lancs.ac.uk/sociology/papers/Law-Urry-Enacting-the-Social.pdf, p. 11.
43. Law and Urry, 'Enacting the Social', p. 11.
44. See, for example, the wide-ranging review offered in Monica Greco and Mariam Fraser, *The Body: A Reader* (London and New York: Routledge, 2005).
45. This site can be found at http://www.people.virginia.edu/%7Emlw5k/.
46. See Bruce Mason and Bella Dicks, 'Going Beyond the Code: The Production of Hypermedia Ethnography', *Social Science Computer Review* 19 (2001): 445–57.
47. Paul Rabinow, *Anthropos Today: Reflections on Modern Equipment* (Princeton and Oxford: Princeton University Press, 2003), p. 99.
48. I am indebted to Andrew Barry for this formulation.
49. Pierre Bourdieu and Loic J. D. Wacquant, *An Invitation to Reflexive Sociology* (Chicago: University of Chicago Press, 1992), p. 235.
50. See Les Back, 'Politics, Research, Understanding', in Clive Seale et al. (eds), *Qualitative Research Practice* (London: Sage, 2004).
51. Walter Benjamin, 'Paralipomena to "On the Concept of History"', in Howard Eiland and Michael W. Jennings (eds), *Walter Benjamin Selected Writings Volume 4: 1938–1940* (Cambridge, MA and London: Belknap Press, 2003), p. 407.
52. Hannah Arendt, *Men in Dark Times* (San Diego and New York and London: A Harvest Book, 1995), p. 11.
53. Arendt, *Men in Dark Times*, p. 11.
54. Arendt, *Men in Dark Times*, p. 23.

55. Said, 'The Public Role of Writers and Intellectuals', p. 35.
56. Albert Camus, *Summer in Algiers* (London: Penguin Books, 2005), p. 14.
57. Raymond Williams, 'The Practice of Possibility', in Robin Gable (ed.), *Resources of Hope: Culture, Democracy, Socialism* (London and New York: Verso), p. 322.

Epilogue: The Craft

1. John Berger, *And Our Faces, My Heart, Brief as Photos* (New York: Vintage International, 1984), pp. 30–1.
2. Michael Burawoy, 'For Public Sociology', *American Sociological Review*, 70 (2005): 14.
3. Thanks to Rachel Dunkely Jones for this insight.
4. *Little Big Man*, 20th Century Fox 1970. Directed by Arthur Penn.
5. C. Wright Mills, *The Sociological Imagination* (New York: Oxford University Press, 1959), p. 197.
6. Jorge Luis Borges, 'The Library of Babel', in *Fictions* (London: Penguin Books, 2000), pp. 65–74.
7. Raymond Williams, 'Culture is Ordinary', in Robin Gable (ed.), *Resources of Hope: Culture, Democracy, Socialism* (London and New York: Verso, 1989), p. 18.
8. Mills, *The Sociological Imagination*, p. 8.
9. Brian Morris, 'Being Human does not Make You a Person: Animals, Humans and Personhood in Malawi', Inaugural Lecture, Goldsmiths College, University of London, 9 March 1999, p. 2.
10. Russell Jacoby, 'Journalists, Cynics and Cheerleaders', *Telos* 97 (1993): 62.
11. Theodor W. Adorno, *Minima Moralia* (London: Verso, 1978), p. 101.
12. Judith Butler, 'A "Bad Writer" Bites Back', *New York Times*, op-ed, 20 March 1999.
13. George Orwell, 'Politics and the English Language', in Sonia Orwell and Ian Angus (eds), *George Orwell: The Collected Essays, Journalism and Letters: Volume 3* (London: Penguin Books, 1970 [1947]).
14. James Miller, 'Is Bad Writing Necessary: George Orwell, Theodor W. Adorno, and The Politics of Language', *Lingua Franca*, January/February 2000: 43.
15. Russell Jacoby, *The Last Intellectuals: American Culture in the Age of Academe* (New York: Basic Books, 2000), p. 18.
16. Stephen King, *On Writing: A Memoir of the Craft* (London: New English Library, 2001).
17. Howard S. Becker, *Writing for Social Scientists* (Chicago: University of Chicago Press, 1986).
18. See Eudora Welty, *One Writer's Beginnings* (Cambridge, MA: Harvard University Press, 1984).
19. Primo Levi, 'On Obscure Writing', in *Other People's Trades* (London: Abacus, 1991), p. 162.
20. C. Wright Mills, 'Letter to William Miller, January 1952', in Kathryn Mills and Pamela Mills (eds), *C. Wright Mills: Letters and Autobiographical Writings* (Berkeley, CA and London: University of California Press, 2000), p. 163.
21. C. Wright Mills, 'Letter to Dwight Macdonald January 17, 1952', in Kathryn Mills and Pamela Mills (eds), *C. Wright Mills: Letters and Autobiographical Writings* (Berkeley, CA and London: University of California Press, 2000), p. 164.
22. Mills, 'Letter to Dwight Macdonald January 17, 1952', p. 165.
23. Jonathan Swift, *A Tale of a Tub* (London: Penguin Books, 2004), p. 31.

24. Brian Morris, 'How to Publish a Book and Gain Recognition as an Academic', *Anthropology Today* 11, no. 1 (1995): 15–17.

25. Quoted from *Pierre Bourdieu: La Sociologie est un sport de combat*, C-P Productions et VF Films 2002. Directed by Pierre Carles.

26. Emma Nugent, 'Building a Creative Person', PhD dissertation, Goldsmiths College, University of London, 2004.

27. Quoted from *Pierre Bourdieu: La Sociologie est un sport de combat* C-P Productions et VF Films 2002. Directed by Pierre Carles.

28. George Orwell, 'Why I Write', in Sonia Orwell and Ian Angus (eds), *George Orwell: The Collected Essays, Journalism and Letters: Volume 1* (London: Penguin Books, 1970 [1946]), p. 29.

29. Nikolas Rose, 'Towards A Critical Sociology of Freedom', inaugural lecture, Goldsmiths College, University of London, 5 May 1992.

30. Zygmunt Bauman, *Liquid Modernity* (Cambridge: Polity, 2000), p. 215

Index